500 Years of
Golf Balls

500 Years of Golf Balls
History & Collector's Guide

John Hotchkiss

Including a reprint of:

The Curious History of the Golf Ball

by John Stuart Martin

ANTIQUE TRADER BOOKS

ISBN: 0-930625-72-2
Library of Congress Catalog Card Number: 97-72625

Editor: *Allan W. Miller*
Assistant Editor: *Elizabeth Stephan*
Art Director & Cover Design: *Jaro Sebek*
Designer: *Darryl Keck*
Production Assistants: *Lynn Bradshaw, Aaron Wilbers*

Printed in the United States of America

To order additional copies of this
book or a catalog please contact:

 Antique Trader Books
P.O. Box 1050
Dubuque, Iowa 52004
1-800-334-7165

Table of Contents

This book is dedicated

to

The Golf Collectors' Society

and its Members

as Custodians of

Golf Ball History

(The Society will share in benefits from this publication)

Introduction

When my brother gave me a replica of the golf ball that astronaut Alan Shepard hit from the surface of the moon on February sixth, 1971, I became inquisitive about what other golf balls might be collectible. Having previously written ten books about collectibles, I started looking for a book on balls. None could be found.

Six thousand golf balls later—these stashed in a closet, under beds and in the basement—I had found only one book, written by John Stuart Martin, a Princeton graduate and the second managing editor of Time Magazine, in 1968. *The Curious History of the Golf Ball*, when found, now sells for from two hundred to five hundred dollars. An exact copy of this book forms the first section of this present book—made available by permission of John Martin's four children: David Martin, Mrs. Barry Martin Osborn, Jill Stuart Ives, and Susan Ashley Ives.

The patent on a one-piece ball issued to James R. Bartsch on April eleventh, 1967, sixty-eight years to the day after Haskell patented his three-piece ball, seemed to Martin a "Third Revolution." The first had been the replacement of the feather ball by the gutta percha ball c. 1850; the second had been the invention of the three-piece Haskell ball in 1899.

Our research indicates that in 1968 a concurrent development—of Surlyn, an impregnable cover material which could be coupled with a solid core—sidelined any real interest in the Bartsch solid one-piece ball. The story of this development, along with other fantastic aerodynamic advancement and chemical magic in the ensuing twenty-five years, forms the Fourth Revolution chronicled in the sec-

ond part of this book. The last chapter takes a timely look at the needs and possibilities for the game of golf in the 21st century.

The third part of this book covers the exploding hobby of collecting golf ball history. For the first time ever the story of collecting antique, classic and logo golf balls with appropriate value guides is being covered in detail and pictures.

A 2000-year Timetable is a flashback on some 200 major events. This is highlighted with illustrations of a range of different costumes of the times.

The Appendix contains diverse supporting information in graphic form, including meaningful charts and tables. It also features a color picture of the famous golf course at St. Andrews, the Mecca of golf, at a time when each hole was played in both directions simultaneously.

Today you as a golfer have a product far superior to that of twenty-five years ago—and with a nineteenth century price. Try to find another mass-produced item with that track record. At one time in the last century, when golf balls were made of feathers, they cost more than the clubs. Today a high tech driver costs over one hundred fifty times the price of a ball.

The information that follows should help you select a ball that will be the best buy to improve your game or enhance your collection.

John F. Hotchkiss
Fort Myers, FL 1997

Foreword

ARNOLD PALMER ON THE GOLF BALL

I have seen a lot of changes in the golf ball over the years. Improved technology has affected every phase of the ball—from its core to its cover and the range of materials, including balata, synthetics such as surlyn, and combinations of just about anything you can think of relating closely to rubber, that have been used to make the outer shell.

Science has influenced the stability and, probably most important, the aerodynamics of the ball in flight, which, of course, is governed by the dimpling of the cover. Even though the manufacturers abide by the Rules of Golf, the dimpling has reached an aerodynamic and scientific point that the ball flies straighter and has more lift than ever before in the history of golf.

To keep the limits and range of golf shots within reasonable bounds, somewhere along the way we are going to have to put some restrictions on the dimpling beyond the sheer number of them, which is now regulated. There also will have to be controls on how the dimples are put on the ball and what they do aerodynamically to its flight.

Clearly, this central object of the great game of golf has come a long way from the feather.

Arnold Palmer

Acknowledgments

The contributions to this book which were made by others came from all directions and in all sizes. Anne Marcus put the book together for the publisher and protected you readers from my creative grammar and spelling. Lynette Pintauro created many of the illustrations and cartoons. Dick Sargent added computer-generated graphics in the Appendix. Dave Kovaleski was responsible for some of the text in the early stages. Lastly but not least, my wife Mimi kept filling in with bits and pieces while substituting for me in my usual haunts and duties.

The largest group is of those who gave me samples in kind, pictures or text about golf balls. For example, Dr. Gary Wiren provided the opportunity to use at least one hundred pictures from his prized collection. John Olman was a similar donor. Historical information came from all the other experts mentioned in the book and below. If by chance you were omitted as a contributor, please accept my sincere apology.

Cuyler Adams
Bill Allen
Bill Amick
Bill Angst
Si Anthony
Archie Baird
Ed Bellows
Karen Bednarski
Patty Berg
Dave Berkowitz
Paul Biocini
Jim Bone
Bill Brown
John Bushfield
Skee Buckland
Amby Carr
Ed Curtis
Ray Davis
Ed Deems
Ed Donoghue
Fritz Ecker
Chuck Farnum
Peter Farricker
Chuck Furjanic
Doc Giffin
Bill Gobush
Bill Grant
Frank Hardison
James Hotchkiss
Jim Hotchkiss

Josephine Hotchkiss
Ted Hoz
Alastair Johnston
Darryl Keck
Bill Keefer
Leo M. Kelly, Jr.
Walter Klie
Scott Kramer
Karen Kuhl
Tom Kuhl
Bob Kuntz
Ed and Carol Lawhon
Don Lawrence
Ralph Maltby
David H. Martin
Rev. George Martin
Mardee McCann
Mike Mickle
Allan W. Miller
Zigmund Mistewicz
Patty Moran
Joe Murdock
Tim Murphy
Andy Mutch
Jeff Neuman
Jay Nuland
John Olman
Morton Olman
Barry Martin Osborn
Arnold Palmer

Bob Pettigrew
Jack Phillips
Charles Potts
George Potts
Trevor Potts
Tyler Potts
Ron Rich
Will Rogers
Dottie Savage
Robert Schiller
Janet Seagle
Bob Schmidt
Jaro Sebek
Kay Shannon
Dolores Sillito
Elizabeth Smith
Elizabeth Stephan
Nancy Stulak
Dick Stranahan
Harry Szmant
Frank Thomas
Judy Thompson
Henry Thrower
Bob Tuttle
Ed Weathers
John Weedon
Jerry Welch
Barry Wright

Other sources of assistance for which the author is indebted and to which he is thankful for a variety of help such as limited use of text, pictures or tables:

British Golf Museum; *Encyclopedia of Golf*, Malcolm Campbell, Random House; *Encyclopedia of Golf Antiques*, John & Morton Olman, 1985; *Encyclopedia of Golf Antiques*, Steel & Ryde, 1975; *Fifty Years of Golf*, Hutchinson, London; *Golf, A Guide to Informational Sources*, Murdock & Seagle; *Golf Antiques*, expanded ed., John & Morton Olman, 1992; *Golf Collectors Society Bulletin* (for members); *Golf Digest*; *Golf in America*, George Pepper and others, 1974; *Golf in the Making*, Henderson, Stirk, England, 1986; *Golf Magazine*; *Golf Weekly Magazine*; *History of Golf*, Robert Browning; Patty Berg Collection, Cypress Lake Country Club, Fort Myers, FL; PGA Hall of Fame (before closing); *Story of American Golf*, Herbert Wind, Farrar-Straus, 1975; United States Golf Association; USGA—Golf House Library, Far Hills, NJ; Manufacturers' Catalogs, Advertisements and Histories from: Spalding, Worthington, Acushnet/Titleist, Silver King, Tryon, Sulcliff, Wright & Ditson, St. Mungo, MacGregor, Burke, Northern Ball Co., Alex Henry, North British Rubber Co., Avon Golf Balls, Wanamaker, Slazenger, PGA, Beckley-Ralston, Billings Ball Co., Bridgestone, Shaler Golf Balls, Wilson, Faultless, Reach Co., B.G.I. Remade Balls, Vulcan Golf Co., U.S. Rubber Co., Titleist.

Part

1

The Curious History of the Golf Ball

Mankind's Most Fascinating Sphere

BY JOHN STUART MARTIN
FOREWORD BY CHICK EVANS

for
JIM and JUDY BARTSCH
fond partners
in life and work who have
so far equalled par
for both courses

Acknowledgments

Of the many people to whom I am indebted for assistance—and encouragement—in pulling this book together, given the honor on the first tee must be Miss Janet Seagle, gracious librarian of the U.S.G.A. in Manhattan. She it was who helped establish the fact that no such book had ever before been done, and who then guided me through the crowded shelves of Golf House to quantities of elusive material.

Brigadier Eric Brickman, D.S.O., secretary (now retired) of the Royal & Ancient Golf Club at St. Andrews, and his deputy Mr. W. N. B. Loudon, furthered the project by putting me in touch with Laurie Auchterlonie, who in 1963 succeeded his father Willie—whom I had met in 1921— as Professional by Appointment to the R. & A. With his bonnie wife Bee, Laurie became my chief of research in the United Kingdom, and was responsible for my rewarding correspondence with George Gibson, longtime secretary of the Professional Golfers' Co-Operative Association Ltd. He in turn passed some of my problems along to Samuel Ball, retired production chief of Dunlop, and to A. E. "Dickie" Penfold Jr., perpetuator of his father's great tradition and business in golf balls; also, to Harry Fernie, son of Willie of Troon, the man who in 1905 helped to stymie the Haskell patent in Great Britain.

Another who steered me to George Gibson and to other fruitful sources was J. Victor East of Evanstown, Ill., a pioneer of golf and golf balls in Australia as well as in the U.S.A.

Special thanks go to Kay Halle and to Winsor French for putting me in touch with Coburn Haskell's daughters and son, who supplied many long-lost facts about their eminent father.

Officials of the Spalding and UniRoyal companies helped not only with material from their archives but by sending me to some of their predecessors, notably John Baymiller, Joseph Brogden, and Dr. Sidney Cadwell.

From Bob Jolly, at his store in Newark, I gained access to the scrapbooks of his late, lively father Jack Jolly; and through him also rediscovered George Fotheringham, my own first golf teacher and U.S. Rubber's first test professional.

James Worthington of Rockfall, Conn., son of the founder, and the late Bob Smith of Elyria, Ohio, a past president, helped me piece out the story of the Worthington Ball Co. Jack Rutherford, former advertising manager of the *Christian Science Monitor* and himself a notable golfer and golf writer, helped me reach some New England oldtimers.

Teru Maeda, of the Far East Rubber Co., furnished background on golf balls in Japan.

Jim Bartsch's creative associate Chet Lee (now with Princeton Chemical Research Inc.) supplied invaluable bits about the Bartsch ball's ice-house days which the inventor was too busy or too modest to remember.

To all these, as well as to my boyhood hero Chick Evans for his fine Foreword, I am most grateful, and herewith attest their scholarly scorecards.

A work like this, especially on the first go-round, must inevitably fall short of perfection. The subject involves so many factors, human and technical, that there will always be room for additions, corrections, clarifications. But that is the beauty as well as "the hell" of it, for this is a game in which all its enthusiasts can join. Readers can undoubtedly improve this first performance at many points by sending me their further recollections, and they are cordially invited to do so. The "Nostalgia and Curiosa" department is wide open. Subsequent editions can and will be so revised and augmented as to represent the lifetime best-ball record of the whole membership.

—JSM Great Meadows, N.J.

Foreword

When you stop and think, it is amazing that no one ever took the trouble to explore and expound the evolution of the golf ball before John Martin undertook the task. Histories of golf have, of course, always described major changes in the ball, but only in passing, and never with the depth and detail needed to reveal the human as well as mechanical factors involved.

If you had asked me a year ago if I knew the curious history of the golf ball, I would have said "Certainly!" but I could have given you only a sketchy account. What my lifelong friend Johnny has done is to give every golfer, including us old-timers, a liberal education in golf from an angle we had never thoroughly considered.

When you think further, as John has done, this angle, or viewpoint, is the most central one of all. The ball is and always has been the game's ultimate focus. You have to keep your eye on it to hit it. The ball's progress from tee to cup is the full name of the game. Controlling the ball's behavior in a thousand subtle ways is the game's whole art and mystery. Upon whether it is a lively or slow ball, large or small, hard or soft, light or heavy, tough or tender, dimpled, meshed or brambled, must depend every nuance of every shot, and very largely the result of every match or medal round.

As John observes, golf is the one game where each player's ball is his very own, his alone to manipulate without physical opposition, interference or assistance from anyone else. I would add that golf is the only ball game not played on a perfectly smooth surface. No putting green, however beautifully rolled and mowed, was ever absolutely flat. From tee to green, courses are now tailored and smoothed like counterpanes, but still they have their deceptive undulations, their hazardous trees, bunkers, water, and a few residual bits of rough. In the old days, golf was a game more of hazards than of fair and gracious turf. But even with the elimination of most hazards, "rubs" of the green remain to cause crazy bounces and cranky lies. Two balls landing but five inches apart may, after certain—or uncertain—gymnastics, wind up fifty yards apart. Accepting these uncertainties, and persevering with the ball to overcome them, is what makes golf the magical study it is.

The golf ball's fascination for me, and my addiction to it, began when I was a caddy at the old Edgewater course north of Chicago. The first ball I remember playing was a solid guttie. It felt heavy, sounded sharply, and did not run on fairway or green. I would clean it beautifully for the member I was caddying for, and can remember the names Ocobo, Musselburg, and so forth. But there is another golf ball that stands out with peculiar vividness.

Mr. Coburn Haskell was a member of Edgewater. One Sunday afternoon I was caddying for him, and I heard him say to Harry Turpie, the professional, that he had a new ball which he wanted him to try. It was a fitful ball, going abruptly and irregularly. It would start suddenly, as if by a leap.

We were on the sixth tee at dear old Edgewater, and no one had ever driven over the top of the big poplar tree near the railroad tracks. The hole bent to the left, so if one could carry over the tree a shot would be saved, and Mr. Haskell asked Harry to try it.

Alas! The Haskell ball went over the fence into shoulder-high grass. We looked and looked and looked, but the first rubber-cored ball was not to be found, and the round was finished with gutties. I was not blind to the brilliancy of that ball. So before going home that night, I went back to the spot where it was lost and, by rolling my whole body over and over until it hit something hard, I found it.

At the club next day, Harry Turpie sifted me thoroughly, and got back his first Haskell ball. (That was always an excellent way to get a good ball: search the caddy!)

Which brings me to a story about a golfer, a ball, and a whole lot of caddies, which I think has never been properly told with all its implications.

I was the golfer, in the National Open Championship at Minikahda in 1916. To the par 5 twefth hole I hit a second shot longer than I had ever hit one before. It was a terrible chance to take because Hagen, Hutchinson and Barnes were on my heels, and I had to carry a creek. But if I brought off the shot I had a fine chance to win, and I did. [Chick's score of 286 stood as the U.S. Open record for twenty years.]

Another fellow evidently thought the same, for on the fourteenth tee he came up to me and put $1,500 in cash into my hand, named the amount, and said that it was mine if I would play the last holes with his Pneumatic Ball, one of which he put quietly into my pocket.

I gave him back his money and his ball, and asked an official to please not let anyone talk to me.

I told my mother about this episode, and she said I had done the correct thing. And as I was waiting for the presentation of the winner's medal, I told Spalding's man about it—he was an old friend, a member at Edgewater. The next morning in front of my mother the Spalding man said he had gotten in touch with the president of Spalding's and was authorized to offer me $10,000 in cash and 20 per cent on all clubs they manufactured with the name Chick Evans on them.

However, the evening before as Mother and I looked into the caddie yard of Minikahda on the edge of Lake Calhoun, we had seen there many boys who would have liked a college education but their home circumstances—like ours—would never have allowed it. Our decision was made then, and we turned down the Spalding offer, which most cer-

tainly would have made me rich, but also certainly professional. I remained for the rest of my days strictly an amateur.

So the uncertain golf ball, specifically that strange Pneumatic one, occasioned a major happening in golf of which I am proud, pardonably I hope. Some years later I was offered $5,000 for a golf instruction phonograph record. This time I accepted the money. I turned it over, in trust, to the Western Golf Association. From that nucleus grew the Evans Scholars Foundation, swelled since into millions by contributions from tens of thousands of everyday golfers. Since their first awardings in 1930, the Evans Scholarships have put 894 ex-caddies through college, and more than twice that many are in college at this writing.

The W.G.A. calls it "Golf's Greatest Charity," but I don't. I call it a golfer's greatest privilege, to help the golfer's best friend: an able and willing caddy who looks after the player's clubs, his frame of mind, and his most treasured possession of many a happy hour—his golf ball.

Having been on hand to witness what John aptly calls the "second revolution" in golf balls, I am naturally most interested in witnessing the third, which is now happening. I have tried the new solid balls and found them most satisfactory. I suppose some work remains to perfect them and to establish quality control over their mass production. But modern technology being what it is, one can expect the best. To my way of thinking, the precision now promised for the golf ball's roundness, center of gravity, compression, and lasting resilience is quite as wonderful as the indestructibility now claimed, particularly if all these wonders can be achieved with an ultimate saving to golfers in the cost of the best balls.

Perfect is as perfect does, and perhaps diminishing the ball's last mechanical uncertainties will help reduce the imperfections of our all too human skills.

—Chick Evans

The Third Revolution

W hen no one answered the doorbell, I ventured on a tour of the grounds. In a rear carriage shed, I suddenly felt like a miser who had stumbled into the back room at Fort Knox.

The earthen floor was entirely strewn, in places piled knee-deep, with small round objects, mostly whitish. Hundreds and thousands more of them overflowed from bushel baskets and apple barrels. They were not, they could not be—yet, lo, they were—a galaxy of golf balls.

To one who had squandered half a lifetime on the fascinating folly that is golf, the sight was as breathtaking as it was incomprehensible. When the lady of the house finally appeared, one question had to pop before any other: "What goes on here?!"

She was a trim and smiling little blonde, entirely delectable, but her answer was crisp to the verge of brusqueness.

"My husband," she stated, "makes golf balls."

When I looked incredulous she added, with loyal assurance, "That is, he re-makes them—so far. But pretty soon he will have invented one of his own—a brand new kind."

I left the place marvelling much, and shaking my head. In this great of Jetflights, astrospheres, Topstreaks and Hummadingers, what brash, nameless dreamer would dare to defy lordly Dunlop and haughty Uniroyal; to challenge wise Wilson and proud Acushnet; to spit in imperious Spalding's eaglish eye? Preposterous!

The man's project was splendidly audacious, but quite absurd. A new kind of golf ball, indeed! Some one might as well try to revolutionize the electric light bulb, I concluded, and put the episode out of mind . . . .

Thus did the author of this history describe for *Sports Illustrated* in 1966 a little experience of 1960 in rural New Jersey, which had brought forth an astonishing sequel. The rash dreamer with the shed full of golf balls and spunky little wife had not only challenged the royal, ancient, and somewhat smug golf-ball industry: he had actually beaten it at its own intricate game. He had done so with little or no knowledge of golf itself, and no prior experience in making golf balls. He was, quite classically, the naive inventor in the rustic byway coming up with a better mousetrap—in this case, mantrap.

Where big manufacturers had tried and tried for decades—and always failed—a modern-minded young rubber chemist had in less than five years wrought the first revolution in golf-ball components, structure, and performance in 68 years (three golfing generations), only the third such revolution in 120 years. He had the test records and the international patents to prove it.

Curiously enough, his performance was precisely analogous to that of the man who did revolutionize the electric light bulb. In the neon tube, a homogeneous gas medium to carry the current was substituted for delicate and finicky filaments. Similarly, James R. Bartsch had taken the filaments out of golf balls and substituted a homogeneous solid as the energy conveyor.

Ever since the Haskell invention of 1898, every golf ball of any consequence has been fabricated by laboriously winding elastic thread tightly around a central core, and then compressing it within a protective cover. Now this elaborate but long-established process has been superseded, with potentially great savings in labor and materials, and immeasurable extension of the product's life. Bartsch's invention returned ball-making to a simple, basic concept which had been followed during the half-century preceding the Haskell patent.

During that long time, golf balls were molded solid, all in one piece, of homogeneous gutta percha, sometimes mixed with Indian rubber, a kindred tree gum. Bartsch's 1966-67 patents, describing the formulation and one-piece molding of a new synthetic elastomer, thus truly paralleled the first great golf-ball revolution in 1846, when a Scottish Divinity student devised the "guttie" to replace the ancient, handsewn leather pouch stuffed with hair or feathers with which men had been amusing themselves since Roman times, before Christ.

The more I thought about it, the more obvious it became that Bartsch's performance merited recording in golf's good-books. This conviction was reinforced, and this book conceived, when the United States Golf Association declared, and the Royal & Ancient Golf Club concurred, that no history book on the golf ball's evolution, per se, had ever been written. That gap in golf's literature was the more surprising when the golf ball's uniqueness, just as a ball, was considered. Among all games played with a propelled object, spheroid or otherwise, golf is the only one (except for target sports like bowling, archery, darts, and gunning) in which the plaything is the player's very own, his alone to possess and control. One golfer does not, must not, touch or otherwise interfere with his opponent's plaything, as in curling, croquet or billiards. In team games "the ball" belongs to and is handled by everybody.

The golf ball is unique in another respect. It is the only ball which is required to behave differently, in itself, at different moments of play. A tennis ball is built and expected to react uniformly off the racket and off the ground on serve, drive, lob, or chop. A golf ball is desired to fly lively off the club yet not bounce so lively upon striking the ground, or spring so fast off the putter. Its varied responses to various impacts must be controllable.

Herein lies the essence of golf's charm and challenge. To control his own ball, all alone without help or hindrance, the golfer must first and last entirely control himself, and himself only. The little round toy sitting so alone and so still, which has so fascinated and tantalized the human animal for more than five centuries, is thus uniquely a psychic as well as physical cynosure of muscular skill and mental concentration.

At each stroke the ball becomes a vital extension, an image of one's innermost self. We remember the arching flight, the uncertain bounce, the final roll toward the hole—or away from it—as an integral whole, a unit of each digit on our scorecards. Yet from the impact of our club until the ball's arrival at its stopping spot, it is the ball itself that describes that hole—the airy parabola, the bounces, the linear ground track. His travelling ball is truly the player himself in motion, in the same sense that a painter's picture is himself on canvas, and a writer's words are himself in print.

We speak of eyeball-to-eyeball encounters between men great and small. Even more searching and revealing of character is the eyeball-to-golfball confrontation, whereby our most secret natures are mercilessly tested by a small, round, whitish object with no mind or will but with a very definite life of its own, and with whims perverse or beatific. Each conjunction of our own efforts and the ball's behaviour freights our memories with regret or jubilation; or, as in the rest of life, with a mixture of both in deserved proportions.

Apart from the mental and muscular efforts it exacts from us, the golf ball exerts potent aesthetic stimuli. When first taken out of its wrap of tissue or foil or plastic, it gleams with a purity more pristine, I think, than any of man's other playthings: than even a new baseball, or shotgun shell, or trout fly. Its perfect roundness, its glossy whiteness, the precision of its dimples, the tiny hallmarks etched so neatly at its poles, even its smell—nowadays so elusive as to be largely imaginary; all these are important elements of that mystique which entrances us each time we step out on a first tee.

For those of us who began our golf as caddies, and between rounds as urchin ball-hunters in deep hay and rank thickets—the untailored "tiger country" of yesteryear—the sight and feel of a new golf ball, or one only slightly blemished, radiated all the magic of a mint-fresh coin. This historian can hark back—or imagines he can—even to the fragrant old gutties and earliest Haskells, which "clacked" harshly before Spalding put balata hides on them.

Many of those old balls were still in play at Garden City, L.I., on the primitive Salisbury links and on the more awesome Garden City Golf Club course, where Walter J. "Old Man" Travis reigned as Mister American Golf. Then the scene shifted to Skokie, nine lush holes beside a broad marsh alive with Illinois wildfowl; and soon after that to nearby Indian Hill, a brand-new 18-holer carved out of hardwood copses and hazel thickets on the south edge of Winnetka, where all was flat except a knoll on which Red Indians slept.

Here the two small Martin boys were taught not only the etiquette of club-carrying and ball-watching for their parents, but also how to distinguish edible field mushrooms—*Agricus campestris*—from the deadly *Amanita*. And here into our young lives came Spalding's brambled "Wizard" and "White," followed by the livelier "Red Dot," first ball in a balata cover. In 1909 came Spalding's delicious new "Dimples": the large floating "Glory"—red, white, and blue at its poles, played by Mother with her upright, pouncy little swing; the smaller, non-floating "Baby" and even smaller, heavier "Midget," played by jerky, flat-swinging Father.

In those days juniors were not allowed to play or even practice on the course except in early morning or late afternoon. So besides gathering mushrooms, many of our hours at the course were spent in collecting birds' eggs and lost balls. Between the thrills of finding a plover's or bob-o-link's nest, or an unscarred "newie," there was little to choose. And sometimes golf balls got mixed right into our oology. I once found a perfectly good ball in a high crow's nest, along with bottle caps, bits of tinfoil, and other bright baubles the crows had carried home. Elsewhere, a pair of brown thrashers had used strands of elastic thread, unravelled by some inquisitive caddy, to line their bundle of twigs in a thornapple bush, instead of the usual wrinkled rootlets.

Taking balls apart to see how they were made was standard juvenile practice. We were warned that some brands had pressurized cores filled with acid, which could put out an eye. I never came upon any, and have since been told that the threat was a myth circulated by ballmakers to discourage the dissection of rubber-wound balls; for bits of those elastics truly could snap into boys' faces and spark damage suits. Carefully unwound to their amazing length and twisted together, the magic strands made fine slingshots, and I doubt that taking balls apart has yet been entirely suppressed.

In those days the young Martins basked happily in the acquaintance of Father's friends the Edwards brothers, Kenneth and Donald, both topflight amateurs. Later, at neighboring courses, we met Charles "Chick" Evans Jr., Kenny Burns, Bob Gardner, Harrison "Jimmy" Johnston, Jock Hutchison, Tommy Armour, Gene Sarazen (who had won his first Open at Skokie in 1922, aged twenty)—champions all.

At nearby Onwentsia, beauteous Edith Cummings whaled the ball like a man; and one summer the family had a cottage beside the Shenecossett course at New London, Conn., where Glenna Collett (later Mrs. Vare) tuned up for her titles under the wise eye of MacDonald Smith.

Still later, in a class by himself, we knew the one and only Bob Jones.

From all of these we learned golf just by watching them play, and in this book will be found reminiscences from some of them about the oldtime balls they remember best. Chick Evans was persuaded to go even further. In the Golden Anniversary of his historic double at Minikahda and Merion in 1916, he furnished our pointed Foreword.

The balls these maestros played will be described in historical perspective, down to about 1936. After that, when balls became tightly standardized, and sophistication if not skill lessened everyone's selectivity among the brands, some of the rarest savor went out of golf. One first-class ball now feels and acts much like another, at least for the week-end practitioner. Only true champions or stickling purists can draw fine distinctions, or pretend to.

So now the golf ball's evolution has come full cycle, in the Bartsch revolution. Back it has gone into a solid phase the like of which has not been seen since McKinley was President, and Walter Travis dealt the old guttie its unkindest cut by winning the U.S. Amateur of 1901 with a rubber-wound Haskell. Sandy Herd completed that job in the next year's British Open, though British golf periodicals suppressed the fact that little Herd played a Haskell in beating the great Vardon.

So now again opened for argument is the question of which is best: the core-wound, covered ball or the solid? Many will cling, if only for old times's sake, to the old style, artfully spun and shelled, one by one. Others will applaud the simplicity and unrivalled durability of the new one-piece ball, precisely engineered in mass batches.

This question is less clear-cut than was the contrast between the obdurate, brittle (or in hot weather, mushy) old guttie, and Haskell's "bounding billy." Rigid regulations now force all balls into fixed performance specifications, at least for tournament play. All that can be argued really are comparative cut-resistance, true roundness, concentricity, and the more subtle questions of "hang" and of side-spin (hooking and slicing), as will be explained.

Meantime, golf marches on. Now it belongs to multimillions of players who are descended from mere thousands within the memory of forefathers still alive and still playing. In an age of space-flight and exploration of the celestial spheres, who can say that the golf ball has achieved its final incarnation? Like the British satirist of 1902 (see Chapter Five), one might predict that it will some day achieve built-in nuclear propulsion, to holes at distances nearing infinity.

Even in such a day, one factor must remain the same: computerized though the judgment and execution of shots may become, and though putts are aimed at craters on the planets, essential to their guidance systems will be the heart and mind of man—the only golfing organism in the known universe.

"Pegasus"—Half Horse, Half Bird

Short of twitting them about wearing skirts, the surest way to infuriate Scotsmen is to suggest that golf, and the ball it is played with, originated somewhere other than in Scotland. Yet that is precisely what leading golf historians have been doing for some time. They trace golf to *paganica*, in the century before Christ. This was a pastime of the Roman legions, who are said to have left it behind them on the empire's northwestern marches after five centuries of occupation.

Paganica means "of heathen or rustic origin;" and the so-named game is supposed to have been invented by the peasants of southern Italy, where legionaries were largely recruited, to dispel the tedium of herding their sheep and goats.

The business end of a shepherd's staff was the curved portion, which was not so much a handle to grasp as it was a hook for collaring wayward animals or fishing them out of crevices and bog holes. Presumably a shepherd, from frequently gripping his staff by the straight end, would become strong and

Golf in the 1st century (a mythical representation)

dextrous at manipulating the crook. He might sooner or later (the theory goes) find amusement in swiping with it at small loose objects on the ground, such as round stones or unripe lemons and chestnut burrs. From there it would be but a short step to fashioning proper balls, and to knocking the balls at targets; and then to placing a competitive premium on the length and accuracy of knocks.

The only trouble with this reconstruction of history is that nowhere in the writings of the two Plinys, or Martial, or any other reliable contemporary commentator, is there mention or implication that any stick or staff, crooked or otherwise, was employed in *paganica*. The idea seems just to have crept in from nowhere and been welcomed because it was so pat.

The Romans had three kinds of heavyish balls: The *harpastum*, a small handball stuffed with hair; the *pila trigonalis*, a slightly larger version, for throwing; and the *paganica*, a still larger ball—four to seven inches in diameter—substantially softer than the other two since it was stuffed with feathers (*pluma facta*). This one was also thrown or batted by hand. Still larger and much lighter was the *follis*, which contained a bladder (sheep's or pig's) inflated with air like the modern volleyball or football. All these Roman balls were used primarily to work up sweats before taking hot baths, not necessarily for sport or to develop skill.

It would be nice to picture Gaius Julius Caesar striding the moors of tripartite Gaul, or trudging a Britannic linksland, and thrashing with a bent stick at a primitive "golf" ball. Before he made himself emperor, General Caesar made a point of fraternizing with his troops, sharing their joys and woes. Surely between battles, when not building stone roads and aqueducts, he would have joined or led his men in a game the like of which would fascinate soldiers, statesmen, and even royalty for centuries to come.

But in the absence of written or pictorial evidence that *paganica* was played with a shafted instrument, this pleasing vision must be dismissed. The fact of the matter is that knocking small round objects about with crooked sticks was begun by persons unknown. Perhaps, to go really far back with the research, some anthropologist can prove that the thing was started by head-hunting savages who added insult to injury by drubbing their decapitated adversaries' skulls hither and yon with their warclubs. In that case, the first golf "hole" may have been a barbecue pit.

Herbert Warren Wind, in his *Story of American Golf* (1948), disposed of the question most happily: "If you follow the theories of the romantic historians, then the first golfer was a shepherd—place him on a hillside in Greece, Palestine, or Scotland, as suits your taste—who was bored with his work. He started to swing his crook at stones, just to give himself something to do, and then, purely by accident, one of the stones disappeared into a hole and a strange, tingling sensation raced up and down the shepherd's spine. He tried hitting a few more stones as close to the hole as he could, and when he had mastered the shot, called over to a colleague and invited him to match his skill at the sport. They became the first twosome and had right of way all over the hillside."

The Gothic word *kulban* meant a knobbed stick. The German *kolbe* was a club or cudgel. An early Dutch game called *kolven* was played with a bent club or stick on ice with a ball struck at posts for targets. *Kolf* was similar, but played on an earthen yard inside walls of stone, or of about wood sheathed with lead, suggesting hockey in a rink. Stick and ball games played in fields by the Belgians and French were *paille maille* (corrupted to *pell mell*) or *jeu de mail*, "the game of the hammer."

"If you follow the theories of the romantic historians, then the first golfer . . . was a shepherd who was bored with his work."

Other names were *croisse,* and *chole* or *choula.* One rugged Flemish version was a team sport played point-to-point for miles along highways, or straight across country. The defenders had a crack at their opponents' ball every fourth shot, when they knocked it backward, or into a ditch or other "hazard" to deter its arrival in a wagered number of strokes at the designated target, such as a church's steps or a pot-house door.

Cambuca was a British game of the fourteenth century played with a tiny ball of boxroot.

Not until a small hole in the ground became the target, and each man stroked his own ball only, was the game called gowf, goff, or golf(e). By then it was established as firmly in the north of Britain as it was in Holland, and was mostly played on "links" (seaside pastures and duneland). In fifteenth-century Scotland it had become so popular that "golfe," along with "futeball," had to be suppressed in wartime because it interfered with archery practice. The arrival of gunpowder restored golf to Scotland's commoners, though Royalty and the nobility played it right along. The first recorded sale of a golf ball was in 1452; the price ten shillings.

As the games had varied, so had the balls in their size, texture, and resilience. Some were as large as five inches but most much smaller. All manner of materials had been tried, from iron to ivory, to flock tightly wound, to beech, boxroot and other hardwoods, which were sometimes turned into egg shapes to improve their trajectory.

Most curious, and of greatest interest today, was the survival, or revival, of the ancient Roman idea of cutting and sewing leather so as to form a globular pouch, and then jampacking it full of stuffing. For this was the structure that somehow prevailed.

The skill and patience required to produce by this process a ball that would fly and roll satisfying distances are measures of how earnestly its early addicts took the game. At this early ballmaking the Dutch first excelled, and their featheries were preferred even in Scotland.

The strong Dutch influence on early golf is still reflected in its vocabulary. A hole in Holland was a put. The player poised his ball upon a *tuitje* (pronounced "toitee"). When he encountered an obstacle, or his opponent's ball on the putting green, he said "Stuit mij" (pronounced "sty my," meaning "it stops me").

In 1618 one James Melvill, a ballmaker of St. Andrews, petitioned King James VI of Scotland (and I of England) to embargo foreign featheries for the protection of Melvill "and other puir people who now for lack of calling wants maintenance." To keep gold and silver from flowing out of his realm to Holland, the monarch obliged. He gave Melvill and his assigns a 21-year monopoly and declared "escheat" (subject to seizure) any golf balls not bearing their bench marks. Half the proceeds from the sale of contraband balls went to the Crown, half to Melvill and friends, whose price for their handiwork was fixed at four shillings.

Who succeeded Melvill as royal ballmaker after 1639 is "wrop in mystery," but in 1642 the town council of Aberdeen issued "license and tollerance to John Dickson to make gouff balls within this burgh during the councils pleasure, and his good carriage and behavior . . . ." How seriously the art was taken is reflected by the fact that in 1637, two years before the end of Melvill's monopoly, a teenage boy was hanged in Banff for stealing golf balls.

Other town councils followed Aberdeen's lead and ball-making soon spread throughout Scotland as a prestige profession. By 1800 the Scottish featherie had become pretty well standardized. It averaged 1½ inches in diameter and weighed 26 to 30 pennyweights, approximately today's specifications. Invariably now it was stuffed with feathers, not hair or flock. The tanned leather

A FATIGUED FEATHERIE.
Wear and weather opened
their seams.
(G. M. Cowie, St. Andrews)

used was most commonly bullhide, sometimes split for flexibility; but often horsehide was substituted. This gave rise to some wit's remark that the golf ball should be called "Pegasus—half horse, half bird."

The leather was cut in four, three or two lobes, separately or fanned out from a common center like the petals of a flower or sections of an orange peel. It was soaked in warm alum water to make it pliable. Later, the finished ball would be rubbed with mineral or neatsfoot oil to render it waterproof, or somewhat so. Chalk or other white pigment was added to raise the ball's visibility.

The sewing was done with a fine, curved needle, using linen thread beeswaxed for strength and lubrication. The stitches were spaced closely but, since they were put into the seams' *inner* side, were left loose enough so that the formed pouch could be reversed at the finish when the final stitches were put in and pulled tight. About a quarter-inch slit was provided in one flap of the leather through which to poke the feathers.

These were most commonly down feathers from the breast of a goose, boiled to make them limp and malleable. Incredible as it seems, "as much feathers as will fill a hat"—a tall beaver hat, that is—would be compressed into a space no larger than a duck's egg.

As the soggy leather and feathers dried out, two things happened: the leather shrank, the feathers expanded. This created two-way internal pressure and rendered the ball (until it got wet again) almost as tight and hard as horn, to which feathers are akin. The basic material of feathers is keratin, a hydrocarbon plastic manufactured by most animals beginning with the vertebrates. It forms the rough epidermis of sharks, the scales of fishes and reptiles. The mammals put keratin into their layered pelts and into horns, hooves and claws. In man it becomes hair, and the nails on toes and fingers. In the birds, which evolved from the reptiles, keratin follicles produce a variety of structures of which down, the avian underwear, is no less fibrous and springy than are the stiff coverts, pinions, tail-feathers, beaks and talons.

Goose-down was the commonest stuffing, but a heroicomical poem entitled "The Goff," written by one Thomas Mathison of Edinburgh in 1743, described much more exotically—doubtless with poetic license—the handiwork of ball-maker "Bobson" (Robertson) who "in Andrea thrives" (St. Andrews), and who:

> *. . . with matchless art*
> *Shapes the firm hide, connecting every part.*
> *Then in a socket sets the well-started void,*
> *And through the eyelet drives the downy tide;*
> *Crowds urging crowds the forceful brogue impels.*
> *The feathers harden, and the leather swells.*
> *He grins and sweats, yet grins and urges more*
> *Till scarce the turgid globe contains its store.*
> *The dreaded falcon's pride here blended lies*
> *With pigeon's glossy down of various dyes;*
> *The lark's small pinions join the common stock*
> *And yellow glory of the martial cock . . . .*

The "socket" was a hard leathern cup which the ballmaker gripped in one palm with the stitched leather "void" lying it, fill-hole up. The "brogue" was an iron rod 16 to 20 inches long, tapered to a blunt point and set at the top into a wooden crosspiece which the ballmaker pressed against his chest.

He started the operation by poking feathers through the slit with a small wooden stuffing wedge. Then he applied the brogue, imparting to it with pressure against his chest a tamping motion. When the brogue could "drive" home no more down, and his calipers showed that the ball was up to size, he used a small, sharper awl to force in a last few feathers before sewing up the slit.

The best of ballmakers could "stuff 'n stitch" no more than four or five "featheries" in a long day. The repeated pressure against his chest, together with feather particles which he couldn't help inhaling, resulted often in lung trouble or asthma. Most ballmakers died young, and many a promising playing career was thus cut short. So a half-crown per ball, or a pound for a dozen, were not exorbitant prices. Even so, only royalty, gentry, and the most affluent of "artisans" could afford them.

The Robertson ("Bobson") family made golf balls at St. Andrews for generations, as did Forgans, Auchterlonies, and Hutchisons. Most famed was vigorous, red-jacketed little Allan Robertson, golf's first acknowledged playing and teaching professional, who died in 1859 at the untimely age of forty-four, unbeaten in any challenge match. Assisted by Tom Morris, whom Allan's father Davie had taught, Allan turned out 1,021 featheries in 1840, 1,392 in 1841, and in 1844 no fewer than 2,456.

The Gourlays of Leith and later Musselburgh so surpassed all in the quality of their work that "a Gourlay" came to mean the finest featherie money could buy. It was "white as snow, hard as lead, and elastic as whalebone."

TOOLS TO MAKE
FEATHERIES.
"Forceful brogues," socket,
stuffing wedges, awls,
calipers (Not shown: needle,
thread, goose feathers,
leather pieces)
(G.M. Cowie, St. Andrews)

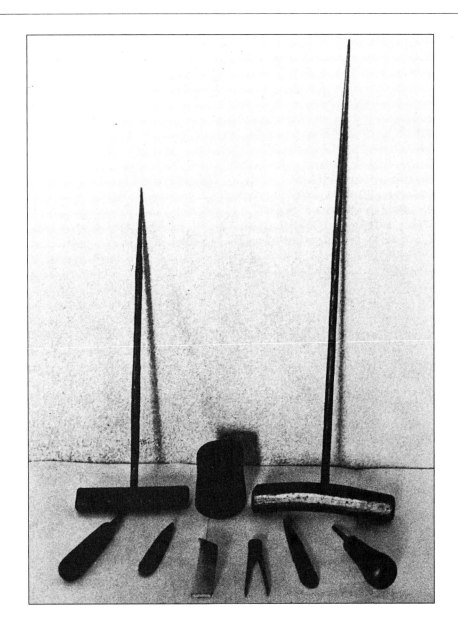

The feather ball, however carefully tapped into shape with hammer before play, was never precisely round. In play it became less so, and in wet or even damp weather it became sodden and useless. Careless strokes with the iron clubs could easily cut it. But when new, crisp inside, and freshly oiled, it would fly surprisingly well, even better than the gutta percha ball which succeeded it.

On what must have been a windy day during a dry spell, the longest hit solemnly measured and attested at St. Andrews was made in 1836 by a Frenchman named Samuel Messieux. He taught French at St. Andrews University and in the process had become a fine golfer. On the Elysian Fields, a long open stretch beside the fifth hole of the original Old Course, it was duly recorded that Monsieur Messieux knocked a featherie no less than 361 yards! In those days, 150-175 yards was acceptable for ordinary men.

As will be related, the arrival of the gutta percha ball in 1846-48 and the consequent passing of the featherie brought great changes at St. Andrews, some of them unhappy but most highly constructive. Before that moment came, the featherie had enjoyed a life of more than four centuries, as curious as they were glorious.

Mother Necessity at St. Andrews

The fifth decade of the nineteenth century was a dour one for Scotland. Though not so desperate as overpopulated Ireland's, where potato blights brought famine, Scotland's economy was so sorely depressed that in 1845 Parliament was moved to pass the Poor Law (Scotland) Act, modelled on similar relief given to England's indigents eleven years before. The proud Scots were not subjected to a workhouse test but, just the same, those days were dark for many a Scottish family, including most in little St. Andrews.

Laurie Auchterlonie's studious wife Bee has summed up the situation: "The town was in debt to the tune of £10,000, a vast sum then for a small community that was dwindling every year. The University had shrunk to a handful of students; there was even talk of moving it to Perth. By 1848 the links, the townspeople's heritage, had been entirely sold to a neighboring landowner, Mr. George Cheape of Strathtyrum. Cholera, the black plague, hit the town. The fortunes of St. Andrews were at their lowest ebb."

For young Rob Paterson, a divinity student whose father's faculty salary scarcely made ends meet, life was hard; and the harder in that, ardent golfer as the lad was, money was lacking to have shoes cobbled let alone to buy feather golf balls at half a crown or even third-hand ones for sixpence.

In its inscrutable way, Providence took a hand in 1843 by causing the arrival at Dr. Paterson's home of a large wooden box from Singapore. In it, sent by an older missionary son, was a statue of the Hindu deity Vishnu, goddess of fertility and preservation. The ornate and graceful four-armed figure in black marble came carefully packed in a mass of blackish-brown shavings. These the learned doctor recognized as gutta percha, dried gum of the Malaysian sapodilla tree.

Since he knew that this exotic material had some value—it was fashioned in those days into whip handles, papercutters, and other knicknacks—Dr. Paterson saw to it that the shavings were not thrown out. They lay around the house for months until the family found a use for them. Heated in hot water they could be formed into sheets which, with glue and a few nails, improved on leather for repairing the soles and heels of the Paterson family's footwear.

When the uppers of his boots wore out completely, young Rob contemplated the hard gum soles. They had scarcely worn at all. Seized by a bold idea, he heated up the stuff and kneaded it into a ball the size of the leather-feather ones he so dearly yearned for. Having watched his mother make dumplings, he found a smooth board and on it rolled his ball under his palm until he got it practically spherical. After it cooled he painted it white lest he lose it in the herbage of the Old Course. For that is where, early one April morning in 1845, he fearfully took his little creation to try hitting it with his golf clubs.

After several strokes, the poor thing disintegrated. But the first few hits had felt and flown not badly at all. So Rob Paterson persevered. He took the fragments home, reheated and re-rolled them. From more gutta shavings he made more balls. Perhaps because he rolled them more carefully, getting all the fissures out, these lasted longer, and Rob imparted his secret to a brother who lived at Lauder, down near Edinburgh.

Robert Adams Paterson finished his studies, became a Reverend Doctor, and emigrated to America. At Binghamton, N.Y., he founded the American Bible College, first of its kind for training female missionaries. Golfless in the wilderness, he served there for more than 40 years. He died all but unaware of the revolution he had started in his favorite boyhood game with his invention, mothered by necessity.

His brother carried on from where Rob had left off. By melting the gutta thoroughly in boiling water to drive out all the air bubbles, and then "cur-

PATTERNSON'S "NEW COMPOSITE." Note flaking paint and lack of surface pattern. (G. M. Cowie, St. Andrews)

ing" it for weeks in a warm, dry place, he so improved "Paterson's Composite—Patented" ball (which he stamped on it) that one or two actually lasted until he lost them. When any broke apart, he just put them together again on the stove.

After the Paterson family's supply of shavings ran out, more gutta was available at Glasgow and other seaports. It came in round bars about a yard long and a couple of inches thick. Chop off a measured segment and you had all the makings of a golf ball. Paterson made up a substantial batch and in 1846 sent them to be exhibited in London. But almost no one there would look at them.

In the spring of 1848, Admiral W. H. Maitland Dougall, R.N., a former golf captain of St. Andrews, visited London and golfed at Blackheath with English friends. He was astonished at the distance and durability of some "Paterson Composites" with which they played in the rain. He had some sent to him in Scotland, as did John Campbell of Glensaddel, another leading Scots golfer.

When Allan Robertson first saw the new balls one day in 1848 at Innerleven, he at once sensed a threat to his trade in featheries, which was just about St. Andrews' only industry. Teeing one up, he intentionally skulled a skimmer, and snorted, "Bah! Thot thing'll never flee!"

John Gourlay of Musselburgh was more prescient. After watching Admiral Dougall, Mr. Campbell and others hit many a fine shot with their gutties, and hitting some himself, he was converted enough to take prompt, prudent action. One of his best customers, Sir David Baird of St. Andrews, had a standing order for all the featheries Gourlay could spare; so he now packed off to Sir David every one he had in stock—no less than six dozen—and quietly went into the guttie business.

Allan Robertson pledged himself and his assistant, Tom Morris, never to use a guttie ball or even to join in a match where one was played. He bought up all strays that were found in the St. Andrews whins and ostentatiously burned them, raising a great stench with "the feelthy stuff."

ALLAN ROBERTSON OF ST. ANDREWS, 1815-1859. Last maestro of the featheries, to him gutta percha was "feelthy stuff."
(Schenck & McFarlane)

One day good-natured Tom Morris relaxed and played a round with a guttie-user. When Allan learned of this, he berated Tom so angrily that Tom quit his employ and opened a shop of his own at Prestwick, where he made both featheries and gutties available. In due time Allan bowed to the inevitable and followed suit. But the two greatest players, teachers, and clubmakers of their day never again joined in business except as partners in money matches, at which they were unbeatable.

That year of 1848 was further signalized as the gutty's birth year by an ode which Dr. William Graham of the Innerleven club sang at its September meeting. Inspired by "The Goff" and other links lyrics, this epic celebrated . . .

> *. . . The change brought round this year*
> *In balls of GUTTA PERCHA.*
> *Though Gouf be of our games most rare*
> *Yet, truth to speak, the tear and wear*
> *O' balls was felt to be severe*
> *And source of great vexation;*
> *When Gourlay balls cost half-a-croun*
> *And Allan's no a farthing doun.*
> *The feck o's [most of us] wad been harried soon*
>   *In this era of taxation.*
>
> *Right fain we were to be content*
> *Wi' used up balls new lickt wi' paint*
> *That ill concealed baith scar and rent,*
>   *Balls scarcely fit for younkers.*
> *And though our best wi' them we tried*
> *And nicely every club applied*
> *They whirred and fuffed, and dooked and shied,*
>   *And sklentit into bunkers.*
>
> *But times are changed—we dinna care*
> *Though we may ne'er drive leather mair*
> *Be't stuffed wi' feathers or wi' hair*
>   *For noo we're independent.*
> *At last a substance we hae got*
> *Frae which for scarce more than a groat*
> *A ba' comes that can row and stot—*
>   *A ba' the most transcendent.*
>
> *They say it comes from yont the sea*
> *The concrete juice o' some rare tree—*
> *And hard and horny though it be,*
>   *Just steep it in hot water—*
> *As saft as potty soon 'twill grow*
> *Then 'tween your loop a portion row*
> *When cool, a ba' ye'll get, I trow,*
>   *That ye for years may batter.*
>
> *Hail Gutta Percha! Precious gum!*
> *O'er Scotland's links long may ye bum.*
> *Some purse-proud billies haw and hum*
>   *And say ye're douf at fleein';*
> *But let them try ye fairly out*
> *Your merits they will loudly tout*
>   *And own they hae been leein'.*

'Tis true—at first ye seem to hing
And try the air wi' timid wing—
But firmer grown, a sweep ye'll fling
  Wi' ony ba' o' leather.
Ye're keen and certain at a putt
Nae weet your sides e'er open up—
And though for years your ribs they whup
  Ye'll never moutt a feather!

But noo that a' your praise is spent,
Ye'll listen to a friend's comment,
And kindlier tak on the paint,
Then ye wad be perfection.
And sure some scientific loon,
On Golfing will bestow a boon,
And gie you a cosmetic soon,
And brighten your complexion.

Paterson's "patent" existed only in his own head. Very soon, as golf's foremost historian Sir Guy Campbell relates, "Revolution was in the air everywhere." All the ballmakers except Allan Robertson started making gutties. They were smooth as eels at first, and the natural gum's brunette "complexion" was seldom given any "cosmetic," such as Rob Paterson gave his first one, because paint just would not stay on. This drawback was worsened by dunking the balls in hot water after a day's play to melt out the nicks and dents. That didn't help the paint stick.

Then it began to be noticed that scarred-up balls "dooked and shied" much less than smooth new ones did. So the gutties were given a few clips with a cleek or other iron club before being put on sale. "An ingenious saddler" of St. Andrews had a better idea. He carried the "revolution" a long step further by using the sharp edge of his hammer's peen (claw end) to whack in shallow meridian grooves, crossed by horizontal parallels all around the ball. This gave it a waffle-iron aspect which was the forerunner of all later surface patterns to improve the ball's grip on the air.

For some time the gutties continued to be "rowed" (rolled) "'tween your loop" (between the palms) and then on a smooth flat surface, until someone— legend says Willie Dunn of Musselburgh—had the wit to make hollow, hemispherical metal molds in which to place the gutty melted "saft as potty" and compress it. A logical next step, more accurate and less laborious than peen-hammering, was to build into the molds raised ridges to imprint the ball's crisscrossing circular grooves.

By popular demand, a white "complexion" came into fashion (and for snowy weather, a red one), so paints were improved and slathered on in several coats. But these filled the surface markings, so the coats were cut to two thin ones, with several weeks between to allow the balls to "season" or "cure." Now every pro's shop became filled with rack upon rack of gleaming, fragrant gutties awaiting their makers' trademarks. By the early 1860s featheries had become collectors' items.

From four or five shillings for finest featheries, or a minimum of 2/6 for culls, the cost of golf balls dropped to a shilling.

....

SOME REAL OLDIES
*Top Row: Gutties from 1848
to 1902 (first three made by
Allan Robertson)*
*Lower two rows: Featheries,
with weights marked in
drams (No. 22 has ruptured)*
(G. M. Cowie, St. Andrews)

Allan Robertson of St. Andrews became reconciled to this when he found that he could make and paint in one hour as many gutties as he used to featheries in a long day. And now, at the lower price, golf suddenly boomed throughout the land. New courses were laid out, increasing the demand for clubs and lessons as well as for balls.

Now tradesmen and artisans, "puir meenisters" and college students could afford the game as well as nobility and the gentry. With the rounder, more durable ball it was easier to learn the game, too, if your time was not unlimited. Players from far and wide swarmed to the links, old and new, but especially to historic St. Andrews.

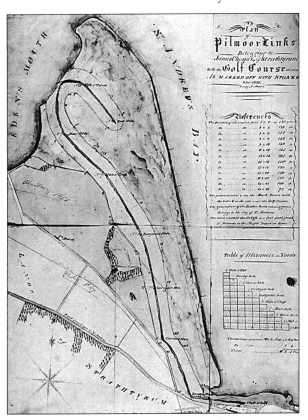

The hegira was sped by extension of the railroad up from Dumfermline to nearby Leuchars, where some of the newcomers built houses. In 1850 they exerted their influence to take the rails on in to St. Andrews. There food, drink, shelter, golf goods, green fees and caddy hire brought such an influx of new money that before long the townspeople were able to buy back their public links from Mr. George Cheape. More, the boom necessitated a marvelous transformation of the Old Course itself.

Originally it was a ten-hole affair which "22 noblemen and gentlemen . . . the Society of St. Andrews Golfers" formalized into a club in 1754, ten years after the Honorable Company of Edinburgh Golfers, who played at Leith, drew up golf's first codified rules. Not until 1834, by gracious edict of King William IV, did it become the Royal & Ancient Golf Club—so named

....

THE OLD COURSE, ST. ANDREWS. *Survey by A. Martin, 1821. Rob Paterson's ball thickened the traffic and doubled the layout.*

because it had been played by Scotland's monarchs since James IV, James V, and Mary Queen of Scots. The holes were strung out in a line from the clubhouse to where the River Eden enters the North Sea.

Upon reaching the tenth green, players would play back to the ninth as their eleventh and so on back, successively, to each hole they had played previously, through the same fairways in reverse. Players "coming in" had priority over those "going out," on the putting greens and everywhere else.

With hundreds of added guttie-whacking starters on the course, this arrangement made for intolerable congestion and hard feelings. The simplest possible solution was adopted. The fairways were greatly widened and the greens were doubled in size, with two holes cut in each. Then as now, more players sliced than hooked their shots, so the British left-lane traffic convention was abrogated. All players out-going and in-coming bore to their right on fairways and greens alike, for the minimum confusion and menace to each other.

Well might the Rev. Dr. Robert Paterson of Binghamton, N.Y. have marvelled to behold two steady streams of golf traffic flowing in opposite directions on the Old Course where, in his youth, there had been but a fitful, eddying trickle. And well might he have congratulated his thrifty fellow townsmen, had he walked through their busy streets, on lifting themselves, as it were, to prosperity by his exotic boot-soles.

The mechanizing of guttie manufacture opened the field to large commercial enterprise. All through the half-century that golf balls were made of the "feelthy stuff" the professionals got increasing competition from companies in the rubber business. One factory-made brand after another came on the market—Eureka, Melfort and White Melfort (brightened with titanium oxide), Henley (marked with St. Andrews crosses), O.K., Clan, Thornton, Ocobo, Musselburgh, to name but a few.

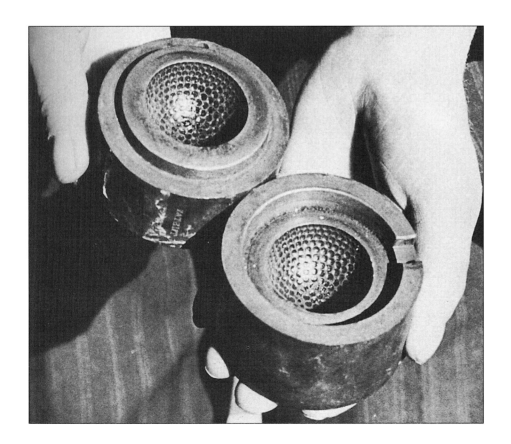

BRAMBLE MOLD FOR GUTTIES. The hands are the late Willie Auchterlonie's.
(G. M. Cowie, St. Andrews)

Historic Spheres from the
Golf Hall of Fame
(Murray)

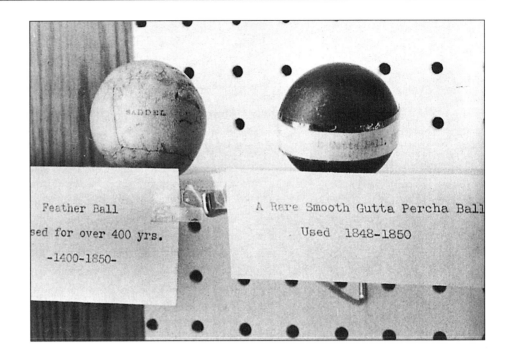

Among the toughest and best was the Silvertown, so hard that it scuffed and even splintered the faces of wooden clubs. The A-1 rivalled the Silvertown for toughness and, in addition, was a floater! Agrippa was the first ball to be given "brambles," bumps like a blackberry's all over it instead of grooves.

All these balls were very light for their size, which was 1.70 inches or more in diameter (compared to today's 1.62-1.68 in.). Re-heating and re-molding shrank and densified them somewhat, and some players considered that this improved their performance. A second remolding made them too small, fit only for practice or for youngsters, and marked down to eightpence each.

The weights of the gutties were designated 26, 26½, 27, 27½, 28 and 29, in pennyweights. These figures covered a range in ounces from about 1.35 to 1.55 (compared to today's minimum of 1.62 oz.).

One bad feature of the gutties was their harshness, of both sound and feel, compared to the kiss of the old feathery which was gentle and sweet until it got damp. In the mid-1880s appeared a yellowish composition guttie called "Eclipse" which contained secret mixtures of India rubber and cork. The renowned writer and golfer, Horace Gordon Hutchinson, who won the British Amateur in 1886 and 1887 playing the Eclipse, wrote: "It goes off the club with the silence of a thief in the night."

Being heavier size for size than the pure gutties, the Eclipse did not carry so far but, being livelier, it made up distance on the run. It bored well into the wind but was more difficult to loft on approach shots. It putted well on greens either slick or slow, seeming by its softness to "creep" over small obstacles that would jar a Silvertown off line. But critics so derided the Eclipse as "the putty ball" that

**Historic Spheres from the
Golf Hall of Fame**
(Murray)

its makers sought to harden it up, and in so doing ruined it. After about 1892 it was forgotten.

In cold weather the gutties got brittle and had a tendency to fly apart. So the rules of golf were amended to cover this contingency. You just dropped another ball beside the largest fragment. Then you picked up all the pieces you could find, took them home, remelted them on your wife's stove, remolded them in your own hand-press. You repainted them by rolling them in your "loof" (palms), and poising them to dry on a triad of nailpoints.

No rule covered another contingency, that of extremely hot weather. One canny Scot who realized this was Willie Park, Jr. In 1894, soon after golf reached America, he teed off for a big money match at Tuxedo, N.Y. on a torrid day in July. When they saw that his caddy was carrying a pail of iced water with a cloth over it, his opponents merely supposed Willie had brought along some cooling drinkables. When they detected him, between holes, exchanging his hot ball for a chilled one from his ice bucket there was nothing they could do about his gamesmanship except play better than he. This they did, and beat him anyway.

The final word in guttie balls—literally the last—was had by England's peerless Harry Vardon. As will be related subsequently, his tour of America in 1900 with his "Vardon Flyer," of purest gum serene, was a triumphal march. It culminated in October when he and the "Flyer" won the U.S. Open Championship at Wheaton, Illinois.

The very next year, Walter J. Travis won the U.S. Amateur using rubber cores, as did the rest of the field. A couple of years after the guttie was as dead as the dodo. 🍂

Ingenuity at Akron

The Great Blizzard of 1888, three nights and three days of snowfall from March 11 to March 14 that lethally buried the entire East, still looms like a grim tombstone in American history. Little noted at the time, but of far more lasting human significance, was a much smaller, happier event which took place in rural Yonkers, N.Y., exactly three weeks prior.

Washington's Birthday was balmy that year, and on it John ("Jock") Reid, a transplanted Scotsman who had made a modest fortune in plumbing fixtures (J.L. Mott Iron Works), entertained some gentleman friends at his Yonkers country home. He had planned his party for March or April, but the fine weather and his impatience to spring a surprise spurred him to advance the date.

The fact is Jock Reid was a "carrier" of that irrepressible parasite which was destined to infest his entire adopted country—the golf bug. A wiry, whiskery, tireless little sportsman who as never quite fulfilled by all his shooting, riding, and tennis, he had commissioned his fellow countryman, Rob Lockhart, to bring back from a visit to their home heath of Dunfermline a set of golf clubs and a few dozen guttie balls. Rob had obliged, and the object of Jock's holiday gathering was to demonstrate his wondrous Scottish playthings to his sporting cronies. This he did so persuasively on that birthday of America's "father," in a cow pasture across the road from his mansion, that in time Jock Reid would be hailed as "The Father of American Golf."

The title is as debatable, if not quite so far-fetched, as Col. Abner Doubleday's to the paternity of baseball, or Adam's to the siring of all mankind. Yet it serves a like purpose, for every human pastime has to "start" sometime and somewhere. And the St. Andrews Golf Club (of Yonkers) which Jock Reid and his friends organized later in that year of the Great Blizzard was definitely germinal. More demonstrably than any other early claimant it precipitated that fallout of golf balls which, sporadic at first and confined to rich men's acreages, has swirled up into today's white maelstrom of 10,000,000 dozen golf balls flying off the clubs of 10,000,000 enthusiasts day in and day out the year long all over the continent.

The St. Andrews (Yonkers) Golf Club was moved and its layout altered four times before it took final root at Hastings-on-Hudson. Actually, it was preceded as an American ground where golf balls were formally struck, followed, cursed at, and prayed over by "courses" dating back a century and more.

A few incorrigible Tories laid out and played some golf holes in 1786 at Charleston, S.C., and at Savannah, Ga., in 1795. Large, muscular Charles Blair Macdonald of Chicago came home from his schooling in Scotland in 1875 and at once went to hitting balls into tin cans sunk on an old Civil War parade ground. (Other Chicagoans thought he was daft.) Even Kentucky (1883), West Virginia (1884), and New Hampshire (1885) have priority claims, to say nothing of Montreal (1873). And so, most definitely, has Foxburg, Pa., north of Pittsburgh at the junction of the Allegheny and Clarion Rivers. Here, in 1884, Joseph Micklen Fox of the old Philadelphia Quaker family laid out some holes on the lawns and meadows of his ancestral summer estate; and then, in 1887, designed a formal little nine-holer, complete with clubhouse (St. Andrews, Yonkers, had but a tent), to which his neighbors came and played at $1 per annum. That Foxburg course has remained in continuous play ever since.

But St. Andrews (Yonkers) was closest to the country's financial, social, and sporting capital, whence its influence and traditions radiated soonest and widest. Within a very few months, similar playgrounds for men (and some women of wealth, leisure and energy mushroomed on Long and Staten Islands, at Tuxedo, at Newport, in New Jersey, and around Boston and Philadelphia. The World's Fair of 1892 in Chicago brought some Britishers who helped bristling, dictatorial Charley Macdonald at last to establish golf near the Windy City, first at Lake Forest on Senator Farwell's lawn, then on a stock farm at Belmont, and finally on a grain acreage (the nation's first 18-holer) near Wheaton.

All the first sticks and balls had, of course, to be imported from Scotland and England; and then dozens of professionals to teach the game, to lay out courses, to make and repair more and more golf sticks, to mold and remold thousands of guttie balls. In 1894, after some intersectional squabbles over early rules and tournaments, the United States Golf Association was formed to govern the game country-wide. The speed of golf's ensuing growth in America can be judged by some turn-of-the-century estimates: 100,000 players on more than 500 courses spending about $10 millions per year on the game.

Under such boom conditions it is not surprising that accurate records on the priorities of golf's birth and rearing in America, and the hot arguments therea-nent, were disregarded at the time. Nor are these pages any place to debate them. But this chapter will now describe in close focus our young country's first basic contribution to the old game. The place was Ohio, that lively mid-sister between the urbane East and brash West—more specifically, the cities of Cleveland and Akron. The year was 1898, just ten years after the Great Blizzard.

By that time, both these places had golf courses—Cleveland's at the fashion-able east end of town on the Lake Erie shore front, Akron's in sheep meadows around the old homestead of the late Abolitionist John Brown in nearby Portage. No golfers emerged thereabouts of a caliber to compare with the top Easterners and Westerners, but two players there made greater golf history than all their contemporaries put together.

Like his father before him, a chunky, energetic Akron youth named Bert (for Bertram) Work labored in the B.F. Goodrich rubber factory at Akron, of which the main output was tires for bicycles and the newfangled motor cars; also over-shoes, rubber blankets, raincoats, and support garments for ladies and gents. It also handled gutta percha, some of which it supplied in bulk to professionals and enthusiasts of the newly imported pasture pastime. It made up a certain number of guttie golf balls in molds of its own.

BERTRAM WORK of Goodrich. Up from the rubber ranks, he encouraged the dilettante Haskell.
(*Goodrich Rubber Co.*)

By 1898, Bert Work had shouldered to the top at the rubber plant, and had taken up golf as much for social as for business reasons. Through it he had formed a close friendship with one of his bicycle tire customers, a young New England sportsman named Coburn Haskell who had come to Cleveland in 1892 and married an heiress, one of the Hanna girls.

Until this book, the annals of American sport were singularly and deplorably devoid of information about this figure who was to make such a lasting mark. All golfers are indebted to his daughter Gertrude Haskell (Mrs. Brigham) Britton of Cleveland, for the following filial memoir she has written expressly for these pages:

"Dad was born in Boston December 31st, 1868, son of William Andrew and Mary Coburn Haskell. He was raised there and went to Harvard, for I don't know how long, but he didn't graduate. He joined a light opera company that went on tour with Gilbert & Sullivan operas.

"From pictures of him in his younger days I thought he was very handsome and dashing—dark wavy hair and a face full of character and humor. When I knew him he was in his forties and fifties and quite portly.

Black Horse Trooper

"His main interests were horses and books and shooting. He belonged to the Black Horse Troop in the National Guard, the Gentleman's Driving Club (amateur trotting horse races in 4-wheel carts, part of the Roadside Club at the Glenville track), and he was a part owner of the Pastime Stables. Their most famous horse was Lee Axworthy, who held a world's record for stallions.

"He was a good shot and belonged to the Cedar Point Duck Club near Toledo, and enjoyed the shooting in Thomasville, Georgia—quail, dove, turkey.

"He had literary tastes—collected rare books, read a great deal, and also collected original illustrations, including works by N.C. Wyeth, Arthur Rackham, Cruikshank, etc.

"His obituary in the Cleveland *Press* (he died Dec. 14, 1922, of cancer), said:

" 'Coburn Haskell was 54 and had been ill many months. He retired from the M.A. Hanna Co. about 20 years ago, and was well known as a sportsman and horseman. He was a member of the Pastime Stables. He invented the golf ball . . . . He was with a ship-building concern before going to the Hanna Co.'

"It was American Shipbuilding, very briefly, I believe. Also, according to my cousin Livingston Ireland, his father R.L. Ireland and mine went into a bicycle manufacturing business together while they were still young bachelors. Evidently his business career lasted only about ten years in Cleveland, and terminated when my mother contracted T.B. and they lived in Switzerland for a while.*

---

* Not understood by his descendants (or this writer) is how or why Coburn Haskell has often been mistitled "Doctor." The Dunlop company's publicity department has even referred to him as "a designing dentist," possibly confusing him with a dentist who did invent the wooden tee-peg. A doctor of no kind was Coburn Haskell, honorary or otherwise, unless perhaps in fun as "Doc" to his cronies, for having made a major scientific advance, or for his solicitous vetting of his horses, dogs, children, and self (he suffered from gout).

"He married my mother, Mary Gertrude Hanna, on June 4th, 1895, three years after coming to Cleveland. His father was a friend of Howard Melville Hanna (who was her father, and a younger brother of Mark), and that is how they met. After Dad's retirement they lived in three places—next door to our present address in Cleveland, in Thomasville in the winter time, and Blue Hill, Maine, for part of the summer. As newlyweds, they rented their first house from John D. Rockefeller, Sr., with whom Dad often played golf.

"By the time I appeared, the golf ball story was that he was the poorest player in his foursome. He thought how nice it would be if he could invent a ball that would sail out beyond everyone else's drive at the first tee, to amaze them—so he did that, with Bert Work's help and connivance."

Stories differ as to just how these two contrasting characters, the sporting dilettante and the factory superintendent, did chance to contrive the golf ball's second revolution. A popular version is this:

One summer day Haskell called for Work at the Goodrich plant to play a round of golf at the Portage links. Delayed at his desk, Work suggested that Haskell take a stroll through the shops. There, on a work table, Haskell saw some piles of elastic thread which the company was trying to fabricate into garters and suspenders. Fingering the stuff, testing its resilience, Haskell (his mind on the coming game) realized that this was the same material (rubber) that went into tennis balls, which were so much bouncier than gutta percha golf balls. When he rejoined Work, Haskell suggested winding up some of that rubber yarn into a golf ball. Goodrich workmen took over and—lo!—the rubber-wound wonderball.

Years after his death Haskell's eldest daughter, Katherine H. Perkins, quoted her father as saying that he first spotted in Work's office "a scrap-basket full of elastic band waste, which he started to wind into a small ball. The ball had become quite sizeable before a slip of the thumb started it bounding across the room. He started on another ball, using more tension, and when Mr. Work appeared he said, 'If you would cover this ball with gutta percha for me, I believe I could win some golf matches.' Mr. Work was impressed with the demonstration of zip and bounce, and told Dad to go ahead and get the idea patented, and that he would put the problem of developing a machine up to his engineering staff. It all worked out . . . ."

In a third version, recorded by the late Dr. William C. Geer, who was Bert Work's brother-in-law and the Goodrich vice president in charge of research, Haskell gave up trying to wind a ball himself, so "some skilled girls were called in . . . . The thread spheres were sent into the factory and covered with gutta percha in a hollow mold. Haskell could scarcely wait for a train to Cleveland to try the ball on his golf course [the Lake Shore Country Club]. He at once found it to be longer in drive and truer in putting . . . ."

Far more circumstantial is an account, preserved unsigned in the Goodrich archives, written by someone in Atlanta*, after a party there evidently about 1920, at which Bertram Work, president of Goodrich, was the guest of honor:

". . . Mr. Work's account of the way the Haskell ball was invented was one particular story I'll never forget.

---

* Bob Jones believes that the author was his own Boswell, the late O.B. Keeler, famed sports writer.

"It was along in 1898, says Mr. Work, that Coburn Haskell . . . was sitting in Mr. Work's office . . .

" 'You ought to be doing something besides just playing golf,' he told Mr. Haskell. 'You've got a lot of ability being wasted. Go ahead and make two blades of grass grow somewhere, or something.'

" 'No thanks,' said Mr. Haskell. 'Golf is all I care about.'

" 'Very well,' rejoined Mr. Work, 'make a better golf ball. Do something for the game, if you love it so much.'

"Now, that was a hunch. Mr. Haskell began to think. After some fairly profound cogitation he said, 'If a good rubber ball could be developed—solid rubber—it would increase the range of the shots.'

" 'Solid rubber won't do,' said Mr. Work, who knew as much about rubber as anybody in the world. 'Too soft. It would yield too much to the blow.'

" 'How about compressing the rubber?'

" 'Can't compress rubber, any more than you can water,' was the objection.

"Mr. Haskell pondered some more. Finally he said: 'Well, if you made the rubber in strips, and stretched the strips, and wound them into a ball in their stretched condition, you could get a ball as hard as you wanted, couldn't you?'

" 'NOW you have said something,' Mr. Work told him, and added that he had better get off his coat and waistcoat and prepare for toil. Mr. Work sent out for a hank of rubber yarn, and Mr. Haskell set to work.

" 'It was a funny sight,' said Mr. Work reminiscently. 'There was Coburn Haskell, perspiring at every pore—it was a hot day—and winding away at the slowly growing core of stretched rubber strands. And just as he would get it about the size of a marble, the blamed thing would slip and the rubber yarn would fly about like a clock-spring released. And he would swear and scramble around on the floor and wind it again, and then it would break loose once more.'

"Mr. Haskell, luckily for golf, was persistent, and toward evening he proudly and wearily presented to Mr. Work a fairly round ball of rubber strands, under considerable tension. It felt firm and solid. 'Now then,' said Mr. Work, 'this thing will have to be covered in some way. The first punch on the exposed strands will set the thing unravelling all over the place.'

"And that was Mr. Work's job. He evolved the cover, of gutta percha then, of balata now, and worked out a plan for heating a slab of 'gutty' and pressing it on to the first rubber core. And when that first ball was finished and painted, Mr. Haskell took it out to his golf club and teed it up, and summoned the professional, Joe Mitchell.

" 'Hit this ball for me,' he requested of Joe. The ball looked exactly like the usual ball, the cover having been pressed in the same mold, and Joe took his stance and walloped it with never a thought that he was assisting at the making of history.

"Out across the fairway of the first hole was a bunker which never had been carried by anybody. It was so far from the tee that only an occasional tremendous poke with the old 'gutty' would send the ball rolling into it, in dry weather. And it was right over the middle of that bunker that Joe's drive with the new ball sailed, high in the air, landing yards beyond.

"Joe Mitchell stood watching the ball with eyes and mouth wide open. Then he let out a yell and began a sort of dance. Then he began to implore Mr. Haskell to tell him if he was dreaming and if not, what was in that ball.

"So that's the way it started . . . . Mr. Haskell may have passed up the notion of making two blades of grass grow where one grew before, but look at what he did for the golfing duffer. He made a hundred thousand grow where one grew previously. And they still are growing."

None of the foregoing accounts gave credit to two Goodrich workmen who actually brought the Haskell ball out of the idea stage and into being.

Emmet R. Junkins is, at this writing, still alive at ninety in an Akron nursing home. It was he, not Haskell, who hand-wound the very first ball to be covered and tested—presumably the ball first driven by Joe Mitchell; and it was he who then taught some nimble-fingered girls how to carry on.

The second workman was John Gammeter, then the genius of Goodrich's tool shop. He it was who figured out a substitute for the girls.

As disclosed in 1951 by Kenneth Nichols of the Akron *Beacon Journal*: "He (Gammeter) was asked by Work if he could invent a machine to wind the balls. Gammeter shifted the wad of tobacco in his mouth and replied, 'Sure.' He was—and is—a sort of Dizzy Dean of mechanics, with full confidence in his own powers.

"Working in a locked room and with the utmost secrecy, Gammeter produced his machine. Its success depended on the use of a core, or center, on which to start the winding."

Before John Gammeter, neither Haskell nor Work had thought of this starting step, but they mentioned it when they applied for their patent on August 9, 1898.

What they claimed was "a new and useful improvement in Balls . . . for use especially in the game of golf." Letters Patent No. 622,834 were granted to them jointly on April 11 the following year. They described a ball of rubber thread "wound under tension . . . upon itself" or on "a central-core-section of relatively non-elastic material," and encased in a gutta or balata shell.

"(The ball) shall possess the essential qualities of lightness and durability and . . . the property of being comparatively non-resilient under the moderate impacts incident to its use, but highly resilient under the stronger impacts."

Translated from the meticulous prolixity of patentese, this language about "impacts" meant simply that the ball should fly swiftly off the club when hit hard, but not rebound too gaily when it struck the ground or was putted.

Two other essential characteristics of all rubber-wound balls to come were also mentioned: ". . . It is an essential feature . . . that the core shall closely fill the interior of the shell and desirable that (it) be confined therein under some compression."

No mention was made of any winding machine because, at the time of the ball patent application, John Gammeter had not yet unlocked his workroom door and brought forth the gadget that would truly and lastingly revolutionize golf. Without it, the hand-wound balls would have failed miserably, through their scarcity and eccentricity.

EMMET JUNKINS, Shop Foreman. His female task force implemented an inspiration. (Taken in 1966, Goodrich Rubber Co.)

JOHN GAMMETER, Master Mechanic. He shifted his quid and went into his shop. (Enlarged detail from a group photo, ca. 1900, Goodrich Rubber Co.

*JOHN GAMMETER'S
BALL-WINDING MACHINE.
1900 patent drawing.*
(U.S. Patent Office)

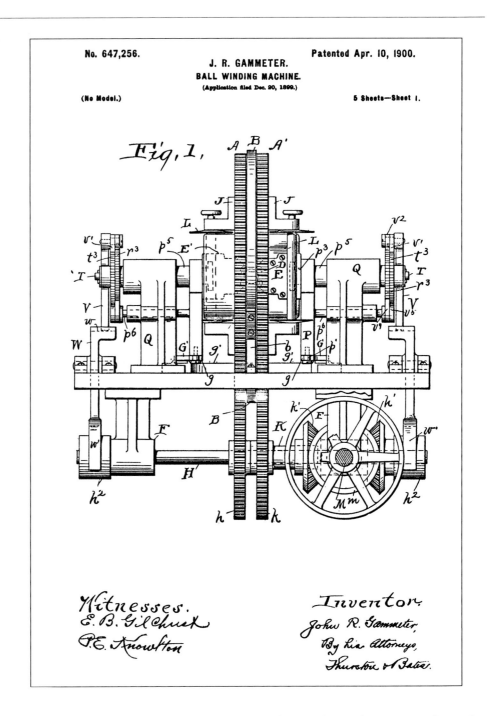

When Gammeter did show what he had wrought, eyebrows must have elevated. The thing was about three feet high and three feet long. It looked more complicated than a 365-day cuckoo clock. It contained more than fifty parts, most of them moving, which it took Goodrich's patent attorneys eight mechanical drawings and seven pages of patentese to describe.

There were "two rotating cord-winders mounted on two concentric circular tracks . . . on opposite sides of a circular frame . . . secured in a vertical position to a bed plate . . . . Each track consists of a cylindrical flange . . . .

"The proximate edges of each flange . . . and associated ring . . . are beveled, whereby there is formed a circumferential V-shaped groove which serves as one part of a ball-race, the other part . . . being formed by a V-shaped groove in . . . the ring-shaped winders . . . mounted on ballbearings . . . . These mesh with two pinions . . . secured to the two concentric shafts . . . .

"To these two shafts are respectively secured the beveled gears which engage . . . a beveled gear fast to the drive shaft . . . . These two winder rings are rotated in opposite directions. Each . . . carries a spool whereon the cord to be used is wound. A needle is pivotally connected to each winder . . . to guide the cord into what I term the 'winding plane' . . . in which the cord is wound upon the ball . . . in a great circle.

". . . The free ends of both needles lie close together, resting upon the ball . . . where they are held, as the ball grows in size, by the pull of the two cords which are being wound upon the ball . . . . The tension device . . . is a small grooved sheave, rotatably mounted . . . . It is subjected to more or less friction, tending to resist its rotation by means of a coiled spring . . . .

"The ball is held in the axial line of the two winders . . . and it is turned to change its position by . . . two parallel rollers . . . . The ball is held with its center in said winding plane between four rollers . . . mounted in pairs . . . . These movements of the ball are alternated and thereby the ball . . . is constantly changing its position . . . with the result that the ball is wound into spherical form."

In other and fewer words, John Gammeter did it the hard way. Instead of spinning on just one he spun on two rubber threads at once, turning the ball constantly in place while applying the threads to it under tension, in a pattern for which his term "great circle" would become a key phrase in the industry.

The whole contraption whirred and growled and gently clanked. Ralph Perkins, who was to become one of Coburn Haskell's sons-in-law and who for a time worked in the Goodrich plant operating a Gammeter ball winder, later recalled: "Imagine, if you can, a machine that would produce a ball of equal and changing radii from a continuous rubber band under equal tension. If the ball ever escaped the four cylinders that kept it revolving, it flew around the shop in a dangerous and unpredictable manner!"

But the thing worked; and it would be years before other geniuses understood it, let along improved upon it. Gammeter was awarded a patent April 10, 1900 (just 364 days after Haskell's) which he assigned to his employers, for whom it long earned royalties.

Until the Gammeter machine was completed, and duplicated many times, golf ball production at the Goodrich plant was painfully slow, limited to the digital efforts of Emmet Junkins' female task force. But even before mass production could be got rolling, the happy inventor displayed and dispensed his creations far and wide. In the Foreword to this book, Chick Evans relates one bit of Coburn Haskell's salesmanship, at the Edgewater club north of Chicago. Haskell was also a member of the Chicago Golf Club, where Jim Foulis was the presiding pro. And it was here that a grave deficiency of the early Haskell balls was accidentally discovered and remedied by Foulis.

The early Haskell was, as noted by Evans, "a fitful ball, going abruptly and irregularly." Although its gutta percha cover was pressed on in the same grooved molds as used for most gutties of the day, it exhibited the same tendency to duck and dart as the earliest smooth gutties had done, before they were grooved.

Jim Foulis happened to possess, and to prefer, a guttie mold of the improved brambled "Agrippa" pattern, with raised blackberry bumps on the ball instead of graving narrow, shallow meridians. One day in his shop at Wheaton, when he was remolding a batch of old gutties, Foulis chanced (without noticing it) to include and to bramble a used Haskell. In play, this ball performed so prodigiously that Foulis cut it open, and discovered what had happened. Unwittingly he had given the Haskell ball the kind of surface its liveliness required to make it fly far and true. Thereafter, all early Haskells were called in to be brambled, and the ball of the future was truly on its way. 🍂

How Haskell's Billies Bounded

First licensees under the Work-Haskell patent after Goodrich were the Kempshall Company of New Jersey and its Scottish affiliate St. Mungo of Glasgow, then Spalding, and then the Worthington Ball Co. of Elyria, Ohio. Retail price set for the balls was $6 a dozen (of which $2 at first but later only 50¢ went to the Messrs. Work and Haskell as royalty). But until John Gammeter's ball-spinner was perfected and installed in numbers, demand so far outran the supply that under-counter prices soared as high as 30 shillings ($7.50) *each* in Great Britain.

When you sclaffed, topped, or only half-topped a shot with the best of gutties, your ball went almost nowhere. The Haskell was so much livelier that even a mis-hit drive or mashie pitch would trickle along to some reward. On well-hit shots, anywhere from 20 to 50 yards of carry and roll were added. Small wonder that duffers, who in those early years of golf outnumbered real players even more heavily than they do today, treasured and coveted the first Haskells as they did their lives and wives.

For reasons that will be explained, the dominant ballmakers of the day, A. G. Spalding & Bros., long held off from taking out a Haskell license. But for this the rubber-core ball might have gone over with an even faster, more furious bang than it did. When the ineffable Harry Vardon toured America in 1900 under Spalding sponsorship, playing exhibitions at 72 courses (and setting records on most of them) before thousands of spectators, he of course used only his own "Vardon Flyer" of finest gutta, also sponsored by Spalding. (Incidentally, the Vardon clubs which he and Spalding introduced at this same time had leather inserts in the faces of the woods to soften the feel *and sound* of impact on the stony gutties.) But there was one amusing, and telling incident on that Vardon tour.

Vardon's touring partner was the mighty John Henry Taylor, who had been British Open champion before him. At the Chicago Golf Club, on Coburn Haskell's invitation, Taylor tried out some Haskell balls. He teed one up at a 220-yard hole on the green on which other players were still putting. To their surprise, and his embarrassment, Taylor's shot ran right up amongst them, obliging him to run after it cap in hand to apologize.

Vardon beat Taylor in the U.S. Open at Wheaton later that year. Long afterwards, in an interview with Henry Longhurst of the London *Sunday Times,* old

Taylor thumped the arm of his chair and growled, "I was too timid, sir! I was too timid! Without a shadow of a doubt I should have beaten Vardon had I played with that ball!"

In a contemporary team match at the Nassau County Club on Long Island, the first ever between British and American collegians, the memorable outcome was decided by a single stroke—or factor—on the third extra hole played by the final pairing. The hole was over 500 yards long and the day a damp one. Though he hit three perfect wood shots the Briton, playing a guttie, got nowhere near home and admitted he could not possibly have done so. The American, even though not a more powerful hitter but playing a rubber-core ball, got home easily with two woods and an iron, holing a 5 to his opponent's 6. The new ball had decided the entire team contest.

Apart from the British view that the new ball was "unsporting" (they called it the "bounding billy," and the Yankees who made, sold, and used it were "bounders"), the Haskell's liveliness did make it harder to control around and on the greens. To a generation who knew nothing about backspin, and who were accustomed to hammering home their dead-ball putts instead of delicately gauging, steering, and easing them in, the new ball was (in Chick Evans' words) "a pill of quicksilver." But at least one patient practitioner had no fear of it, and he did more than any one man to establish the rubber-core's pedigree.

This was Walter J. Travis, a transplanted Australian who, though he did not take up golf until 1896 in his thirty-sixth year, reached the semifinals of the U.S. Amateur in 1898 and again in 1899, beaten each time by the burly transplanted Scotsman, Findlay Douglas. In 1900, Travis won the Metropolitan at Tuxedo and then the U.S. Amateur at his home course, Garden City, this time beating Douglas in the final. When congratulated, Travis remarked, "I am only just learning this game. I am just scratching on the outside . . . . If I don't improve my game by at least another three strokes in another year, I shall be very much surprised."

WALTER J. TRAVIS, ca. 1904. The British didn't care for his putter. (Culver)

As can be imagined, "Old Man" Travis was not a popular figure. He then wore a scraggly beard, long pants, and a Rough Rider hat. He chewed cigars and was taciturn to the point of rudeness in competition. He was short and slender, but wiry and determined. He practiced incessantly. The short game was his forte, especially putting, but in an amazingly brief time he brought his drives up from 175 to 200 yards and more. *Golf Illustrated,* the pontifical British weekly, discovered how. It revealed that in his win at Tuxedo, Travis had played a rubber-core ball made by Kempshall. This was a pulpy, loosely wound thing by comparison with true Haskells, but its very mushiness served the "Old Man's" purpose: it chipped, pitched, and putted much less skittishly than a true Haskell, yet went nearly as far on full shots. What ball Travis played at Garden City did not come out.

But the next year at Atlantic City, in the U.S. Amateur of 1901, where the "Old Man" won the qualifying round and then went on to retain his title, it was common knowledge that he played Haskells. So did 24 of the other 27 contestants, including Findlay Douglas, whom Travis this time disposed of in the semi-finals. After that, so far as America was concerned, the "bounding billy" was in like sin.

Overseas it was different. Beginning in 1901 when the first rubber cores began reaching Great Britain, *Golf Illustrated* was full of quips and cracks about the new Yankee monstrosity. The jokes ranged from the jocular to the satirical to the downright bitter. Examples: "A gutty on the green is worth two billies in the bushes." "A good ball for a tired man." "Next they'll be playing 'golf' with tennis racquets."

As recalled by the present sage of St. Andrews, Laurie Auchterlonie, his father Willy, the sage before him, declared: "The Americans have spoiled the game. That devilish rubber ball just goes too far. The game will never be right again till they come back to the solid ball. When you played with a guttie, the ball said, 'Hit me true and true I'll fly.' But the rubber core, you can hit a dunt anyhoo an' it'll fly. A half-hit shot is a half-hit shot. With a rubber core, it could go in the hole!"

John D. Low, *Golf Illustrated*'s seer of seers, opined that the rubber core would favor weak drivers and timid putters and hence be a detriment to the game, an unfair handicap levied against the strong. It was "too elastic for the short game" to be played properly. "When a club and ball are produced which will make it possible to drive over the road on the last hole at St. Andrews, or to the edge of the bunker at the last hole at Hoylake, our present golf courses will be spoilt, and the evil implements will be ruled out of court."

Mr. Low's editor, however, admitted with some satisfaction that he could get 15 or 20 yards farther with Haskells and Kempshalls, which in his estimation was "not enough to make nonsense of our courses." And he printed (perhaps wrote himself) a satirical parody entitled "Golf in the Next Century," which was as goodnatured as it was fanciful.

In this little masterpiece, the American champion challenges the British to a 36-hole match in the 2002 A.D. Two 18-hole courses are laid out—cross-country— between London and John o'Groats (the northernmost tip of Scotland), up along the west coast and down along the east. Each hole is miles long over hill and dale, mountain and moor, with the cups cut in the bottoms of quarries, sand pits, rocky ravines, and the like.

Both champions are equipped with the latest, most improved American clubs, their explosive heads charged with "refined picric acid." But the sly American brings along, instead of "the standard eight-mile ball," some new ones designed to fly "at least two miles further."

The English champion has the honor and opens on the first tee with a splendid shot off his driver, which is made of pure condensed argon from Jupiter. The American passes him by a mile or more and then reveals, for the first time, that his ball, made from "the red spectra of Mars," will presently be marketed in Great Britain.

Followed by a massive gallery travelling aloft in "aerials," the players line up their shots to the horizon with "spectrographs." The American produces a hydraulic mashie for a spectacular recovery out of a bog. The Britisher plays manfully, getting the most out of every supercharged club in his bag, but one hole after another goes the way the first one did, against him. The American's ten-mile Martian spectral ball is just too much. When they reach the turn at John o'Groat's, the American is 12 up with 18 to play.

After lunch, the American wins four holes hand-running and the match is all over, 16 and 14, on the 22nd green at Edinburgh. There, all hands repair to the Golf Museum, where they muse over exhibits from the ancient days. These include a curious American ball dating back to 1900 called a Haskell and containing a rubber-wound core . . . !

Early in the spring of 1902, Spalding opened a store on Fetter Lane in London, featuring their "Vardon Flyer" guttie golf ball and also offering some of the new rubber-core Haskells, specially imported for Britain's tournament season. (The Kempshall Company missed this boat. Its store in the Strand did not open until three months later.) Spalding's Haskells soon sold out entirely, and it became obvious that many players were planning to try out the "bounding billies" in the Amateur Championship, to be played in May at Hoylake.

Deeply perturbed, the powers-that-were held long meetings to discuss whether or not this should be permitted. In the upshot it was, and as at Atlantic City the year before, more than half the field teed up rubber cores. *Golf Illustrated* reported that "most of the successful players" at Hoylake, including Hutchings, the winner, played Haskells. "All these players seemed to be able to stop the ball with the mashie and [in the final] the putting was enough to make the future of any ball."

In all fairness *G.I.* said that, after failing to win with a Haskell, the redoubtable Mr. John Ball, former double champion, had reverted to the guttie. "Mr. Ball finds the Haskell a little too playful in its manners."

But *G.I.*'s editor, whose bread was now being buttered by Spalding and Kempshall advertisements, interjected: "The Haskell's liveliness, not to say skittishness, is interesting, just as a spirited horse is more fun to drive than a quiet one . . . . The Haskellisation of the golfing community proceeds apace, and the eagerness to possess and to try the new ball has been accentuated by the impossibility of doing so, for love or money, during a whole fortnight. Not a 'Haskell' was to be got. The championship had cleared them all out before there was time to renew supplies from America."

With the British Open coming up next, also at Hoylake, *Golf Illustrated* invited opinions from some of the leading contenders. Harry Vardon, with his gutta "Flyers" to sell, of course condemned the Haskell out of hand. More interesting was powerful ex-champion James Braid's comment: "I have tried three Haskells and split them all, one at the second shot, another playing the third hole, and the other at the third hole of the second round. I found very little difference in the length of drive . . . . Perhaps they run farther but they certainly don't carry as far . . . . They are also more difficult to stop when approaching, and on the putting greens are very liable to jump out of the hole."

Even more emphatic was little Sandy Herd, who had often been best man but never the bridegroom in a British Open. Said he: ". . . A very difficult ball . . . . It drives all right, but that is about all . . . . As regards putting, especially on hard, bumpy greens, it is simply off altogether . . . . I hope all the professionals play with it at Hoylake—except myself. So much for the Haskell."

"The Haskell's liveliness is interesting, just as a spirited horse is more fun to drive than a quiet one."

So the Open of 1902 was played mostly with gutties, and it was full of surprises.

Harry Vardon was so unfortunate as to drive twice out of bounds from the very first tee. Then he settled down, went out in 35 thanks to four consecutive 3's, and brought in a record 72, five shots ahead of the field. His next round was 77 but he was still four strokes in front. Then he skied to an 80, while Sandy Herd shot 38-35 to go three under the maestro. In the final round Herd, whom *G.I.'s* writer observed had often been "wanting in dash and power just at the telling moment," faltered with a 40-41—81. But he backed into the championship when Vardon missed a six-footer on the 72nd green which would have tied Sandy's 307 total. Vardon was forced to share second at 308 with big James Braid.

Golf Illustrated was cozy about the whole thing. In its detailed wrap-up report of that Open, and indeed in the following issue full of other pros and cons, not once did it mention what every golfer soon found out: That sly little Sandy Herd had, after all, played all his four rounds with one *single* Haskell ball, which he had scrounged at the last minute off the disgruntled Mr. John Ball. Furthermore, throughout the final nine this ball was cracked open, with some of its entrails hanging out.

When little "old" Walter Travis went over for the British Amateur of 1904 and won it with a Haskell from Ted Blackwell, longest hitter in the land, all argument subsided over the new and old ball's merits. Instead, great diversionary grousing ensued over the center-shafted "Schenectady" putter which Travis had so magically used, and which the Royal & Ancient soon afterwards outlawed.*

The added distance that Travis got from rubber cores on his long shots would never have been enough in itself for him to win so consistently from more powerful men. What he whittled them down with, besides his putting, were his deadly run-ups from off the green with the relatively straight-faced irons of his day. As rubber cores were wound tighter and tighter and their covers proofed against cracking, they became livelier and livelier and restored to strong hitters much of their old advantage, taking away from the pitch-and-run men much of theirs. For now golf courses began to be lengthened out by as much as 100 yards per hole, with much tougher pars replacing the old bogeys on scorecards. And in further response to the lively ball, clubs were redesigned, especially the short irons.

Their faces were laid back further to throw the ball higher, and the best golfers had to learn to swing more steeply, to "cut the legs off the ball" and stop it quickly after its flight. In other words, as the rubber cores were improved, they ushered in the era of backspin. Mashie faces were ribbed, and then slotted to enhance this action. Between the mashie and the niblic was inserted the mashie-niblic (No. 7 or 8 in today's parlance). Through the fairway the lofted spoon became more and more useful, for its high parabolas held greens better than low-trajectory long-irons like the old cleek.

In a word, by winding up that wad of suspender yarn, Coburn Haskell had revolutionized not only the golf ball but golf itself. After the first decade of the 1900's, the old game's face had been entirely lifted. 🏌

---

* This aluminum putter was designed by A.W. Knight of the General Electric Co. in Schenectady, N.Y., and patented in 1903. Devereux Emmet introduced it to Travis.

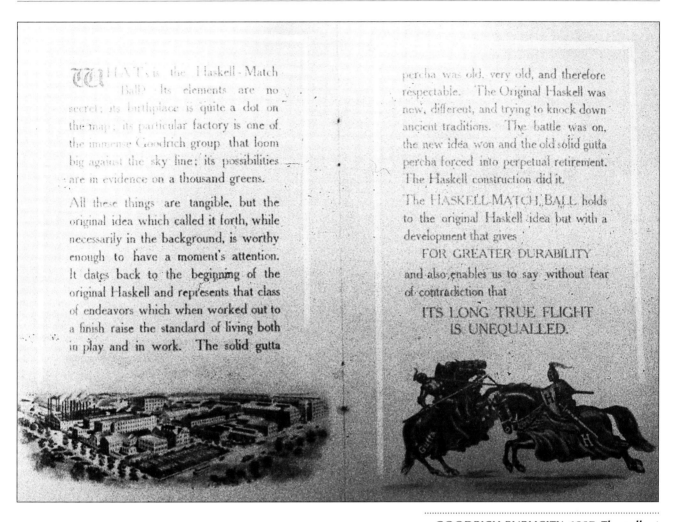

WHATS is the Haskell-Match Ball? Its elements are no secret; its birthplace is quite a dot on the map; its particular factory is one of the immense Goodrich group that loom big against the sky line; its possibilities are in evidence on a thousand greens.

All these things are tangible, but the original idea which called it forth, while necessarily in the background, is worthy enough to have a moment's attention. It dates back to the beginning of the original Haskell and represents that class of endeavors which when worked out to a finish raise the standard of living both in play and in work. The solid gutta percha was old, very old, and therefore respectable. The Original Haskell was new, different, and trying to knock down ancient traditions. The battle was on, the new idea won and the old solid gutta percha forced into perpetual retirement. The Haskell construction did it.

The HASKELL-MATCH-BALL holds to the original Haskell idea but with a development that gives

FOR GREATER DURABILITY

and also enables us to say without fear of contradiction that

ITS LONG TRUE FLIGHT
IS UNEQUALLED.

GOODRICH PUBLICITY, 1907. The gallant Haskell unhorses the lowly Gutta.
(Goodrich Rubber Co.)

Evolution at Chicopee

Before and during the Civil War, organized baseball had been largely confined to the larger seaboard cities. But now, within weeks of that April finale at Appomattox, the returning soldiers took with them to their farflung homes, and to their kid brothers, the bat-and-ball game they had played at their training grounds, in their bivouacs, and in prison camps. They formed baseball teams in every town and hamlet, and challenged each other with no less gusto than they had put into the grim game of war.

The National Baseball Club of Washington, D.C. called itself the best in the land, and in 1867 it set out on a country-wide tour to prove this claim. All comers fell before the mighty Nationals until, in a tournament held at Chicago, a stocky Illinois schoolboy stepped to the pitcher's mound and whipped the champions roundly.

His name was Albert Goodwill ("Al") Spalding; his age, seventeen. His team was the Forest City Club of small Rockford, out on the Black River in cow and corn country. This Spalding lad had been Forest City's top pitcher for two years. He was also the team's captain and, when not pitching, was its sluggingest outfield.

Professionalism was already entering baseball, though frowned upon by many. Among the severest frowners was phenomenal young Al Spalding's widowed mother, a dominant lady of old New England stock. When her son was offered salaries as high as $2,500 by several big-city teams, she would hear none of it. (A parallel with Chick Evans' mother here comes to mind.) So he dutifully took other employment, first in Chicago and then at home in Rockford. But he kept his hand in by continuing to pitch for Forest City, sometimes accepting a modest honorarium.

Through no fault of his own, failure proceeded to haunt every business enterprise to which Al Spalding attached himself. Seven of them collapsed within five years, much to his mortification. If anyone had told him in 1872 that he would some day be known as the founder of one of his country's longest-lived, most illustrious and profitable corporations, Al Spalding would probably have tugged at his boyish mustache in disbelief. If they had further told him that he would be instrumental in popularizing and perfecting in America a precious and purely British pastime called golf, he might have done a backflip.*

No one, of course, told Al Spalding any such thing. And when a prominent Boston insurance company became the seventh on his list of bankrupt employers, he at last contravened his mother's pious wish. He turned baseball pro.

With those great, barehanded Nationals of 1867 had played George Wright, whose equally accomplished brother Harry in 1871 organized the Boston Red Stockings. At George Wright's urging, and that of Henry Chadwick, a newspaperman whose devotion to early baseball earned him a fair share of Colonel Doubleday's "father" image, Harry Wright had kept after Al Spalding to join his new team. When he finally consented, all he did was pitch 301 games in four years, winning 241 of them and four straight national championships for Boston.

In 1876, unhappy about conditions in pro baseball, Al Spalding went with other reformers to New York City where they founded the National Baseball league. He then proceeded to Chicago where he joined a new team called the White Stockings, whom he pitched to the National League's first championship. Simultaneously he did something else which would benefit all sports far into the century that lay ahead.

With his brother J. Walter Spalding, an able merchant, Al Spalding formed A.G. Spalding & Bro. to deal in sporting equipment, chiefly for baseball. They put up only $400 each for working capital, and in that first year grossed a little less than $12,000. But with Al throwing their "official" ball like a bullet in the game's biggest league, and with Walter minding the store, their success seemed assured. After two years they took in their banker brother-in-law, William T. Brown, and pluralized "Bro." to "Bros."

Will Brown so expanded their capital and operations that within a few years they were able to absorb their prime competitors in the East. These were the A.J. Reach and Wright & Ditson sport goods companies, also founded by celebrated baseballers, the latter by Al Spalding's early admirer, George Wright.

Albert Goodwill Spalding's remarkable ability, interest and leadership remained focussed chiefly on baseball to the end of his days in 1915. After taking charge of that first Chicago ball club, he took it and a picked team of other National Leaguers on the first round-the-world baseball tour in 1889. When a second league, the American, was formed in 1900 he saw to it that Spalding made its "official" ball also.

---

* As late as 1875 the American edition of *Hoyle's Games* described golf as: ". . . a celebrated Scotch game, almost peculiar to that country . . . played with balls and clubs. The club tapers, terminating in the part that strikes the ball, which is faced with horn and loaded with lead. But of this there are six sorts used by good players, *viz.* the common club, used when the ball lies on the ground; the scraper and half scraper, when in long grass; the spoon when in a hollow; the heavy iron club, when it lies deep among stones or mud; and the light iron ditto, when on the surface of chingle or sandy ground.

"The balls are much smaller than those used at cricket and stuffed much harder; they are made of horse leather, and stuffed with feathers in a peculiar manner, and then boiled . . . .

"When playing with the wind, light balls are used; and heavy ones against it.

"At the beginning of each game the ball is allowed to be elevated to whatever height the player chooses, for the convenience of striking; but not afterward. "This is done by means of sand or clay, called a teeing.

"The balls which are played off at the beginning of the game cannot be changed until the next hole is won, even if they should happen to burst . . . ."

The motto on A. G.'s desk, "Everything is possible to him who dares," was heartily subscribed to by his partners. While he was otherwise preoccupied, and America's games were proliferating, Walter Spalding and Will Brown enlarged the company's stock in trade to accommodate and dominate sport after sport. In 1890 they founded the American Sports Publishing Co., which issued "official" guides, records and rulebooks, thus copper-rivetting their arbitral position. Their company having been founded by a superstar, they enlisted top performers as buyers, salesmen, and designers of all their lines from the very first. They made "finest quality" the Spalding hallmark on the sound axioms that the best that money can buy will bring in the best money; and that sportsmen, true or tinhorn, will not stint on the gear of their games.

In 1885 they recruited to their sales force a tall, handsome Yale oarsman and footballer, Julian W. Curtiss. In 1892 they sent him abroad to buy merchandise and to learn how English footballs were made. In England, Curtiss saw golf played. Though quite without authority to do so he bought some $400 worth of clubs and balls and shipped them home. Their reception, and his, at the head office was anything but cordial. Golf was so far only a socialite fad in America, beneath Spalding's notice.

Undaunted, Julian Curtiss rallied some friends, laid out five golf holes on his family's acreage at Greenwich, Conn. (which later became the Greenwich Country Club), and set about learning the game. To his relief, the items he had so rashly imported soon sold out and had to be re-ordered. Still, he would scarcely have bet that within only a few years golf accessories would account for more than half of A. G. Spalding & Bros.' total sales and that he would become president of the company.*

Not for four years after the Curtiss coup were "golf sundries" dignified by a page in the Spalding catalog. But during those years a lot happened to golf in America. New courses popped up like mushrooms. In 1894 the U.S.G.A. was formed. In 1895 the first U.S. Open was played, at Newport. Cautiously, quietly, Spalding started making the first American clubs and balls at its Chicopee shops. Its first announcements were given a respectfully British inflection, and were confined to balls and their unkeep gadgets (paint, ball-holder, press, cleaning sponge)

> *"The 'Silvertown' ball, is almost exclusively used on the principal links of Scotland and England, and is universally conceded the best ball made . . . ."*

"The 'Silvertown' ball," said the catalog of 1896, "is almost exclusively used on the principal links of Scotland and England, and is universally conceded the best ball made . . . . We have exclusive control of this ball for the United States." The Silvertown was priced at $5 the dozen. Given second billing was a "highest quality" ball at the same price, branded "Spalding" but without saying where or by whom it was made.

The next year (1897) this second ball was reduced to $4 per dozen while the Silvertown stayed at $5 and was accompanied by the "Henley," another British import, marked with St. Andrews crosses. In 1898, no less than ten different balls, mostly British, were offered in the catalog, again led by the Silvertown. The company was still feeling its way, biding its time. But the groundwork was being laid for a major promotional effort which would benefit American golf scarcely less than the company.

---

* In 1957, President Eisenhower threw out Spalding's ten-millionth baseball to start a game at Washington. The following year, "The General Motors of Sport" sold its quarter-billionth golf ball. inflection, and were confined to balls and their upkeep gadgets (paint, ball-holder, press, cleaning sponge).

Unbeknownst to all concerned, this effort was on a collision course with developments out in Akron, Ohio, and would so remain for four years before it was altered. In 1897, J. Walter Spalding visited England where he took pains to watch peerless Harry Vardon play the game, and to make his acquaintance. Before coming Mr. Spalding had signed up Vardon to inaugurate the new century three years hence by touring America, and to collaborate with the Spalding Company on clubs and balls, with emphasis on the latter. Even while the Haskell rubber-wound patent was being processed in Washington, a Spalding catalog was in the works to clarion:

"THE VARDON FLYER, Vardon's own ball, manufactured in England for him from 'Special Gutta' . . . is without doubt the longest flying ball in the market today. It is a bramble-marked ball. Vardon claims for this marking a longer and truer flight than can be obtained from the smooth markings . . . .

"The man is a marvel; the ball is second only to the man!"

Alas for this brave balloon! Within two years Spalding would have to start shooting it down, along with all its own guttie balls made at Chicopee. As related in Chapter 5, the exploits of J. H. Taylor, Walter Travis, Sandy Herd, and other prominent advocates of Haskell's "bounding billies" were just too much, too incontrovertible. The new American golfing public went mad for a ball that would romp home though only half hit. The gutta percha ball was doomed.

A test suit was brought, claiming that Haskell's thread-wound ball was unpatentable because baseballs had been similarly wound, using worsted yarn around a rubber center, for many years prior. But the judge tersely ruled that Haskell and his licensees were "making golf balls, not baseballs."

After that, though it meant a lot of expensive retooling at Chicopee, Spalding accepted the inevitable and took out a Haskell license. Such were the company's perspicuity, prestige, enterprise, and eloquence that, for the half-century from 1903 onward, the history of the evolving golf ball would be written largely by Spalding, with few innovations of lasting importance by others. This was true world-wide, for Spalding grew to encompass the globe, including Africa, Australia, and New Zealand.

When Spalding at last plunked for the rubber-cored ball it did so lyrically, and in a manner calculated to steal the stage from all predecessors. The catalog of 1903 trumpeted on a full page:

"THE SPALDING 'WIZARD' GOLF BALL"

"Well drove 'twill fly from tee to green"	"It is not an experiment but a pronounced success"

Like the "Vardon Flyer" (and the early Haskell that Jim Foulis had accidentally remolded at Wheaton) the "Wizard's" cover was brambled. It was "manufactured from gutta percha and other resilient materials from a recipe known only to ourselves." This referred to Spalding's absorption of a Massachusetts rubber company named Stoughton which had succeeded in so refining gutta that it came out pure white. And among the "other materials" was balata (bully-tree gum, imported from nearby Latin America instead of far Malaysia) which Stoughton had found to be less frangible than gutta. Spalding guaranteed that Wizard covers would not "crack open or break during eighteen-holes-play [as Sandy Herd's Haskell had done in the 1902 British Open]. If they do, send them back and we will replace them."

But the "Wizard" could boast still more: *The Core Is Wound to a Higher Tension* than is possible on any machines other than the ones we use [the latest Gammeters], and the highest tension must produce the best ball."

For reasons best known to itself, Spalding nowhere mentioned Haskell in these first advertisements. Perhaps this was to avoid offending guttie diehards and anglophiles, to whom "Haskell" was still a nasty word. Or perhaps Spalding thought that the rubber-wound patent might yet be found invalid. But the next year (1904) Spalding acknowledged its debt to the Haskell Golf Ball Co. (a Goodrich subsidiary). Furthermore, though this edition still listed "Vardon Flyers," Spalding "Brambles" and "Silvertowns," all molded of gutta, Spalding went whole hog with this statement:

"American manufacturers are progressive, and the `Wizard' golf ball's 'durability' is as great an improvement in its way as the rubber-cored ball is over the now obsolete solid gutta ball."

By 1906, Spalding had adopted "Dot" as a label for some of its balls, and to its Wizard ("Blue Dot") had added a line called Whites of which one, the "Red Dot," was destined to survive for many years. With one or another of these, major championships of 1905 had been won—the U.S. Amateur by Chandler Egan, the U.S. Open by Willie Dunn, the World Open by James Braid. To blanket the field, that 1906 edition also offered Haskell and Kempshall rubber-cored balls, and echoed a new bit of golf ball mystique invented by the Kempshall Company expressed by the world "click." This was that undefinable sensation which players get when a ball receives the clubface with a sweetly crisp sound and feel, in contrast to the stony harshness of the old gutties and early Haskells. "Click" has stayed in golf's lexicon ever since.

During the guttie era, bashed-up balls had been remolded as a matter of course and thrift. This practice was continued into the rubber-cored era, as we have seen, by pressing new shells onto used interiors. Even mighty Spalding offered this service, at a mark-down to $4 per dozen (from $6 for most of its new ones), or $2.50 if you furnished your own oldies of approved makes and vintages. The 1906 catalog thus kept respectable the ancient art of golf ball renovation. At the same time it put a telling finger on the rubber-wound ball's built-in weakness. It said: "These balls are recovered, not merely remolded, and fresh elastic is added to take the place of the small quantity immediately under the cover *which deteriorates during its life as a new ball.*"

Two areas in which, after Haskell, there was plenty of room for the golf ball's further improvement, were thus clearly defined: 1) toughness of the cover, 2) tensile strength of and tension upon the winding thread. No. 3)— composition of the core, the better to transmit energy and to regulate weight, sphericity, and concentricity—would be studied in due time. Meantime a fourth aspect was investigated by an Englishman, and by him improved and patented. Spalding twigged quickly to what he had done and was the first American maker to license and produce the Taylor "dimple."

No kin of long-hitting John Henry Taylor, one William Taylor of 57 Sparkenhoe Street, Leicester, was an engineer with a keen understanding of aerodynamics. In 1906 he applied for and in 1908 received a Crown patent having "for its principal object to obtain better results in the flight of the ball, in the direction of a sustained, hanging flight giving a flat trajectory with a slight rising tendency, particularly toward the end of the flight, than have been possible with balls of known types.

"Formerly the most common marking . . . consisted in numerous grooves . . . intersecting each other and leaving between them polygonal portions of the spherical surface of the ball . . . . It has been proposed to invert this marking so that the spherical surface . . . consists of numerous ridges . . . enclosing isolated polygonal cavities [i.e. mesh marking, later introduced by Silvertown].

"Another common marking consists in forming the surface with numerous separate prominences resembling those on the surface of a blackberry . . . .

"The characteristic of the marking which constitutes the present invention may be described . . . as an inverted bramble pattern . . . of isolated cavities . . . substantially circular in plan . . . evenly distributed shallow, and their sides, particularly at the lip of the cavity, must be steep.

"Steepness of the cavity is essential to the hanging flight, but excessive depth, besides promoting the collection of dirt, is detrimental to length of flight by offering greater resistance to the passage of the air. Consequently the cavity must be shallow, and the steepness of its walls confined to the immediate neighborhood of the lip.

". . . Preferably the cavities should occupy not less than a quarter nor more than three quarters of the entire surface of the ball . . . diameter . . . not less than nine-hundredths nor more than fifteen-hundredths of an inch . . . .

"Nor should they be of greater depth than fourteen-thousandths of an inch, and in any case their depth should not exceed one-eighth of their diameter."

Inventor Taylor claimed that besides improved flight in cored balls "pitted" as he proposed, "the shell has thereby given to it an added tensile strength and elasticity . . . which tends to prevent bursting, and permanent set or slacking of the shell."

While still continuing its brambled Dots, Spalding introduced its first Taylor-patent Dimples in 1909. The red-white-&-blue dotted Glory was a floater, the Black & White a slightly smaller sinker, both priced at an unprecedented $9 per dozen.*

Without going into Inventor Taylor's more technical explanations and claims, the catalog simply announced that indented balls had longer flight— "because club comes in contact with body of ball . . . straight flight—no ducking . . . flight unimpaired by use (i.e. no protrusion to get flattened) . . . . Increased strength and durability."

Though special attention was not called to it, the small, heavier Black & White was given about 10 per cent more dimples than the Glory, smaller, shallower, more closely spaced. Both new patterns became popular at once, and while some brambled patterns were long continued, notably the Red Dot, brambles would eventually give way entirely to dimples and other recessed markings.**

---

* The 1909 catalog somewhat sadly offered "Vardon Flyers . . . the best solid gutta balls ever made . . . excellent for practice," for $2.

**For a discussion of dimple and other markings, see Chapter 8.

Spalding was trying, through aerodynamic studies, to match its balls to its customers' strength and skills. Ladies and light hitters would do better with large floaters, strong men with smaller, denser sinkers. By 1913, when Spalding brought out its first catalog devoted exclusively to golf, these distinctions were elaborated still further into Large, Medium, and Small balls. A family called Domino (with four dots at each pole) was introduced—the Black (big and heavy), the Blue (medium and heavy), and the Red (medium and quite light). Smallest of all were the Baby and Midget Dimples, the former with two red and two blue dots, the latter with two green and two orange. Baby was of medium weight. Midget was the heaviest little wind-cheater yet designed and caught on immediately in gusty Great Britain, where it won both the Amateur and Ladies' Championships of 1914. In 1915 Spalding transferred the Midget's manufacture to its new factory in London.

The Dimple and Domino families were followed by the dimple Spalding Honors, with four dots repeated six times, at the poles and around the equator for quick identification. These were balls of various sizes and weights with cores of a new softness supposed to give them greater resilience, longer roll. Smallest and heaviest was the Bullet Honor, another wind-cheater, with dots of battleship gray. The 1915 catalog explained:

"Other things being equal, the heavier the ball, the longer the roll." This catalog also carried a somewhat plaintive note: "Don't hit the ball on the [pole] dots every time you tee it up, and then blame the manufacturers if you lose direction and finally distance. Play fair with the ball and it will play fair with you." (Evidently some of the new covers, thinner for liveliness, were coming unstuck at the seam.)

Cores had long occupied ballmakers' attention. Rubber, cork, steel, celluloid, various doughs and pigments were tried. But away back in 1906 one Frank H. Mingay of Berfield, Scotland, had reasoned that "any convenient uncompressible liquid such as water, treacle, glycerine or the like" would, if encapsulated at a ball's center, best receive and translate into motion the energy of a blow on the ball's surface. In 1908, the same year as William Taylor's dimple patent, Frank Mingay had obtained a patent on putting liquid into "a suitable receptable or shell made of elastic material, preferably vulcanized India rubber or the like, and also preferably of spherical shape, and with or without an orifice . . . .

"The liquid is forced or inserted in the receptacle by means of the sharp nozzle of the filling instrument or by means of a needle or piercer.

". . . When the rubber is expanded by the liquid it, of course, by its contractile action, presses on the fluid and thereby insures, practically speaking, a solid although mobile core."

Foresightedly, Spalding had acquired rights to Mingay's invention, but not until 1919 after much experimentation did it bring out a liquid-core ball. The name chosen was "Witch" and its liquid component was glycerine. But no great fanfare accompanied this development. Other ballmakers had already taken up the idea, so the liquid core was not a Spalding "first" like the dimple. Later, for glycerine was substituted a wide variety of ingredients including castor oil, honey, mercury, frozen or deliquescent pellets to obviate the use of sacs and hypodermic needles, eventually even finely pulverized metals and earths, to create "a solid although mobile core."

"Other things being equal, the heavier the ball, the longer the roll."

Compression was yet another field of study for all ball-makers, and here too Spalding pioneered. Its 1915 catalog had explained, "Compression figures indicate the comparative hardness of balls, the higher figures representing the softer, the lower the harder balls.* Hardness furnishes the greatest steadiness in the 'short game.' " In 1919 the catalog listed balls in a bewildering variety of size and weights whose compressions ranged from 8 down (or up) to 4½.

As the 1904 catalog had noted, "the bugbear of all manufacturers of rubber-cored balls . . . has been to produce a cover which . . . will stand any amount of 'topping.' " As compressions went up, and balata covers were made thinner and thinner, balls were getting tenderer and tenderer. Late in the 1920s two distinguished rubber chemists at last slew the "bugbear," or almost did. They figured out how to vulcanize— i.e. harden by heating—a balata cover right on the ball.

One of the chemists was the afore-mentioned Dr. William Chauncey Geer of Goodrich. Geer covers were put on a new ball called "Kro-Flite" of which the 1930 Spalding catalog boasted: "The Kro-Flite ball has completely disproved the old theory that great distance and extreme durability could not be built into the same ball. The combination of great distance and maximum durability belongs only to Kro-Flite. No other ball has it.

This drew fire from the U.S. Rubber Co. whose research chief, Dr. Sidney Cadwell, had independently but almost simultaneously devised a cover-vulcanizing process so similar to Dr. Geer's that it was hard to say who was infringing whom. Several years of argument ensued as to which had priority. The matter was eventually settled by merging the claims (*see Chapter 7*).

The early Geer covers did not in fact combine *maximum* distance with the new durability. During vulcanization, the heat somewhat softened and loosened the rubber-thread windings within, robbing them of tension and the ball of bounce. In driving-machine tests, the Kro-Flite actually fell ten yards short of Spalding's tightly-wound "Tournament" ball with an *un*vulcanized cover (which continued in preference for championship play). Not until the mid-1930s were faster accelerators for the vulcanizing process evolved, which permitted curing at reduced temperatures and creation of the ultimate in thin-covered distance balls. Thereafter the "Tournament" became the celebrated Spalding "Dot" of today.

Meantime, during the 1930s, an engineer named Harry Davis provided Spalding with an interim method of livening up the tough-skinned "Kro-Flite." He molded the ball to a smaller diameter and, after vulcanizing the cover, injected water into its core by hypodermic needle to swell it to standard size with high pressure, thus re-stretching the windings and regaining their resilience. This "needled" Kro-Flite was abandoned after cool vulcanization was achieved.

Another short-lived innovation of this period, invented by Dr. Geer of Goodrich, was Spalding's paintless "Top-Flite" ball. White pigment was added to highly refined balata and the covered ball, instead of being vulcanized, was treated in chemical solutions (tin tetrachloride followed by acetone) to harden its surface to a depth of about .002 inches. The ball was then polished to a high lustre with no further coating. Perfected in 1932 by Spalding's John Baymiller, "Top-Flite" was put into production for a couple of years in Canada, England,

* In later years this obtuse nomenclature was reversed.

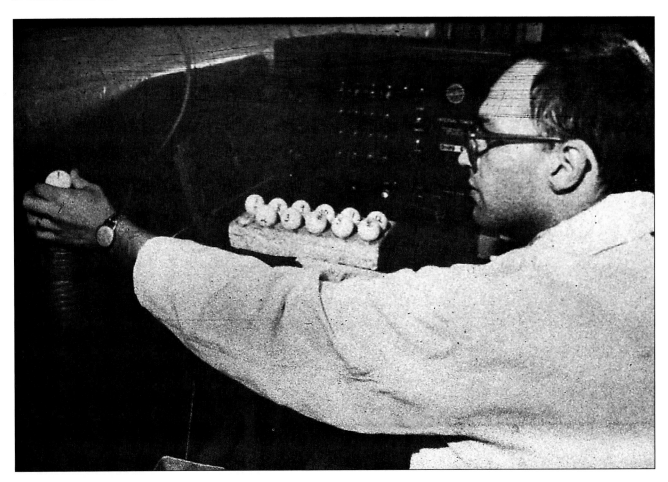

U.S.G.A. INITIAL VELOCITY TESTER. Electric eyes time the ball as it is airblasted through the tube. (Sports Illustrated)

and Australia as well as in the U.S., but its high cost made it a casualty of the Depression.

That 1930 catalog heralding the tough-hided Kro-Flite was full of other wondrous things. In it Spalding could boast: "In the last 16 years Spalding balls have won three times as many major championships—at home and abroad—as all other makes of golf balls combined." It also announced compliance with a new ruling announced by the U.S.G.A. to correct a situation for which Spalding was largely responsible.

So long and lively were golf balls becoming that no limit to their performance seemed in sight. They were reducing par 5 holes to par 4's, and 4's to a drive, pitch and putt. Golf courses were being stretched out *ad absurdum* to make room for siege gunnery. To check this "alarming" trend the U.S.G.A. ruled that after Jan. 1, 1931, no ball would be eligible for official American tournament play that weighed more than 1.55 oz. or measured less than 1.68 in. diameter. These specifications were calculated to reduce the carry and roll of a 250-yard shot by about six yards, and to curb the ballmakers' ingenuity.

The new sphere thus ordained was found somewhat less than fascinating to all but duffers. The "balloon ball," as it was called, so shortened the best efforts and exaggerated the worst mistakes of real hitters that big Jess Guilford spoke for them all when he called it "larger, lighter, and lousier." Particularly incensed were the British, on whose windswept links a smallish, heavyish ball had always been best, and which they would like to play when they competed in America.

So in parleys between the U.S.G.A. and the Royal & Ancient, a compromise was reached. As of Jan. 1, 1932, the British fixed the minimum and maximum for their official ball at 1.62 oz. and 1.62 in., which was the Canadian standard. The Americas accepted 1.62 oz. as minimum weight but retained 1.68 as the minimum diameter. These specifications have stood ever since and they explain what is meant by the "small" British and "large" American balls.

With that flap settled, Spalding and all other ballmakers returned their attention to refining their products within the limits set. By winding them up ever tighter, they continued to increase the balls' range and to batter away at golf course architecture. This progress went unchecked until, in 1941, the U.S.G.A. devised a machine to test initial velocity which, as of Jan. 1, 1942, was limited to 250 ft. per second (plus $2^{1}/_{2}$ %) at 70° F., sea level.

This regulation, still in force for official play, made true a 1935 statement by Spalding's venerable Julian Curtiss, who said: "Golf balls have reached their limit, so far as distance is concerned . . . . If possible we will make them more durable."

And that area was precisely wherein, 30 years later, the next great golf-ball revolution would take place. ✎

The Great Rubber-Core Parade

After Coburn Haskell started rubber cores rolling, there ensued a parade of them that has never stopped, and perhaps never will. In the very year of the invention, one of the men who would lead this parade, a young Scot from St. Andrews with his clubs over his shoulder and a hungry look in his eye, walked up lower Broadway in Manhattan and into golf-ball history.

KEMPSHALL, ST. MUNGO, AND JOLLY

His name was Jack Jolly and a jolly little jack tar was he. Born in 1880 he had gone to sea at thirteen and now, by 1898, had sailed the seven oceans. Having learned the game well—and a great love for it—on the Old Course at home, he took his sticks everywhere he went and played golf around the world wherever Britons had planted it.

At New York he had come down with malaria, and his ship sailed without him. This was just as well for Jack Jolly, for on that next voyage the vessel foundered in a storm with the loss of all hands. Walking up Broadway, Jack was looking for a job, this time ashore.

In a shop window he spied a golf magazine, and went inside to buy it. Whom should he find there but Jamie Smart, a St. Andrean not much older than himself. One good thing led to another, and Jack Jolly was just the chipper, congenial, terrier type to make the most of them. Through his friend Smart, he got odd jobs at the golf courses then springing up in Manhattan's suburbs. He played exhibitions with compatriots already established as professionals and soon made a name for himself. When Alec Pirie, another St. Andrean, in 1901 left his post as professional at the Forest Hill course in Bloomfield, N.J., Jack Jolly stepped into it.

One of the Forest Hill members was Eleazer Kempshall, a Bostonian who had made a fortune in celluloid, chiefly out of color-fast eyelets for shoes, and men's indestructible collars. At his factory in Arlington across the Passaic River from Forest Hill, Mr. Kempshall had gone into making golf balls, the third such enterprise in the land after Spalding and Goodrich. To a large number of patents of his own devising he had added a license for the Work-Haskell rubber-core patent, on which he was trying to improve. Naturally he hired his club's new professional to try out his new models.

Within a year Jack Jolly forever left off manicuring greens, raking bunkers, putting sand into the tee boxes, and biting his lip over duffers. He moved into Mr. Kempshall's plant as the full-time ball expert and country-wide sales chief.

Mr. Kempshall's pet notion of somehow putting celluloid into golf ball cores, or covers, or both, was quite literally a bust. His best efforts cracked or flew apart. So Jack Jolly had a better idea. The main troubles with Haskell's "bounding billies," he opined, were that they were a bit too hard, too light, too lively, and their centers of gravity were uncertain. Jolly figured that he could beef them up, slow them down, and balance them more perfectly by putting some kind of liquid into their cores, and winding them more softly. The problem was how to get the liquid in there and make it stay.

Going out for lunch one day in 1902, Jack saw some baby-bottle nipples in a druggist's window. He marched in and bought the man's entire supply. Back at the plant he filled the nipples' tips to bulging with plain water, tied them tightly and snipped off the necks. Then he had his shopwomen hand-wrap his little waterbulbs with broad rubber tape before putting them on the Gammeter-patent winding machines to receive the tight thread. Then he pressed the wound centers into guttie covers as usual.

Compared to Frank Mingay's injected liquid cores of 1908 (*see previous chapter*) Jolly's contrivance was a bit crude, but he got a U.S. Patent on it and collected royalties for 17 years. And before he was through he would give Spalding and others a good run for their money on liquid cores, and many another kind.

The St. Mungo Golf Ball Co. of Glasgow, named for that old city's patron saint (an Irish missionary of the eighth century) was the Kempshall company's British associate and outlet. It had the biggest golf ball factory in Scotland. In 1910 it bought out Kempshall and put in Jolly as operating vice president of its American subsidiary. In 1915 it built a big new plant on Sylvan Avenue, North Newark, with a production capacity of 1,000 dozen balls per day. Besides its own line of mesh-marked "Colonel" balls, it manufactured some 30 other brands for other people, mostly with liquid cores.

Jolly was among the first to make a liquid core stay put for winding by freezing it with dry ice (solid CO^2). Like others he tried caustic soda solution as a filler to densify it. He changed to harmless glycerine when too-inquisitive people damaged their eyes by cutting into the pressurized sacs. He introduced mercury-filled cores and also steel ones, including a noisy contraption called the "Fast 'n Slo" Colonel which had a ball-bearing rattling loose inside its hollow core, supposedly to impart backspin or topspin as desired.

About 1930 he tried a liquid core with a gooey white pigment suspended in it. When a batch of these proved faulty and were being cut open for examination at the plant, some of the juice spurted onto a bystander's polished shoe. The man couldn't remove the stuff with any amount of washing and scrubbing, so he learned the formula and proceeded to get rich out of "Shu-Milk," a dressing for white buckskins.

In his travels around America selling his wares and obliging people, lively little Jack Jolly became as widely known and as popular as any pro before or since his time. (He survived until 1964, aged eighty-four). Nor was he any slouch with his sticks. He held several course records from time to time, and was runner-up to Alex Ross in the first North & South Open at Pinehurst in

1904. But it was as a promoter and missionary of the game that he shone most brightly.

Besides four of his brothers, he brought over and placed scores of other talented Scots. When he revisited St. Andrews for the first time, in 1936, the members made him an honorary vice-president of the Royal & Ancient for life. Scots still chuckle over how he introduced one of his products to Scotland when dealers there were reluctant to stock them. He took hundreds of his "Jolly Colonels" aboard railroad trains and, whenever he passed a golf links, threw them out the windows as free samples to every amazed player he could see.

The St. Mungo Company at Newark expired in 1932 but Jack Jolly continued making "Jolly Colonels" there for a few years on his own account. Then he conducted a jobber business with his son Bob, who still has the store.

◼ GEORGE WORTHINGTON

Fourth licensee of the Haskell rubber-core patent, after Kempshall, St. Mungo, and Spalding was a dynamic, mustachioed friend and golfing companion of Coburn Haskell named George Cushing Worthington. He lived in nearby Elyria, Ohio, where, with his brother-in-law Arthur L. Garford he (like Haskell) manufactured bicycles; also tricycles, velocipedes and wheel chairs. All these vehicles required tires, so George Worthington was pretty much in the rubber business.

Worthington was inventive by nature and training. After grade school and Andover Academy he had studied mechanical engineering and draftsmanship at Yale's Sheffield Scientific School. With a young associate he had invented a control system for trolley-cars which, when his father refused to back them, they sold outright for a pittance to George Westinghouse, over in Pittsburgh, only to see it installed on trolleys the world around without any benefit to them from the massive royalties.

Next, George Worthington had invented tubular framing for his assorted vehicles, to give them strength with lightness. Here again he missed out on a fortune though tubular frames became universal.*

Undaunted, he bought into his friend Haskell's golf-ball idea because he thought he could improve it; and, before he was through, in many ways he did.

Legend says that one day in 1904, armed with his Haskell license, his golf clubs, and a collection of rubber cores made by Goodrich, Kempshall, St. Mungo, and Spalding, George Worthington strode out on the Cleveland links and drove one ball after another off each of the 18 tees. He made notes about the feel and performance of each ball, and next day at his plant in Elyria had them all sawed in two, to compare their construction. He placed the halves in neat groups on his desk, along with his notes. He then called in his tire production staff and gave them a summary course in golf ball making, highlighted by his own ideas for advancing the art.

---

* One thing that George Worthington did not invent was a pump. His son, James M. Worthington of Rockfall, Conn. says: "He had nothing to do with the Worthington pumps. I have been asked that question 101 times."

He built a small shop for this purpose, which grew over the years into the country's oldest and largest manufactory of golf balls exclusively—the Worthington Ball Co. On its golden anniversary in 1954, the following were some of the claims made for Worthington's contributions to ballmaking:

". . . First to produce a white covered ball . . . first with the diamond stud mesh . . . with the large, thin-walled liquid center . . . first to develop hardness and ball compression tests, first with the dip process one-piece cover; first to design and develop the winding machine, and first to use tape winding."

Few if any of these "firsts" stand unchallenged by other ballmakers, but that is beside the main point, which is that if George Worthington never led the rubber-core parade, he was always abreast of its front rank. For example, it is certain that instead of licensing John Gammeter's winding machine, which was patented in 1900, he devised one of his own, which his son describes as follows:

"[It] consisted of two discs or jaws which rotated the ball placed between them (held together by a strong spring) in such a way that the thread rubber was wound onto the ball uniformly in all directions. Two pedals operated the machine, one for opening the jaws, the other for rotation. They were operated by women who placed adhesive tape on the thumb and first finger to keep the rubber thread from burning their fingers as they kept the thread under tension as it wound onto the ball."

On one occasion George Worthington stepped out so far ahead of the parade that, though he soon had to fall back again, he really put his company on the map. This was in 1910, when Worthington galvanized the golfing world by announcing a ball into whose rubbver core, to enliven it, he said he had mixed some particles of radium!

As everyone now knows, radioactivity could have no effect whatever on a rubber golf ball except to damage your fingers if it were strong enough. But 1910 was the year in which Mme. Marie Curie, the Nobel prize winner, first published her classic treatise on the subject. In the public imagination of 1910, there was no miracle that radium might not perform.

Worthington even got a patent on his gimmick, which he called the "Radio" ball; and he collected from at least one big infringer—for a short while. But when fact caught up with fancy, as it has a way of doing, radium supercharged balls disappeared as suddenly as they had popped up. Nevertheless, as James Worthington recalls: "John Wanamaker, who bought a large quantity of 'Radio' balls, backed my father [in the infringement action]. Fortunately, my father won, and this was the real starting point for the success of the Worthington Ball Co."*

Another patent situation, controlled by Spalding, long prevented George Worthington from marking his balls with dimples. The mesh pattern was pre-empted also. But these were no impediments to a man of his inventive powers. Some of his happiest hours were spent in dreaming up and designing cover patterns of his own, which varied over the years in a dizzying array.

---

* Quite predictably in our present era of nuclear miracles, at least one fanciful manufacturer advertises (at $25 for "a set of 12") an "atomic" golf ball. Claiming to "own its source of cobalt 60 under AEC license," this genius says: "Through the use of Gamma radiation, special steel center of ball has been energized for livelier performance, greater distance! Tougher cover, too! Harmless, of course—except to opponent's game!"

He started in 1904 (four years before dimples and eight before mesh) with a diamond stud raised within a diamond crater. This was soon followed by a circular crater around a diamond stud, then by a smaller diamond crater with no stud. Next came still smaller and fewer empty diamonds, and then star-shaped craters, Next came oblong raised blobs like dumbbells, linked in pairs; and next, some little buttons which anticipated if they did not inspire U.S. Rubber's early "Nobby" design.

The man's ingenuity was boundless. Whether he was always aerodynamically sound is not a matter of record, for like all ballmakers George Worthington kept his test data close to his chest, and his assistants in remote Elyria were not as migratory and unloyal as those of some other ballmakers. But the variety of Worthington's dozens of patterns over 50 years, ending up with the standard dimple, was fascinating. There were assorted meshes, a mesh enclosing bars, a reversion to the bramble, recurrences of the diamond motif, and one masterpiece in which substantial domes were enclosed by ridges, like eggs in a carton. All this virtuosity paid off, not in any one celebrated ball under Worthington's own brand, but in a huge volume of balls spun and molded for other people under names and in patterns of their choosing. Worthington always made more balls for other people's imprint—pros, clubs, merchandisers—than for its own. Thus, for example, when the Wilson meat-packing company of Chicago decided in 1914 to branch out into sporting goods,* starting in a little red schoolhouse near the stockyards, Worthington was ready and willing to supply its golf ball line (later shared by U.S. Rubber).

No reproduceable print or negative can be found of the 50-year succession of Worthington golf balls published in eulogy by the *Sporting Goods Dealer* (St. Louis) in 1954. But some idea of their variety can be gained from the photos in this chapter, of two dozen assorted oldtimers, obtained from the Atti Engineering Co. of Union City, N.J., which for many decades has made cover molds for most U.S. ballmakers large and small, custom and trade. Among those strange and forgotten brands and patterns—Burbank, Cavignac, Mohansic, V.L.&A., Bull's Eye, Gargoyle, Gem, Long Flash, etc.—there are doubtless many Worthington products in disguise.

The Worthington Ball Co. was absorbed in 1966 by Victor Comptometer Corp. and moved to Morton Grove, Ill. There, Victor's new 80,000-sq. ft. golf-ball plant is one of the world's most modern. It is currently producing balls at an annual rate of 1,400,000 dozens, and is capable of two million dozens, one-eighth of foreseeable world demand.

██ How the British Stepped In

Word of the outrageous new Yankee golf balls crossed the Atlantic long before the British got their hands on one. Just who conveyed the first description before or after Haskell's patent was granted and published in 1899 is not

---

* Contrary to canard, Wilson went into sports equipment as an expression of faith in a healthy, vigorous, fun-loving America, not as an outlet for the hides of its slaughtered creatures. That story gave rise—considering the horsehides on baseballs—to rude quips about the true nature of some of Wilson's "beef." Fact is, Wilson bought its pig, sheep, calf, cow, and horse leather from tanners, who bought their raw hides in the open market, and still do.

known. It could have been any one of a dozen or more transplanted Scottish professionals, writing home in horror. The first English pro known to have tried out a Haskell was J.H. Taylor, when he toured the U.S. with Harry Vardon in 1900 and made his own eyes pop with one shot he hit (*see chapter 5*).

However much they were deplored and derided by British purists, the construction of the "bounding billies" was well understood by British ball-makers before Spalding and Kempshall started selling them in London and they won the two big British championships of 1902. After that, with all golfers clamoring for rubber cores, it is not surprising that, regardless of patent considerations, some of the bolder British ballmakers moved to cash in.

Elastic thread was in good supply. So were rubber for cores and guttie for covers. Lack of winding machines was no great obstacle. In fact, the traditional British preference for hand-made goods over machine-made converted this lack into a virtue, even worth advertising. When the Haskell Golf Ball Co. turned its attention to the British market and its patent status there, it found competitors already in the field with a variety of brands like "White Heather," "Tube Core," "Farsure Meteor," "Elastine," "Rompo," "White Imp," and a family called "Kite," "Eagle," and "Hawk" (all birds of prey).

These last three were among the best sellers, so in 1905 Haskell's lawyers zeroed in on the makers—Hutchison, Main & Co.—with an infringement action. The case was heard by Mr. Justice Buckley who, after eight days of exhaustive argument, found for the defendants, with costs to Haskell. The next winter an appeal was heard by Lord Justices Romer and Cozens-Hardy, who entirely upheld the lower court. In this upshot it turned out that not the alleged infringers were on trial but the Haskell patent, which was found invalid in Great Britain on the ground that at least two prior users of the claimed novelty had been shown. Herein lay some forgotten golf-ball history.

A Captain Stewart, R.N. (retired), testified for the defense that away back in 1873-79 he had, as an enthusiastic amateur, wound rubber bands around various cores, under tension; covered the resulting spheres with gutta percha; and played many of them as golf balls "in public," even selling some to friends for a shilling each. Prosecution tried to suggest that, at seventy-one, Captain Stewart's memory if not his veracity might be faulty. This the Justice would not concede. He thought that the old boy had stood up jolly well under a barrage of technical questions, more than 500 of them.

A second witness was more devastating. He was Willie Fernie, most distinguished member of that great golfing clan, long the pro at Troon, winner of the British Open in 1883 and second five times since.

Willie Fernie said that in 1893 his brother George had secretly cut some slender triangles, 3/8-inch wide at the base, out of burst football bladders. He had stretched these rubber bits over wee balls of cork, keeping them in place under tension with "Irish" (linen) thread as he built up spheres to golf-ball size. These he had dipped repeatedly in melted gutta percha, and finally pressed them in patterned guttie-ball molds.

Willie said his brother George had made at least two dozen golf balls thus in 1893 and sold them for eightpence as "remades." But the venture was not successful. The Fernie balls soon cracked open. So George had told and sold his secrets to Brother Willie and, after a time, had gone to live in Ireland. Subsequently he (Willie) did little about the matter until after the rubber core furor of 1902. Then, encouraged by Hutchison, Main & Co., he had revived the rubber-core art, Fernie style, and in 1904 had obtained a "provisional" patent on it, unspecific and good for only one year. Even so, the pedigree of the "Kite," "Eagle" and "Hawk" balls could be viewed as antedating Haskell's inspiration of 1898 by at least five years.

Willie Fernie's surviving son Harry, now seventy-three but still the pro at St. Anne's-on-Sea in Lancashire, says: "I was only twelve years old at the time but my father's evidence is clearly in my mind. His ball was hand-wound. The center was cork, and the winding was broad elastic. The cover was fairly thick." Harry Fernie recalls that his father never did get a definitive patent, and therefore no royalties. But neither, in Great Britain, did Coburn Haskell.

Also present at those Haskell hearings was Horace G. Hutchinson, a top English amateur and foremost golf writer of the day. He was called as a witness for the plaintiff because he had been the first man to play the Haskell ball in England, and was loud in its praises. Writing more than ten years later* he recalled:

"I suppose other trials are sometimes as humorous, but I could not have believed that there could be such good entertainment as I found in that court. The judge, Mr. Justice Buckley, was not a golfer, yet the way he kept his eye on the ball . . . was above all praise . . . . For there were many balls of different sorts brought into court . . . . They were constantly running off the judge's desk, and tumbling and jumping about in the body of the court, where the learned gentlemen knocked their wigs together as they bent down to search for them.

"There was an old lady who said that she had made balls which were practically identical with these Haskells all her life—balls for boys to play with. So she was commanded to go away and come back with her apparatus and to show in court how the balls were made.

"She returned, and it appeared that, after some winding of thread about a core, the next proceeding was to dip the balls in a molten solution of some boiling stuff that smelt abominably. She cooked this up in court, and the whole business was very suggestive of the making of the hell-broth of the witches in *Macbeth* . . . .

"The balls were apt to escape from the old lady when they were half cooked, and to go running around the court where the barristers, retrieving them, got their fingers into the most awful sticky mess, and their wigs seemed to be the appropriate places on which to rub the stickiness off . . . ."

Some nice *obiter dicta* in what *Golf Illustrated* headlined as "The Great Ball Patent Case" were enunciated by Lord Justice Cozens-Hardy. Appellant's counsel (Mr. Astbury, K.C.) had argued that, in contrast to the Haskell ball, which had sold as high as £1 per copy when in short supply and was "the greatest invention since the pneumatic tyre," the earlier, primitive rubber cores were commercial flops. His Lordship observed that the latter had doubtless suffered "lack of success . . . because . . . sturdy champions of the game scorned to avail themselves of expedients designed for the use of incompetent persons."

In 1906, such sturdy scorn was rare. Even proud Harry Vardon was weakening. After the lowering of the bar, and all that publicity, the rubber-core parade that had started in America became in Britain a headlong rush. With the design declared open to all comers, every one and his aunt got into the act.

---

* In *Fifty Years of Golf*—H.G. Hutchinson (1919).

New rubber cores sprouted like mushrooms, most of them ill-made. "There were," says Laurie Auchterlonie, "literally hundreds of them, a new one nearly every week."

Some that Laurie remembers were the "Pimpernel," "Scarlet Runner," and "Iris," brought out by McDaid of Edinburgh. Cochrane of Edinburgh produced "Challengers." Leham of Willowsden Green called his offerings "Zenith," "Zenith Orb," and "Bogey" (for the Colonel whom duffers adored). Metropolitan Ball Co. of London had a pair of brands niftily named "Pal," and "Opal." Wilfred Short thought he had something tremendous when he announced that into his "Gravitator" he had put "a core of Indian Ox-horn, instead of celluloid."

Martin of Birmingham, where the golf-ball industry was centering, scored well with "Zome" and "Zodiac," two of the best. Their putty core was dipped repeatedly in latex to form a multi-walled sac, then wound with oiled rubber thread, then dipped again in rubber to form another sac, then wound again and given a gutta cover surprisingly thin for that era. And in 1908, Martin announced an "important invention": a ball named "Marzo" whose cover was made of rubber and gutta tape, vulcanized and pressed into a wound center containing "1,152 ft. of tensioned rubber."

Even austere Willie Auchterlonie, who had declared the rubber core a menace (and who regarded Willie Fernie's testimony at the Haskell hearings as unlikely, to say the least), surrendered in the end. In his shop at St. Andrews he wound some curious balls patented by a man named Singer, of which the novel feature was a buckshot-size steel ball-bearing rattling loose inside a round kernel of vulcanized gutta percha. This was hand-wound with wide rubber tape and then pressed into a gutta cover a quarter-inch thick. These balls were called "Ortogo" because they "ought to go," which they soon did—the way of other primitives.

With their long headstart in America, the Haskell, Spalding, and Kempshall balls held an advantaage over all early British rubber-cores except St. Mungo's. Affiliated with Kempshall, this old Glasgow firm had had early access to the Haskell mysteries, and its "Colonels," "Admirals," and "Captains" were favored by Britons if only for their names. But even these leaders were presently overhauled by a company which had quietly abetted Messrs. Hutchison and Main in stymieing the Haskell patent.

This was the India Rubber & Gutta Percha Co. (which later became British Goodrich, and then British Tire & Rubber Co.). Its plant was in the industrial area of Woolwich (near London) called "Silvertown," and that was the name it had given its great ball of the guttie era (see Chapter 3).

Presiding genius of Silvertown in those years was an eminent scientist named Dr. Rollo Appleyard. His understudy, who after technical schooling had been apprenticed to the company in his early teens, was a stalwart, square-chinned London youth who would do more to, and for, British golf balls than any Englishman before or since.

ALBERT EDWARD PENFOLD, 1884-1941. Than he, no man did more for British golf balls. (Penfold)

▇▇ THE PRODIGIOUS PENFOLD

His name was Albert Edward Penfold, born in 1884 and loyally christened in honor of the then Prince of Wales. The young man's mental muscle seems to have been as strong as those in his corpus, for besides playing good golf as well as the "manlier" games, he became a master of chemical analysis and innovation. His job under Dr. Appleyard was in research and development, chiefly inspecting and refining the raw materials imported world-wide for the company's many products, from "tyres" to erasers.*

Throughout the long technical Haskell hearings, young Albert Penfold sat by attentively. He learned a lot, perhaps even more than he had from Dr. Appleyard, whose specialty was gutta percha. After the case was won, Silvertown took its time preparing its own entry in the rubber core stampede, but when it did, in 1911, young Albert Penfold was put in charge.

To echo its great guttie's name, the title "Silver King" was chosen. To echo the old ball's cross-hatched cover, Penfold designed a pattern of parallel ridges circling the ball at right angles to each other, but with the square areas between ridges *recessed* about .013 in. (whereas the old "Silvertown's" squares were *raised* between parallel grooves.)

Such a pattern had been described, but not claimed, by William Taylor in his patent for round dimples. In 1912, Penfold got a patent on his "mesh" pattern, and also on a "lattice" design wherein the longitudinal ridges were slightly curved. He assigned his "mesh" to his employers but retained rights to his "lattice."

Also in that period, Albert Penfold succeeded in so refining gutta percha as to render it snow-white (as Stoughton of Massachusetts had done) and so tough that it could be molded onto the wound core much thinner and tighter than before. For his core's liquid center he used a thin-walled latex balloon (like Jack Jolly's bottle nipple) instead of Mingay's thick-walled, injected sac.

The resultant "Silver King" fully lived up to its name in performance and popularity, on both sides of the Atlantic. It reigned until long after Albert Penfold left Silvertown in 1919 to proceed to further personal triumphs.

In 1888 a Scottish veterinarian who had settled in Belfast equipped his son Johnny's tricycle with some pneumatic rubber "tyres" of his own invention. This event, in the infancy of the bicycle and automobile industries, led to prodigious developments in the rubber trade. For the vet's name was John Boyd Dunlop, and the concern which some Irish cyclemakers founded to patent and exploit his invention swiftly grew into vast Dunlop Rubber Co. Ltd. with a home base in Birmingham, plantations in Malaysia, and (today) factories around the globe.

Dunlop joined the rubber-core parade in 1908, two years after Willie Fernie cleared the way. Its first products were only so-so and are long-since forgotten—the "Orange Spot," "Junior," and "V." Its "29" and "31" of 1912 were better. And then, in 1919, Dunlop secured the services of Albert

---

* "During his second visit to America, Columbus was astonished to see the native Indians amusing themselves with a black, heavy ball made from a vegetable gum. Later explorers were equally impressed by these balls, and an historian of the time remarked that they rebounded so much they appeared to be alive. Three centuries elapsed before the material was brought into commercial use . . . to rub out lead pencil marks—hence the name india-rubber or rubber." —*Encyc. Brittanica.*

Edward Penfold. He directly set about evolving a ball to rival his famous "Silver King."

He built into it further refinements of core, thread, windings, and cover, and he called it "MaxFli," meaning maximum flight. What probably most enabled it to zoom Dunlop from near obscurity to front rank as a ballmaker was its creator's "lattice" cover marking, contrived by him years before.

Penfold left Dunlop in 1927 to form his own research company, Golf Ball Developments Ltd. But the "MaxFli" flew on. With ever-sharpening technology, Dunlop thinned its skin and tightened its windings still further, and in 1934 brought out the "MaxFli 65," commemorating a record-breaking round fired by Henry Cotton in the British Open at Sandwich. Cotton's record still stands, and the "MaxFli" still flies, little changed after 33 years.

Albert Edward Penfold put yet a third major rubber company on the golf-ball map when in 1928-29 he overhauled and re-designed the North British Rubber Co.'s plant near Edinburgh. But by then his own plant, in Bromford Lane at Birmingham, demanded more and more of his attention. In 1930 he brought out a "latticed" ball bearing his own name which was an instant hit on both sides of the Atlantic. It was the third of his creations to gain top billing in the U.S., where it commanded a 25¢ premium over other balls even during the Depression. The Penfold was the first ball to be sold exclusively to, and through, professionals.

Albert Edward Penfold's career was cut short in 1941 when he was drowned off the Irish coast in the torpedoed *Siamese Prince,* on his return from a war mission to the U.S. His son and namesake continues the family business in the forefront of the golf-ball industry by dint of following Penfold Sr.'s guidelines: refined research, precise workmanship, quality control.

INGREDIENTS OF THE DUNLOP "65."
(Dunlop Rubber Co.)

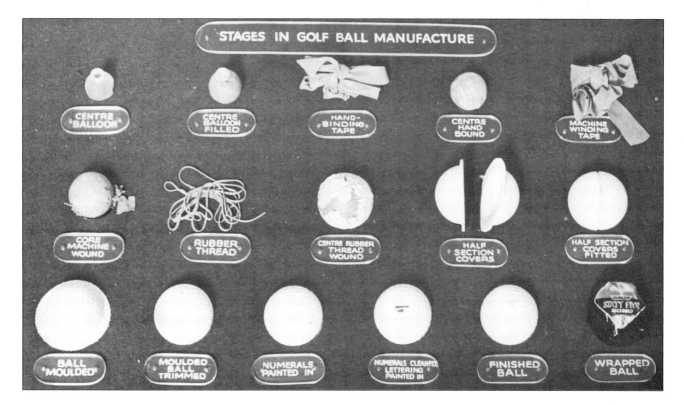

■ THE LATTER-DAY AMERICANS

In the second decade of the new century, events conspired to stimulate golf and the making of rubber-core golf balls in the U.S.A. Courses had continued to multiply, and British professionals continued to swarm into the country. Even the White House lent a hand. Theodore Roosevelt had been a tennis-playing President but William Howard Taft, despite his corpulence, enjoyed ambling around the fairways and so, more effectively, did angular

Thomas Woodrow Wilson. Photographs of chief executives playing it gave the game a new dignity.

Still stronger stimuli came from two American boys who had grown up beside golf courses, learned the game as caddies, and now proved that golf properly belonged to the common people (as in Scotland), not just to the privileged few; nor to the middle-aged, nor to professionals.

Jerry Travers and Bob Gardner had proved that golf belonged to the young by winning the Amateur from their elders in 1907 and 1909 at twenty-one and twenty, respectively.* But both these boys had wealthy fathers. Now upon the scene came Charles "Chick" Evans, Jr., who, to preserve his amateur standing, had quit caddying at Edgewater the day before his sixteenth birthday in 1906, and gone to work as an office boy on the Chicago Board of Trade.

Thereafter, in his late teens and early twenties, Chick burned up the nation's courses with a game that was unbeatable, except on the putting greens. "The kid with the grin" won everything in sight regionally, with a style sweeter than any since Vardon, and until Jones. But time and again he blew national championships, until 1916. Then, at Minikahda and Merion, he won both the Open and the Amateur, the first time this had ever been done (and the last, until Jones in 1930). Chick's record 286 in the Open stood for 20 years.

CHARLES "CHICK" EVANS, JR. U.S. Open and Amateur Champion, 1916.
(Western Golf Assn.)

The emergence of Francis Ouimet, another amateur, was even more sudden and dramatic. In 1913 at Brookline, aged but twenty, he stepped "across the tracks" onto the exclusive Country Club course where he had carried bags and, in a sensational play-off, whipped Harry Vardon and Ted Ray, the two top British pros, for the U.S. Open. The next year Francis won the U.S. Amateur (beating Travers).

Heroes like these spot-lighted golf, made new golfers, sold more and more golf balls.

---

* And Jerry had repeated in 1908.

As the Haskell rubber-core patent approached its 1916 expiration, the nation's largest rubber company bestirred itself to review the rubber-core parade. The United States Rubber Co. (now UniRoyal) was, like other turn-of-the-century "trusts," an amalgamation of many small companies put together by dominant financiers, in this case by Charles R. Flint, a shipping magnate and importer of Brazilian crude rubber. Its mass products were footwear, clothing, and such mechanical adjuncts as hoses, belting, bicycle and then auto tires.

Winding little golf balls with rubber thread had seemed comparatively small potatoes, and U.S. Rubber had had no desire to pay royalty to its big independent competitor, the Goodrich Company, under the Haskell patent. But in 1915, in view of the impending expiration, the manager of U.S.R.'s plant in Cleveland, Haskell's home town, sparked some promising experiments with golf balls, and presently the company employed Ernest S. Bradford, an astute market analyst, to survey the field.

Bradford's findings, dated Feb. 6, 1917, give us a clear picture of the then state of the game. There were 1,200 courses in this country alone, used by 250,000-300,000 players. They were buying more than a half-million dozen balls from only ten manufacturers. These were priced from 50¢ to 85¢, and demand was outrunning supply. Bradford went into great detail about the qualities most popular in golf balls, and how best to package, advertise, and distribute them. Much impressed, his big client promptly moved its development work from Cleveland to its sundries plant in the old Banigan shoe factory at Providence, R.I., and went full out into golf balls.

Experts from Leicester, England, were imported to show U.S.R. how to make the finest elastic thread. And on the mechanical staff was just the man to figure out how best to wind it without paying royalty on Gammeter machines, the patents for which still had some time to run. This was Harry Z. Cobb, opposite number of Goodrich's ingenious John Gammeter and long

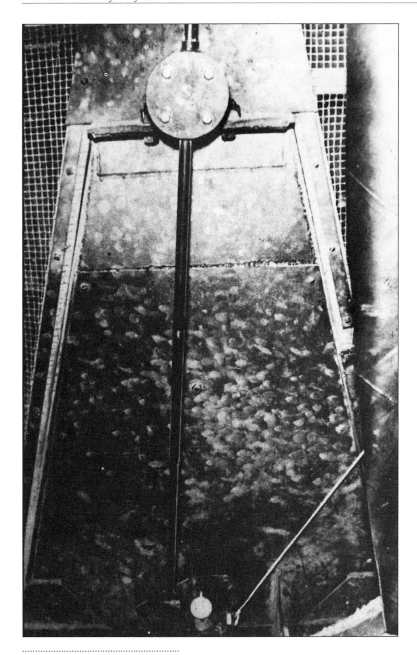

UNIROYAL'S TESTING MACHINE. It's strength is as the strength of ten. (UniRoyal)

his bitter rival. Time and again these two had, in solving their employers' fabricating problems, come up independently with devices so similar that litigation had ensued.

This time there was no conflict. Harry Cobb devised a ball-winder entirely novel, and much simpler than Gammeter's. Instead of carrying two strands of thread around a positioned core, Cobb rotated his ball with four little rollers, causing it to wind itself up in a single thread under tensions readily controllable. Moreover, he made possible a "basket-weave" pattern whose interstices, more open than in Gammeter's "great circle" pattern, would give the cover a firmer grip when molded onto the wound core.

Having no license for the Taylor dimple patent as exploited by Spalding, U.S.R. was content to mark the cover of its first golf ball with raised buttons, simulating in miniature those on its successful Nobby Tread tires, and to christen it the "U.S. Nobby." For the core it first used solid rubber, but then switched to a steel pellet and renamed the ball the "U.S. Royal." This engendered a quaint controversy.

U.S. Rubber's first test professional was George Fotheringham, a pioneer of golf in South Africa (and the present writer's first golf teacher, at Indian Hill in 1915). Every week George took the night boat up from New York to Providence for two days of hitting experiments. Ever the blunt Carnoustieman, George speaks today (at eighty-four) with wry amusement about his and the technicians' sessions with that early "Royal."

To begin with, George never did like the name. He considered it out of place on any American ball. Secondly, he thought the steel center made the ball feel dead. When challenged on this, he said, "Very well, blindfold me! Mix up a dozen Royals with some Spaldings, Dunlops, Silver Kings, and whatever, and tee them for me without saying which is which. I'll pick out the Royals every time, just by that heavy feel." And so he did.

Thus it was that the "Royal" was soon switched permanently to liquid centers, using water, oil, or a metallic paste, frozen stiff before winding—but the name was never changed. In fact, the company is now named UniRoyal.

George Fotheringham—spare, sandy-haired and circumspect—left U.S.R. in 1922 to become professional at the Norwood club in New Jersey and later at nearby Hollywood, where he is still professor-emeritus. He was succeeded at Providence by a character who could not have been more contrasting—a swarthy, slick-haired, brash embodiment of the racy 1920s named Walter Hagen, then just entering his great winning streak of four British Opens and five P.G.A.'s within seven years. To the U.S. Royal "the Haig" (as in Haig & Haig) contributed massive publicity, but little technology. His technique both off and on the course was purely personal.

Joseph Brogden, then head of U.S.R.'s thread department and later superintendent of the whole "Royal" ball works, had the duty of chaperoning Hagen on testing and exhibition trips to Atlantic City, Pinehurst, Florida, and wherenot. Himself a life-long non-drinker and non-swinger, Joe Brogden recalls vividly, but not with pain, two of Hagen's salient characteristics: He was seldom less than a half-hour late for any appointment; and when they arrived at any hotel it was seldom more than five minutes before local ladies started phoning for gallant "Sir Walter."

Hagen eventually blossomed out with a ball company of his own, backed by the Kelsey ("clincher") wheel and tire people of Ohio. But by that time the last thing U.S.R. needed was flamboyant representation. From the first the company had recognized that, of all rubber products, cored golf balls require finest precision in the 80-odd operations required to put one together.

Perfect concentricity, the exact formation and positioning of the wound center, is the heart of the matter. To check on this, U.S.R. engineers exmployed X-rays, and in 1926 the company scored a triumph by publishing internal photographs of six "Royals" beside six other makes. The hearts of all the "Royals" showed up perfectly round, and right where they belonged. The others showed hearts more or less deformed and misplaced. For the next two years the "Royal" advertising theme was, "You can't putt straight with an egg."

Mention has been made of how Goodrich's Dr. William Geer toughened the cover of Spalding's "Kro-Flite" in the late 1920s, and then U.S.R.'s Dr. Sidney Cadwell came along and improved on Dr. Geer's process. An historian of U.S.R. has now told* precisely how these important, intricate effects were achieved and inter-related:

"Geer . . . invented a method of partially curing the cover at a temperature of about 210° F to 220° F for about three minutes, after which the balls were cooled and allowed to air-cure at ordinary room temperatures from four to seven days. The curing was achieved by using a rapid accelerator in the balata compound . . . . But balata was an expensive material and the flash that formed when the . . . halves of the ball cover were pressed together could not be reworked. The flash and any imperfectly formed balls had to be scrapped.

"Cadwell . . . succeeded in vulcanizing the cover at still lower temperature, *after* the ball had been molded. In this process, the cover stock contained only part of the ingredients needed for vulcanization . . . . After the balls had been molded, they were subjected to an emulsion of carbon disulphide, which diffused into the cover stock and . . . produced a cover so tough that it withstood cutting to a remarkable degree. Since it was also possible to reuse the unvulcanized flash . . . cost savings resulted. The patents obtained by Geer and Cadwell were so basic and so valuable that all golf ball manufacturers took out licenses to make the famous Cadwell-Geer golf ball cover. After Geer's patent expired, licenses to manufacture under Cadwell's patent continued to be taken . . . ."

To test its golf ball's durability in all respects, U.S.R. contrived a striking machine one blow of which would equate with ten hits by an expert golfer. If

> *"Geer invented a method of partially curing the cover at a temperature of about 210° F to 220° F for about three minutes, after which the balls were cooled and allowed to air-cure at ordinary room temperatures from four to seven days."*

---

* *History of the United States Rubber Co.* by Glenn D. Babcock (University of Indiana, 1966).

after 100 strokes on this machine any ball shows any damage, that ball and all its batch are scrapped.

When mesh marking became available, it was adopted for the "Royal." U.S.R. also tried an attractive sunken square pattern, which is described on a later page. But when conventional dimples prevailed generally, U.S.R. joined the trend.

U.S. Rubber was the first to boast, and still does, that every particle of its golf balls except natural jungle gums is manufactured in its own plants, even down to the paint.

By no means are all U.S.R. golf balls sold under the UniRoyal brand. Millions more are "proprietaries," made for customers to their own specifications. Among the largest of such customers has long been Wilson Sporting Goods Co., of Chicago, whose "Staff" brand ranks among the world's eight top rubber cores both as to quality and volume.

■ PHIL YOUNG AND BILL BOMMER

Among the last, but far from the least, to join the ranks of major U.S. ballmakers was the concern which is still called Acushnet Process Sales Co. How it got that name is one more example of how necessity mothers invention, especially in the rubber trade.

When World War I sent Brazilian rubber prices skyward, Philip E. Young, night superintendent of the Goodyear plant at Dedham, Mass., turned his attention to guayule, a lowly shrub which thickly blankets Mexico and lower Texas. An M.I.T. graduate, Young knew that guayule's stiff stems contained a gum so rubber-like that the Aztecs used to make it into handballs. He figured out an economical process for extracting guayule latex in quantity, and offered it to his employers.

When Goodyear declined, Phil Young found an angel in Allan Weeks, an affluent yachtsman of Marion, Mass., whose one stipulation was that their factory be located on Buzzard's Bay, his favorite sailing water. So a spot was found on the Acushnet River just upstream from the old whaling port of New Bedford.

Dr. Lothar Weber, a brilliant student of vulcanization and of accelerators to improve it, was drawn into the picture. Some of his improvisations were, to say the least, exotic. Besides guayule he found uses for scrapped tires and even for dog manure (a source of ammonia). Acushnet Process made yacht models, hot water bottles, douche bags, syringes—and then rubber tees, for Young was a golfer.

Playing golf one day with his dentist, Phil Young looked askance at his ball. It was, he swore, out of round and its gravity was off-center. In the dentist's chambers they X-rayed the offender, and proved Young right. That such a thing could happen in the advanced year of 1931 (just after the Jones "grand slam"), when the ballmaking art was supposed to have been just about perfected, filled Phil Young with something akin to crusading zeal.

He knew another M.I.T. graduate, Fred William Bommer '18, who had also specialized in rubber and who also was sports-minded. In fact, after setting up plants for others at Lambertville, N.J., and Malden, Mass., Bommer had started one of his own in Dorchester where he was making, and re-making, golf balls for Wilson, MacGregor, Sears Roebuck, et al.

In 1932, Phil Young persuaded Fred Bommer and his superintendent, Carl Saunders, to join him at Acushnet. They added Stanley Szulik, a dynamic rubber chemist and salesman, as their laboratory chief, and concentrated their work on golf balls.

At first (1933-34) they made only private brands, including some for pro shops. In 1935, when the Geer and Cadwell patents were merged, they adopted that thin-but-tough cover technique, tightened up their windings around solid cores reduced to as small as $^5/_8$ in. diameter ($^{17}/_{16}$ths was standard) and produced a ball whose stepped-up compression made others feel "like old puddin' bags." Later they changed to a non-compressible liquid core, still kept small to make room for plenty of winding, ("the motor under the hood," as A.E. Penfold called it).

With this product they followed Penfold's "for pros only" policy, but with correct assurance to amateurs that light hitters *can* get *some* added distance with high-compression balls. They named their ball "Titleist" and, to bear out their boast that this was "the best ball ever made," they instituted and advertised two highly visible tests.

First of these was the test made that day by Phil Young and the dentist: every wound center was fluoroscoped for perfect roundness and concentricity before being covered. All culls were scrapped. Second, a double-action driving machine was built (and sent out around the country) wherewith two Acushnets out of any dozen (or one Acushnet and one brand-X) could be driven simultaneously at the same target to prove perfect uniformity (or clear superiority) in distance and direction.

They also took advantage of Dr. Harold Edgerton's new stroboscopic camera, developed at M.I.T., to study and compare the deformation and recovery of golf spheres during the instant of impact. And when the U.S.G.A. in 1941 imposed the initial velocity rule (255 f.p.s. at 75° F sea level) they built a replica of the official testing machine to keep their increasing accelerations within bounds.

The pay-off of all this technology was general acceptance of Acushnet's claim that, for something like 18 years now, "Titleist" has been played by more top pros and amateurs in major tournaments than any other ball—and no one is paid to play it or given any balls free. Acushnet subsidizes nobody.

Another point-with-pride by Acushnet is that, like UniRoyal's, theirs is a fully integrated operation: the company itself makes every element of its balls. This is almost but not quite literally true. Bill Bommer, Jr., who succeeded his late father as president in 1957, and Stan Szulik still rely partially on certain wise heads at nearby Bristol, R.I.

There, a company named Carr makes special rubber thread exclusively for Acushnet, as it does also for Wilson, Hagen, MacGregor, and Victor. This specialty concern was created in the 1950s by the late Arthur Carr and the aforementioned Joseph Brogden, after long years together at U.S. Rubber.

ENTER: THE JAPANESE

Like juggling, gymnastics, and karate, golf is an athletic art-science peculiarly suited to the Japanese, who compensate for lack of stature and brute strength with their inborn co-ordination, dexterity, and self-discipline. In recent years the old empire of the Rising Sun has become a new democracy of the Flying Golf Ball.

Golf in Japan dates back to 1903 when some British residents of Kobe built themselves a nine-hole course on the summit of nearby Mount Rokko. Soon after, some other foreigners laid out a little course inside a Yokohama race track. The first course founded by and for Japanese was the Tokyo Golf Club in 1914, whose members had caught the bug as students or businessmen in the U.S. and England.

By 1924 there were seven golf clubs in the empire and they organized the Japan Golf Association, adopting Royal & Ancient rules. In the same year they played their first Amateur Championship and three years later their first Open, which was won by Rokuro Akaboshi, a stalwart amateur who had captained the golf team at Princeton.*

In 1930 the J.G.A. got Joe Kirkwood and Walter Hagen to tour Japan, and then "Wild Bill" Melhorn and "Wee Bawby" Cruickshank. These visits so spurred interest that 30 new courses were soon built and golf became a prime pastime of affluent Japanese.

The nation's military adventures, culminating in World War II and disaster, enforced a long hiatus. But the U.S. presence and Japan's democratization brought a renaissance. By 1950 the J.G.A. was functioning again, now under U.S.G.A. rules. American experts again toured the land, and native pros proliferated. In 1957 the Canada Cup matches were played at Tokyo and who should win from 29 visiting teams but the Japanese pair, Torakichi Nakamura and Koichi Ono. They handily whipped the likes of Sam Snead, Jimmy Demaret, Peter Thompson, Dai Rees, and Gary Player.

By 1962, Japan had more than 300 courses with more than a million patrons. Now, some years later, there are nearly 500 courses but still the facilities by no means meet the demand, even with night-lighting. The basic problem is to find available real estate.

By law, lands at all suitable for agriculture may not be used for golf, and the cost of leveling the rocky hills with dynamite and bull-dozers is prohibitive. Local taxation further elevates the price of play, even on the "public" (commercial) courses. So mass enthusiasm is expended and skills are sharpened at a myriad of practice ranges, often built in tiers and even on rooftops in the hearts of cities, floodlit until all hours. Hung on bicycles, motorbikes, pedicabs, and on the shoulders of pedestrians, the golf bag now rivals the briefcase and shopping bag as travel equipment.

EICHI MAEDA of Osaka. He quit shipbuilding to make golf balls.
(Far East Rubber Co., Ltd.)

Parallel to this growth of the transplanted game, the energetic, imitative Japanese cultivated a golf-ball industry of their own, the only one to flourish outside the English-speaking countries.

In 1927 at Tomano City, near Okayama in southern Japan, a born sportsman named Eichi Maeda founded a little firm called Far East Rubber Co. He

* Where the present writer knew him as Akahoshi (the English spelling).

was an electrical engineer with the Mitsui Shipbuilding Company, but addicted to golf. He bought golf balls from the leading overseas manufacturers and, for five years, diligently studied their construction and flight characteristics. Unembarrassed by patent problems, he selected what he considered the best features to imitate. He ordered raw materials and designed his own machines to put them together.

For his core Maeda adopted a thin-wall latex balloon filled glycerine (like Jolly's and Penfold's). He wound over it, by hand, a wide rubber tape and then, with a hand-driven spinner of his own inventionm, built up his center with fine rubber thread. Again following western technique, his covers were pre-molded gutta percha or balata hemispheres pressed together.

In 1928, following the Kirkwood-Hagen tour, two other golf-ball firms were started up, Seiko and Tani, with machinery purchased in Scotland from North British (whose plant A. E. Penfold had just re-designed). In 1934 the Bridgestone Tire & Rubber Co., largest in the Orient, went into golf balls; and in 1939, Dunlop built a Japanese ball factory.

During the war, all golf-ball production ceased in Japan. After it, the Far East company was the first to resume, sparked by U.S. Army orders in 1947. Bridgestone resumed in 1948 and Dunlop a bit later. In 1951 an American firm called Caprico (now Kabriko) International contracted to distribute Far East's balls in the U.S.A. under brands such as Strato Plus, Hummingbird, Steel Flite, Nylo Flite, Tempo, and Electra (with a "bouncing putty" core by General Electric, priced at $2 a copy!). Not all these balls conformed to U.S. tournament standards but the deal marked Japan's entry into the international market and, coupled with an expanding domestic market, skyrocketed Far East into one of the world's largest golf-ball businesses. A Japanese syndicate bought the Dunlop name and plant in 1960, and now contributes about equally with Far East and Bridgestone to Japan's annual output of some two million dozen golf balls, one-eighth of world demand. Of these, some 700,000 dozen are exported, about 400,000 dozen by Far East to the U.S. through Kabriko. About 150,000 dozen Japan-made balls are exported to Hong Kong, Italy, Germany, Great Britain, Denmark, Sweden, Australia, South Africa, and Canada.

Like so many of Japan's consumer goods, the emphasis in its golf balls has been on cheap imitations, chiefly for range use, including quantities of solid clunkers concocted from ground-up tires and fish glue by companies large and small. But this is changing. Operated by the founder's three sons—Masayasu, Teru, and Kazio Maeda—the Far East Company now uses electronically controlled rubber-core machinery perfected by its own staff of 100 engineers. It has branched out into four plants across south Japan, centered at Osaka. Like big Dunlop and Bridgestone it now not only aspires to, but confidently claims, parity with top-quality occidental balls.

The new philosophy of Japan's major industrialists is, "Find out the best practice in the world, and improve on it." That the leading Japanese ballmakers may be adopting this view is suggested by the fact that their scouts were among the first in 1966-67 to buy options on the American patent for a new solid, one-piece, high-performance sphere that promises to revolutionize the art entirely (*see Chapters 10 and 11*).

WHAT HAPPENS WHEN A BALL IS HIT—
without a resistant core

I. Aluminum projectible impacts coreless rubber ball.

II. Ball flattens on the side struck, and . . .

III. . . . instantly pancakes, but soon . . .

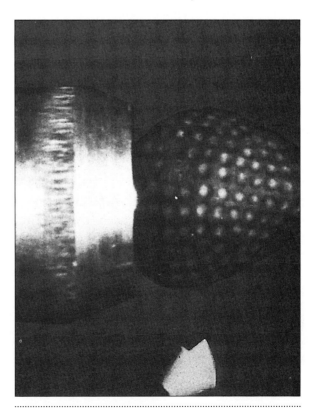

IV. . . . bulges in front before departing. The bulge represents lost energy.

WHAT HAPPENS WHEN A BALL IS HIT—
with a resistant core

I. Projectile impacts cored ball, which . . .

II. . . . starts flying before flattening, and . . .

III. . . . it pancakes only partially, due to internal resistance.

IV. When it flies it is pulsating, only slightly, having retained the impact's energy. (Dunlop Rubber Co.)

**HOW GOLF BALL
THREAD IS MADE. A
wide ribbon of elastic
is sliced finely by
disc knives.**
(Dunlop Rubber Co.)

**THREAD-WINDING
RUBBER CORES. Each
lady tends a bank of
machines, which
function automatically.**
(Dunlop Rubber Co.)

HOW RUBBER CORES ARE COVERED

Pages 65-67

(A picture sequence by A. G. Spalding & Bros.)

I. *Blocks of gutta and balata, with vulcanizing agents already mixed in, are trundled to . . .*

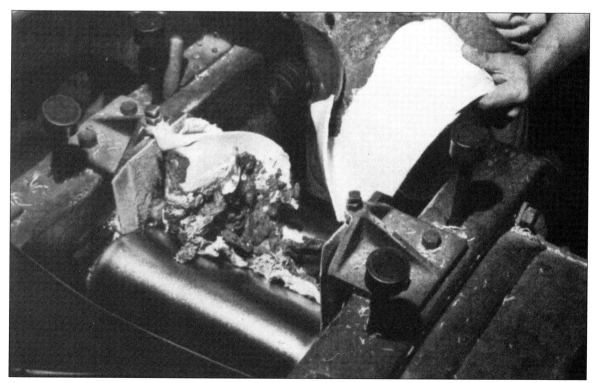

II. *. . . a milling machine, where scraps of the blocks are judiciously ground together.*

TWO PHASES OF THE GUTTIE

Hand-hammered
(G. M. Cowie, St. Andrews)

Machine-molded
(G. M. Cowie, St. Andrews)

One Dozen Early Cover Patterns from the collection of Atti Engineering Co.
List on facing page.
(Jerry Focht)

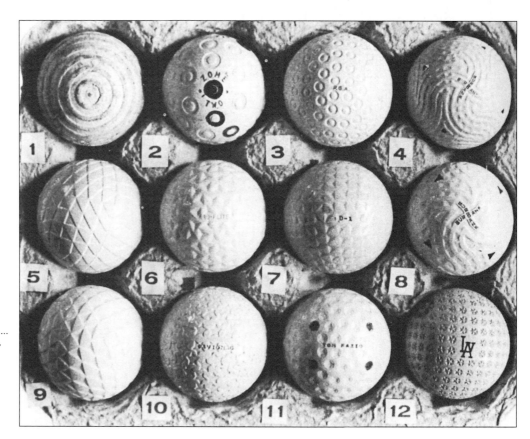

One Dozen Early Cover Patterns from the collection of Atti Engineering Co. *(Jerry Focht)*

1. Experimental guttie (1890?)
2. Zome (ink-marked)
3. Goodrich (late 1920s)
4. Burbank
5. Maker unknown
6. Needled KroFlite (Spalding)
7. Maker unknown
8. Burbank
9. Maker unknown
10. Cavignac
11. Mohansic
12. Von Lengerke & Antoine

13. Click Colonel (Jolly)
14. Maker unknown
15. Maker unknown
16. Latticed Dunlop
17. U.S. Royal (Electronic)
18. Maker unknown
19. Maker unknown
20. U.S. Royal Special (Dr. F. S. Martin's design)
21. Star Colonel (St. Mungo
22. Vardon Flyer
23. Haskell No. 10
24. Dunlop dimple

The Art at Peak

We have seen how the golf ball evolved from a lump of hardwood, sometimes carved eggshaped, into a feather-stuffed leather sac, and then into a solid blob of jungle gum. Then it became and has long remained an elastic sphere assembled in three parts—core, winding, and cover—each engineered with intricate, expensive delicacy. By the time of today's third revolution in golf balls, wherein all the advances thus far achieved in the cored-wound-covered ball are translated into a homogeneous, one-piece artifact whose characteristics summarize and may surpass all its predecessors', the rubber core's refinements are fine indeed.

Before examining the new-era solid ball and how it came into being, let us pause and retrace the rubbercore's arrival at the peak to which science brought it. The concentric headings for such a summary are Core, Thread-Winding, Cover, Markings, and Paint.

CORE

When the Messrs. Haskell and Work adopted a "small central-core-section" for their new ball in 1898, it was only as something on which to get a starting purchase for their suspender thread; to wind the rubber *around* instead of "upon itself." (Captain Stewart and Willie Fernie had also used cores, but Haskell and Work had never heard of them.) Actually, credit for the central-core concept should undoubtedly go to Emmet Junkins or John Gammeter for it was they, the two shopmen, who translated the dilettante's bright idea into a reality.

Junkins had to teach his girls—Gammeter his mechanical fingers—how to handle, under tension, that filament so prone to "fly about like a clock-spring released." One or other of them discovered that a starting core was helpful if not indispensable.

Solid rubber was used for the first cores as much because that stuff was handy and plentiful in the Goodrich shop as for its resilience, or "to regulate the weight of the ball." After licensing the Haskell patent, Eleazer Kempshall at once tried substituting cores of his celluloid, for which he was ever seeking new uses.

Nobody appears to have perceived, until Jack Jolly did in 1902, that apart from helping to form the wound ball and perhaps add some bounce of its own, the core's higher function was to *resist* the winding's elasticity; to give it something to press *against* when impacted. Only thus could the clubhead's entire energy be captured within the ball and translated into motion.

Jolly adopted water for his resisting agent because he knew that, like most liquids, it is incompressible. Within its container (the bottle nipple) it would arrest the clubhead's shock wave and make the rubber windings spring back.*

Jolly was no part of the physicist that the later Frank Mingay was, who in 1906 explained his patented liquid core most accurately. His key phrase was "solid although mobile." Those words well define the prime characteristic of every efficient core thereafter. The range of highest core efficiency was found to lie between the most solid of solids and the most mobile of liquids, i.e., between a metal such as steel, and a gas such as air—both of which were tried and found wanting: the one too hard and heavy, the other too soft, light and potentially explosive (*vide* the pneumatics).

After Jolly and Mingay, experiment with "vernals" focussed on three factors: the size of the hollow inner sphere, the thickness of its walls, and the nature of the filler. The Haskell ball's solid rubber core was only $^3/_4$ inch in diameter. Subsequent hollow cores, usually of rubber, have ranged up to $1^3/_8$ inch diameters with walls up to $^1/_4$ inch thick. Fillings have run through a wide and exotic spectrum, from mercury to castor oil to honey and even wine, but with little demonstrable improvement over plain water with some heavy powder in suspension to add weight.

From a purely scientific point of view (disregarding the cost factor), one of the most efficient core-fillers ever used is "bouncing putty," a silicone so viscous that it looks, feels, and acts like a solid though it is actually liquid. A free pill or ball of it will bound and rebound phenomenally, as in the "Super Ball" and "Silly Putty" now marketed as children's toys. Confined within elastic windings under high pressure, bouncing putty's "solid mobility" appears to add yardage to hand-hit golf balls without increasing their initial velocity on testing machines.

THREAD-WINDING

Dissection of a Haskell "No. 10" ball, made about 1902, reveals a flat elastic thread .072 in. wide and .025 in. thick—considerably coarser than the gauges used today. At the Haskell hearings in London (1905) it was testified that 126 ft. of such thread was stretched to 820 ft. and exerted 3,000 lb. of pressure on the core. This would indicate a stretch factor of about seven in the elastic, for the Haskell patent said: "The highest resistance . . . is attained when the thread is under a tension close to the elastic limit . . . the full strength of the material."

Wild Amazon latex was used in that early thread. The subsequent cultivation of plantation rubber, in Malaya and elsewhere, provided latex which was cleaner if not stronger, and improved methods of vulcanization brought the stretchability of natural threads up to eight times their length. Still later, admixtures of synthetic rubbers to natural have brought this factor up to ten and more.

To save on expensive fine threads, early ballmakers used strong rubber tape, as wide as $^1/_2$ inch, for their inner windings, with the finer thread on top. As late as 1933 a specification in Jack Jolly's factory for a 1.68 in. "Colonel" with a 1.125 in. core called for 78 feet of tape and then 54 feet of thread, both

---

* In passing British judgment on the Haskell patent, one of the Justices used the word "vernal," as a noun, in place of "core." Whether this was an archaic usage or a deft pun, from the seasonal adjective, it was most apt. "Vernal" might well be adopted today to end the confusion between "core" and "center."

capable of 850 per cent elongation, for a total of 1,122 feet of windings in some 11,000 wraps.

Top quality rubber cores today contain no tape, only finest threads. The smaller the core, the more room there is for thread ("The motor under the hood"). Thus, cores of $^{17}/_{16}$ in. can be given 35-40 yards of thread, $^{5}/_{4}$ in. cores 30 yards, $^{11}/_{8}$ in. cores only 20 yards. Threads are from .07 down to .0625 in. wide and from .020 in. down to .016 in. thick. Stretch factors go as high as 10.5; but in practice, on high-speed winding machines, threads are seldom elongated to that limit. Some ballmakers put their finer threads inside, their coarser outside, to leave larger interstices in the weave for the molten cover-stock to grip.

The pressures imposed by windings may build up to 5,000 p.s.i. or more. The more thread and the more tension, the higher the compression, as in an elastic bandage, and the farther the ball should travel from an adequate impact.

The "compression" scale is an arbitrary one. Its degrees are purely relative, from "60" for soft range balls up to "100" for hard-hitting experts. Novelty ballmakers wind up "hot" products of 120 compression and more for super-sluggers who are not interested in tournament rules. But such balls handle poorly in the short game.

▰ COVER

Just about the last word on covers was written by Dr. Sidney Cadwell, in his improvements on his joint work with Dr. William Geer back in the 1930s (*see Chapter 7*). The great desideratum was toughness coupled with thinness, to resist cutting while transmitting maximum clubface energy into the winding, which is analogous to a dynamo's armature. Here was the last obstacle to improvement of the rubber core. It may now have been bypassed by the new polymeric, one-piece balls, which dispense with the cover entirely yet are impervious to cleavage.

▰ MARKING

When the first guttie balls made their public appearance in 1846, graven upon them were shallow facsimiles of a featherie's stitched seams. This was not because the Paterson boys knew anything about the aerodynamics of a sphere. It was pure camouflage, an apologetic bid to gain acceptance for an imitation which flouted centuries of Scots tradition. The innovators well knew that sharp pros like Allan Robertson and the crusty gentry to whom they catered would be critical enough without being asked to try a ball as bald as an egg.

But putting the things in a vise and scratching the "seams" on with a stylus took a lot of time. So after the balls caught on a bit and the idea and feel of gutta percha were accepted, the graving was omitted in favor of quicker, cheaper production.

Now dawned a dim notion of how useful those seams and stitches on the leather hides had been. Without some approximation of them, an entirely smooth new guttie "whirred and fuffed and dooked and shied" worse than the most beat-up of featheries. Full enlightenment came, as it so often does, from the school of hard knocks. The truer flight of beat-up gutties led to the wilful scarring of new ones with iron clubs before putting them in play; and then, to the hammering in of lines and grooves; finally, to molded designs.

Who first conceived of molding raised bumps ("brambles") instead of sunken grooves is not recorded. Perhaps this idea occurred severally, for it seems never to have been patented. Why the first brambled ball was called "Agrippa" is not known, either. The only conspicuous bearers of that name were an ancient Greek skeptic and a line of Roman rulers one of whom tried to put Jesus to the sword as an infant, and later did crucify Him. It is just possible that the name was meant to suggest "a grip on the air," which is what brambles gave the golf ball better than any other marking until dimples came along. They saved the Haskell rubber core at a critical early moment in its life.

Also unknown is just how William Taylor of Leicester, the dimple's inventor, arrived at the specifications stated in his patent application of 1906 (see Chapter 6). He must have worked with some sort of wind tunnel, and he must have been a close student of Peter Guthrie Tait, the eminent Scots physicist who died in 1901 and whose technical papers on the flight of golf balls were promptly republished in extenso by *Golf Illustrated.*

Taylor's findings have stood up remarkably well to this day. He laid it down that dimples should have "a depth not exceeding one-eighth of their diameter . . . . A diameter not less than .09 in. nor greater than .15 in. . . . . A depth not exceeding .014 in." He did not state how many dimples the ball should have, but did say: "Preferably, the cavities should occupy not less than a quarter or more than three-quarters of the entire surface."

These figures gave much latitude to early ballmakers who, unlike Spalding, did not license Taylor's dimple patent. Between the years 1908 and 1925, when dimples became public domain, some pretty wild cover patterns were brought out, many of them purely as eye-catchers. But even to these parvenus Taylor's equations were helpful.

After about 1930 all markings but the round dimple went by the board, more or less permanently, and the consensus on optimums for standardized balls (1.62 in. and 1.68 in.) is this: 332 to 338 dimples of .127 in. (plus or minus .002) diameter and .012 to .0135 depth—squarely in the middle of Taylor's scale. Dunlop made full-shot tests with its 1.62 in. Maxfli "65," the results of which were summarized thus:

Dimple Depth	Carry	Carry Plus Roll
.001 in.	117 yd.	146 yd.
.004 in.	187 yd.	212 yd.
.007 in.	212 yd.	232 yd.
.010 in.	223 yd.	238 yd.
.013 in.	238 yd.	261 yd.
.016 in.	225 yd.	240 yd.

(Other experimenters, using smaller increments of depth, have found the optimum to be .012-.0125 in. for the 1.62 in. ball.)

Dunlop explained: "It will be noticed that the maximum distance occurs at a depth of .013 inches, and deeper recesses only reduce the flight again. The pattern gives the ball stability in flight and also lift . . . . A normal [i.e., unmarked] projectile with the speed of a ball and its angle of projection . . . would stay in the air only 2 seconds, but it [the dimpled ball] stays in the air 5 seconds for a good wood shot. This is purely due to the backspin in conjunction with the pattern . . . . "

Inventor Taylor's emphasis on the steepness of the dimple's walls, and the shape of its edges, led John Baymiller to study these relations closely. In *Golf Digest* he recently wrote: "After a modern ball has been hit 20 or 25 times with full shots, the dimple edges become rounded and the ball assumes a slightly higher trajectory, with about five yards extra of carry . . . . It follows that if a ball were manufactured with rounded dimple edges . . . we might have a farther flying ball.

"However, there would be negative aspects . . . . After about 50 more blows the dimple edges would become too round, thus reducing the dimple's depth. The ball then begins to 'peak' . . . and it will have a relatively erratic flight. Therefore, if the edges of the ball's dimples were rounded in the first place, it would have a shorter life at maximum efficiency. Also, a round-dimpled ball would appear to be over-painted, and might not be attractive to the buyer."

(Herein may lie food for thought by the new polymeric ballmakers. If their balls are so tough that the dimples cannot be hammered out, perhaps they should round the edges.)

Mesh and lattice patterns, popular from their appearance in 1912 until well into the 1930s, fell out of favor largely because dirt tended to collect in the corners of their square indentations. During the 1950s, U.S. Rubber tried to revive mesh-marking, and Dr. F. S. Martin designed a pretty one wherein the dent's four sides sloped gently to converge at a shallow central point, like an inverted pyramid, offering no lodgement for dirt. But the "Royal Special" did not catch on. The public eye had become so accustomed to round dimples that they now appear to be immutable.

◼ PAINT

James Worthington recalls how golf balls were painted in his father's factory at Elyria "by women, who put white paint in the palms of their hands and rolled the ball until it was entirely covered. This seems unbelievable, but I remember seeing it done."

Also slightly unbelievable are the illustrations in Spalding's old catalogs, under "Golf Sundries," showing equipment for renewing golf balls in the home. For $2 you could buy a "painting machine" which consisted of a metal "U" on a stand with pins inside the top, one of which screwed in to hold the ball mid-air yet let it rotate. For $1 you got "Macpherson's Golfer's Companion": a rack with three spring-clips to hold balls after painting, and a can of "specially prepared 'Foo-Chow Enamel,' with a brush affixed to the lid, which being self-closing keeps the enamel in good condition any length of time." (Red enamel was also available, for snow time.)

From those days till now, the whitening of golf balls has come a long way. Today they roll out of conveyor channels to be caught on mechanical talons, arranged in threes, which slowly twirl as they travel the balls past atomizing nozzles that spray a mist of paint from above and below. A girl picks them off at the end of the line with pin-clips held between thumb and forefinger, and places them on drying racks. Each ball gets a primer coat and then one or two coats of tough polyurethane enamel. Then, after going through machines which print on the brand and identification marks, in color, each gets a finish of clear urethane varnish, proof against scuffing and stains. Truly the poet's prayers in 1848 have been fully answered:

> . . . *And sure some scientific loon*
> *On Golfing will bestow a boon*
> *And gie ye a cosmetic soon,*
> *And brighten your complexion.*

CHAPTER 9

The Foes of Folderol

Even without the boosts given to the rubber core by Walter Travis in 1901 and Sandy Herd in 1902, there would have ensued a rush on the U.S. Patent Office following issuance of the Haskell specifications in 1899. Haskell's bold thinking was infectious. It aroused American ingenuity. It triggered enterprise. "Improving the golf ball" became an obsession almost as compulsive to inventors as the game itself was to initiates. Any man who could spare the ballmakers the expense of the elaborate elastic thread- spinning process would surely be rewarded. A common aim was to find substitutes for gutta percha which would permit a return to the shaping and compressing of an uncomplicated ball, preferably one-piece.

Prominent among the aspirants was the aforementioned golf and celluloid enthusiast, Eleazer Kempshall. On Haskell's heels, Mr. Kempshall filed applications for scores of golf-ball ideas, most of them harking back to the solid-ball principle. To Kempshall's practical mind (as to James R. Bartsch's many years later), all that rubber-yarn core-spinning was so much troublesome and expensive folderol. Some of his notions were inspired, and some almost worked.

One of Kempshall's earliest applications was dated Sept. 25, 1901, and a patent (No. 695,866) was granted on it March 18 the next year. He described a solid filling of "any suitable material . . . elastic in all directions . . . preferably gutta percha or one of its substitutes" which he would compress within "a shell . . . of a relatively hard but springy material"—celluloid, of course.

"A ball thus produced is not only waterproof, fast color, and practically indestructible," announced Inventor Kempshall, "but also [it] drives a phenomenal distance and is excellently adapted to the game of golf. It overcomes the defect of prior golf balls of being easily cut by a blow from an implement. The ball cannot easily be knocked out of shape, as is the case with former golf balls.

"The shrinking of the celluloid, which continues for a very long time after the ball is completed and even after it goes into the hands of the players, tends to reduce the capacity of the shell"—thus rendering the ball livelier as it aged! Inventor Kempshall even opined that his new construction would make fine balls "for use in playing billiards and analogous games."

Then the fertile Kempshall mind had an even better idea. On Dec. 18, 1901 he applied for, and on March 25, 1902 was granted, Patent No. 696,366. (This was one week later than his previous patent. Why it should have received a number exactly 500 digits lower is a minor mystery.) Now the gutta percha "sphere" was to be enveloped with "hemispheres of soft rubber . . . preferably vulcanized, and of a firm texture." The ball thus formed would be placed between "two hemispherical segments . . . of celluloid . . . somewhat green or not completely cured," and the whole then compressed in steam-heated dies. He now had a solid gutta-rubber-celluloid ball, again without any bothersome thread-winding. But still he was unsatisfied, and soon he tried again.

On March 15, 1902, with improvements added March 28, Kempshall applied for a patent on a simple, solid gutta percha ball with this one new wrinkle: that the gum should be re-heated and re-pressed two or more times. "I apprehend," he wrote, "that the reheating of the ball after being once compressed relieves substantially all of the strains among the molecules . . . so that upon again heating the finished ball there is not sufficient tendency . . . to recover their normal condition, to effect a distortion of the ball . . . . I consider within my invention balls made by subjecting the gutta percha to a third or subsequent heating and compression."

Kempshall's only aim here appears to have been to proof ordinary guttie balls against softening in hot weather. This was not considered a notion novel or substantial enough to warrant a patent, and he was not granted one.

But on October 21, 1902, he was back in the game again, this time with specifications invented and assigned to him by one Francis R. Richards of Hartford, Conn. The Richards' idea was to stir granules of leather or rubber, or both, into melted gutta percha and mold a solid ball of the mix. "Pressure is maintained while the sphere cools and hardens . . . . The gutta percha, being in the form of a honeycomb, acts better under a blow than in solid form."

If desired, this rubber-leather-guttie ball could be used for golf as was, or it could be encased in a gutta percha cover to toughen it further. Better yet, at the heart of the ball could be placed a "center piece" of Eleazer Kempshall's old standby, celluloid.

While Kempshall's patent attorneys kept the Patent office doors swinging, there was plenty of other golf-ball traffic there. And many of those other petitioners, too, brought ideas calculated primarily to eliminate elastic windings.

Richard B. Cavanagh, of Washington DC, obtained (and assigned to Kempshall) a patent dated Oct. 7, 1902, for wrapping a "center piece" or rubber or hard wood in "a thick sphere . . . of paper or paper pulp," compressed in a gutta percha shell.

That same November, John H. Stevens and Charles H. Turner of New Jersey obtained (and assigned to Celluloid Co. of New York, one of Kempshall's competitors) letters on a "pyroxylin article" designed to overcome "inherent objections to golf balls made of gutta percha . . . due to the naturally dark color of these balls, which limits their whiteness to the paint on their surfaces; and also to their natural softness, which causes them to be marred or dented by a blow . . . ."

"Celluloid can be made in a permanent and brilliant solid white, or in different colors . . . . We enable the player to substitute colors which will give an individual character to the different balls in play (as in croquet) . . . ."

These inventors proceeded by "seasoning" a solid molded glob of celluloid (letting its solvents evaporate) "until it has an outer skin or rind of fairly hard material about one-eighth of an inch." The ball was then to be steam-heated in a die so that the inner solvents vaporized and created a "porous interior in the ball." Thus semi-finished, the ball was then "seasoned" some more, to toughen it further. And "in cases where the operator through lack of judgment . . . cannot be depended on to make a ball which will remain round

"Celluloid can be made in a permanent and brilliant solid white, or in different colors which will give individual characters to different balls in play."

after leaving the die, we recommend the formation of a ball a trifle larger than the size required, as such ball can be thereafter turned or molded to the right size after it is seasoned . . . .

"By reason of our invention we are enabled to control the specific gravity of the ball, so that we can make it light enough to float on water, or as heavy as or heavier than the popular gutta percha ball."

What became of any and all celluloid golf balls is not exactly known, but legend and reason tell us they simply cracked up.

Search of the patent files reveals many another earnest effort to escape from toilsome thread-winding, for which you had to buy a license that cost good money, apart from the added costs of labor and materials. No dream-ball is more fascinating than the one described in Patent No. 906,664, granted to James W. Smith of Lynn, MA, on Dec. 15, 1908.

"My invention," asserted Mr. Smith, unabashed by his own temerity, "consists primarily in providing yielding or resilient means for connecting together a pair of hemispherical shells made of suitable resilient material, such as steel."

As everyone knows who has ever marvelled at those displays put on by ball-bearing makers, wherein a number of bearings are caused to pursue each other perpetually around an intricate steeplechase course, apparently defying gravity and not losing altitude while bouncing unerringly off a steel base-plate through holes of their exact diameter, steel is just about the most resilient substance known, especially its beryllium alloys. But hemispherical *shells* of steel! What manner of golf balls might those make?

Inventor Smith came up with answers so breathtaking that he may be suspected of having inspired some of the wondrous cartoons of Rube Goldberg, who in 1908 was an alert lad of twenty-five.

For his "resilient tie or bond" between his steel shells Inventor Smith submitted three designs in his application diagrams. In one design, a pair of annular (ring) springs, in planes perpendicular to each other, were connected to the shells' inner surfaces by two arms, which screwed into nubs on the shells and into holes in the springs. In addition to these arms, "a plurality of struts are arranged between the framework and . . . the shells. Any number of such struts, and any desired arrangement of them, may be employed as desired, but I believe that four in addition to the arms . . . will suffice . . . .

"At the base of each strut is a foot or extension which serves as a counterweight to balance the ball about its center and [to] offset the weight of the nubs . . . ."

In his second design, Smith elaborated his first by adding a spring-metal band around the inside of the ball where the shells were joined, to reinforce the joint and replace feet for the struts in that plane.

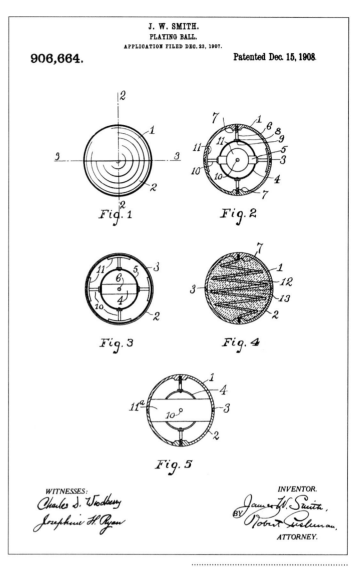

J. W. SMITH.
PLAYING BALL.
APPLICATION FILED DEC. 23, 1907.

906,664.

Patented Dec. 15, 1908.

Fig. 1 Fig. 2 Fig. 3 Fig. 4 Fig. 5

WITNESSES:
Charles S. Woodbury
Josephine H. Ryan

INVENTOR.
James W. Smith,
BY Robert Cushman,
ATTORNEY.

J. W. Smith's Steel Ball Concepts, 1908. With springs and hoops and armatures, Mr. Smith would have created resilience.
(U.S. Patent Office)

In his third design, Smith simply tied his shells together with one spiral inner spring, whose ends screwed neatly into the shells at their poles but were fastened nowhere else. What happened when you hit the ball on its equator, or anywhere other than at a pole, Smith did not explain. But he did add: "While no filler for the ball other than the spring frame itself will usually be found necessary, it is desirable under certain conditions, as where the spiral form is used, to fill the interior of the ball with, and embed the spring frame in, a plastic, resilient material"—such as gutta or rubber.

Whether or not Smith's little steel monsters ever left the ground, filled or unfilled, is lost to history.

In this book's Foreword, Chick Evans tells about the brash salesman of a "Pneumatic Ball" who tried to buy publicity for it at the U.S. Open of 1916. This was but one of many inflated rubber products, pumped up hypodermically, with which manufacturers tried from time to time to circumvent the Haskell patent. Chick does not recall his annoyer's name or auspices but the ball involved was probably what Dick Tufts of Pinehurst remembers as "the Chicago Pneumatic, a very expensive ball that gave fine results until it lost pressure."

Tufts relates: "A rather canny golfer was playing in a close match against an opponent who did not know the Pinehurst courses. Having the honor on the old par 3 hole of the No. 2 course, he took out his driver and, using a somewhat deflated Chicago Pneumatic, dropped it into the middle of the green. His opponent put his mid-mashie back in the bag and, using a driver, cleared the green and landed in the tree-tops beyond."

(The "mid-mashie" mention would seem to date this episode somewhere in the early 19-teens, after which that club was called the mashie-iron.)

Laurie Auchterlonie recalls an even earlier and more dramatic happenstance. In an exhibition match at St. Andrews, Willie Dunn struck a new British "pneumatic" off the first tee, slicing it toward the gallery. The ball exploded mid-air, a fragment damaged a lady—and that was the end of its maker's noble experiment.

Perhaps that was the same maker whose creation figures in an anecdote by the venerable J. Victor East of Evanston, Ill. Before coming to the U.S. and working for Spalding, later for Wilson, Victor East was a pioneer of golf in Australia soon after the turn of the century. He relates:

"Years ago the Prince of Wales' birthday was celebrated in British countries with displays of fireworks and the like. On one such occasion and public holiday, a special event took place at the Killara Golf Club in New South Wales, Australia.

"The player who led off at the first hole teed up a pneumatic ball which, when he drove it, exploded with a resounding, rifle-like 'crack.'

"Thinking the player had planned an appropriate celebration in honor of the P.O.W., other people reacted with an outburst of applause. When it later became known that it was but a freak coincidence, the chatter crystallized into, 'Well, it was a damned good show just the same!' "

The absence of large Goodyear Tire & Rubber Co. from "the great rubber-core parade" (*Chapter 7*) may strike readers as strange. It is accounted for this way:

In 1903, having prospered in larger and costlier products, and not about to pay royalties to his rival, B. F. Goodrich, under the Haskell rubber-core patent, Goodyear Tire's founder, Frank Seiberling, brought out a pneumatic golf ball patented in 1902 by one T. A. Saunders. Goodyear advertised: "Compressed air is the perfect resilient . . . lively when it should be lively, as in driving, but in putting as dead as gutta percha."

In 1906, Goodyear was able to boast that its Pneumatic Ball had finished 1, 2, and 3 in a championship, played over the Inverness course at Toledo. But after that— silence. In 1909 Frank Seiberling tersely wrote: "Retiring from golf ball business, can't make any money on it."

Where pneumatic balls were concerned, Goodyear's experience apparently tallied with that of its British peer, Dunlop. That great company's retired production chief, Mr. Samuel Ball, summarizes the matter thus: "There have been many patents for pneumatic golf balls, but they would in actual practice be of no use. Those we made for experimental purposes *burst in stock!* We hastened to destroy them."

Not until 1922-23 did any one come up with a formula that really bore promise of a solid, unwound, uncovered ball whose durability and bounce-to-the-ounce might rival conventional balls. In those years thomas W. Miller of Ashland, Ohio, whose smallish Faultless Rubber Co. had a high reputation for hot water bottles and other household accessories, filed specifications for which he was granted Patent No. 1,477,516 on Dec. 11, 1923.

He described a one-piece, molded ball compounded of rubber, zinc oxide, sulfur, and glue. After vulcanizing under pressure in registering molds (to form dimples or brambles), he said he would remove "any salvage or overflow" at the equator of his ball, then boil it clean, then dip it in a solution of balata or gutta percha, and then in lacquer or varnish.

"It will be understood," Miller said, "that the unfinished ball as it comes from the mold will have the true design of the finished ball and substantially its diameter, as in ordinary practice the thickness of the cover will be negligible."

Mr. Miller is said to have made and sold large quantities of his solid Faultless balls, but they never caught on widely except at driving ranges, and were discontinued.

Later in the 1920s, when golf's rulemakers were seeking some way to curb the ever-lengthening range of rubber cores, and their painful effects on golf architecture, some British ball-makers urged a return to the lethargic old guttie. They produced a few with modern refinements and added ingredients. During one of his visits abroad Bob Jones, then approaching his peak, tried out some of these balls and later, in one of his 1929 syndicated columns, wrote wryly as follows:

"I [got] the impression that I was pounding futilely upon a sphere of wood . . . . After playing seven holes with one, I found flat places all over it . . . . Probably it would have been almost cubic if I had hit it on the pole every time."

Known efforts to return the golf ball to a solid state thereafter ceased until the 1960s, when word of James R. Bartsch's work in New Jersey got around. Then, just beforer his labors were rewarded with Canadian, British and U.S. Patents, Spalding divulged that since as early as 1958 it had been trying to get away from cores, threads, and covers. Spalding beat the first solid Bartsch balls to market with a one-piece product called "Unicore," and then with the same thing encased in a cover and named "Executive."

The very appearance of these novel balls from so elite a source told the golfing world that another revolution must indeed be in the making. For how events unfolded, see the next two chapters.

"There have been many patents for pneumatic golf balls, but they would in actual practice be of no use."

The Ball That Was Born in a Barn, Sophisticated in an Icehouse

In 1846 and again in 1898, when first Rob Paterson and then Coburn Haskell in turn revolutionized the golf ball, the wish of each was parent to his inspiration. Golfers both, they had their goal clearly in mind when they started tinkering, Paterson with the stuff in his boot soles, Haskell with the stuff used in garters and suspenders.

No such clear-cut purpose existed in the mind of young James Richard Bartsch when, one day in March of 1959, his eye fell on a small insertion in the *Wall Street Journal*. The ad read:

Golf ball business for sale. Materials on hand will gross $15,000. $^{3}/_{4}$ work finished. Order coming, late orders received. Appointment. Phone NEtcong 2-2264 (N.J.)

Jim Bartsch knew nothing and cared less about golf, let alone golf balls. He was just a hard-working young chemical engineer with a bride to support and children in the offing. Eight years out of the Choate School after a gentle upbringing in Essex Fells, N.J., four years out of M.I.T. after specializing in polymers, two years out of the Army (Intelligence branch) and two into matrimony with a little goldilocks from Duluth named Judy Kirby, he was a dark-haired slimjim of twenty-seven now commuting between their farmstead in Stanton, N.J., and a duPont plant in lower Philadelphia.

His salary as an expert in paints and coatings was one at which few young men would sneeze. But those 140 daily miles of breakback motoring, two hours each way through the Delaware Valley's whimsical weather, were just about getting Jim down. One of these days (he had been telling himself and Judy) he would let big industry go hang. He would start a little business of his own—something he could crank up at home, out in the country, and take into town when he got it rolling.

Tough-minded young Jim Bartsch knew the *kind* of business he wanted. Having so far enjoyed little of it himself, but seeing it proliferate all around him, Jimmy had become impressed by Leisure Time. When he started working for himself, he said, it would be in the area of America's fun and games— its mass pastimes. Among these (he thought as he read that newspaper ad) what was more typical or more thriving nowadays than golf?

Millions of golfers needed multi-millions of golf balls, each costing at least 50¢. That is a nice mass-item price from which to extract a profit. And golf balls are made of rubber, about which Jimmy Bartsch knew a good deal. So he rang the Netcong number and made an appointment with the golf-ball man, one Norman Van Ness, whose operation was at Stanhope, N.J., about 30 miles north of Stanton.

Mr. Van Ness proved to be a middle-aged jack-of-all-jobs no small part of whose equipment was a gift of gab. With only his son and daughter as helpers he was, he said, retreading about 12,000 dozen beat-up golf balls per year, grossing about $40,000, and netting about $20,000. The machinery he wanted to sell was housed in and over his garage, and in due time he would show it to him. Of greater importance, he emphasized, were his mailing lists—his sources for used golf balls and his customers for remade ones. These were mostly golf professionals at public courses, who charged him 15¢ per dozen for "oldies" and paid him $3.25 per dozen for remakes. Mr. Van Ness treated his visitor to a spiel on golf-ball technology and statistics which lasted two hours, with a promise of more at any time.

Much impressed, and little suspecting that he would have to unlearn most of what he had been told, Jimmy Bartsch closed with the man for $25,000 cash on the workbench, and went home in the golf-ball business.

For the next several weeks Jimmy commuted to Stanhope to learn his new trade under Van Ness's tutelage. He had to pay the son and daughter for their work, and Mrs. Van Ness for bookkeeping. He paid Mr. Van Ness for an inventory of balata cover stock, only to find that it had to be converted from bricks into sheets, for which there was a hefty surcharge. He paid for a large quantity of "finished goods," but the paint fell off these and he had to have them repainted at 50¢ a dozen.

Meanwhile, Jimmy had to remodel his own barn, which had been used by a previous owner for breeding chinchillas.

At last came the day when he trucked home Mr. Van Ness's bits and pieces of machinery—two thread-winding machines to renew the old balls' outer threads; a blade for cutting balata sheets; a press stand and 50 molds to form cover half-shells and dimple them; a stamper to put names on them. To vulcanize his products, Jimmy found to his chagrin that he must build his own cooker and furnace, with thermostatic controls. To blend, roll and sheet his raw balata bricks, he would have to construct his own rubber mill.

Jim took this last problem over to his father's big machine shop in Newark, the Enterprise Tool Co. (whose building, by chance, had housed Jack Jolly's golf ball business). Here Arthur Gustav Bartsch, an astute mechanical engineer who had immigrated as a young man from Germany in 1914, turned out specialties for the aircraft, telephone and other major U.S. industries. In the many equipment problems his son James was to encounter, Vater Bartsch was to be an ever present financial help and indefatigable improviser.

And now began a long love affair between charming, day-dreaming, but hardheaded Jimmy Bartsch and the nation's leading suppliers of materials that go into golf balls. From duPont he got new accelerators to improve his balata formulations, with an eye to toughening his covers. Glidden helped him set up his painting assembly, and experimented for him with oleo resins that would make his ball coatings more durable.

Compared to breeding chinchillas, who have their own tried and proven techniques, the early creative efforts in Jimmy Bartsch's barn were fumbling and chaotic. But it was a happy chaos for Jim and Judy, and out of it in the late summer of 1959 came their first balls, rewound and soundly recovered to Jimmy's near satisfaction. He had a variety of cover formulas by now, from which he would pick and improve.

At that time of year it is fairly torrid in New Mexico, but Judy's father had a ranch there, near Albuquerque. So thither the pair of them trekked with several dozens of their new products, in assorted grades. What better place to test new golf balls than a sandy, rocky, blazing desert? To study how his various covers took punishment, Jim left them all unpainted, but each was numbered indelibly.

For one so small, Judy Kirby Bartsch hits a pretty wicked wood shot. Hour after hot hour she ran her slender husband ragged shagging balls amid the cactus, jackrabbits and rattlesnakes. But James sweated it out. These were his first brain-babies.

And the trek paid off. When they went home, Jimmy knew just which of his covers were toughest, and Judy told him which felt and sounded best off the club. And he knew another thing: No longer would he mess around recovering other makers' golf balls. From here in, he would build his own from scratch, the Bartsch golf balls.

He decided on a hollow rubber core, filled with glycol by hyopodermic, and ordered a quantity of such from the (aforesaid) Faultless Rubber Company of Ohio. From the Easthampton (Mass.) Rubber Thread Co., biggest in the business, he ordered topgrade elastic filament. He took his winding machines over to his father for improvement and duplication. He designed an automatic cover-blank cutter and an automatic cap press, and got his father to build them. He experimented with compressions.

By the spring of 1960 he was able to offer his golf pro customers a line of custom-made and marked Bartsch balls ranging from $4.50 per dozen for light hitters up to $9 for sluggers.

But the pros wanted a yet cheaper ball with even less performance. Impatient with their niggling, Jimmy took one more plunge. He turned his back on the pros, hired a promoter, and set out to sell "personalized" golf balls to the general public.

A certain type of mentality, he had learned, will buy golf balls with their own name stamped thereon in preference to the finest standard brands. To solicit the Christmas trade of 1960, Jim and his new sales manager, Fred Swackhammer, put ads into the *Wall Street Journal, New York Times,* and *Sports Illustrated.* Orders flowed in, topped by a monster from a mail order outfit in Birmingham, Ala. called Select-A-Gift. These people talked about taking 100,000 dozens. Among other customers especially pleasing to Jim and Judy were some Benedictine sisters who wanted several thousands christened "L'il Angel" to sell in their Alabama gifte shoppe.

The chinchilla hutch could hardly house such mass production, so Jim went on the prowl for larger quarters. All he could find was a rambling old ice plant, formerly a sausage factory, in an alley at Lambertville, down the Delaware. This he could get only by buying the whole shebang, which he did, converting parts of it to his uses while continuing the ice business for many months as a community service.

Thus far his labor force had consisted only of Judy, himself, and a Stanton lady named Olive Fuhr, who had become a proficient ball spinner, balata cook, and dimple presser. Olive's husband Owen was now enlisted as handyman and overseer, and 30 Lambertville girls were trained to operate the ball-forming machinery.

The new plant, which they opened in early autumn with Christmas only three months away, was a monument to Vater Bartsch's ingenuity and to Jimmy's courageous imagination. The improved winding machines had higher speed, finer alignments, more accurate brakes for compression control. The new balata mixers, cookers, mills and presses all worked smoothly, night and day. Upon the potholed alley Jim conferred a splendid name, Golf Ball Plaza.

To "personalize" each order of golf balls meant changing the dies in the stamping machine that Jim had acquired from Mr. Van Ness. This operation took the better part of half an hour, often for just a few balls. To speed up, Jim and his father rebuilt an expensive electric typewriter, putting heat and added symbols into the keyboard, at a cost of $17,000. Now Jim could switch labels on one ball or ten thousand within 180 seconds, simply by punching out a new tape.

With a sleepless Jimmy bossing all operations and the girls working in shifts around the clock, production rose from a few score dozens per day to hundreds of dozens per week, then to 10,000 dozens per month. Fulfillment of the Christmas orders was well in sight—when disaster struck.

Select-A-Gift cut its orders back to a few measly thousands of dozens. The nuns did not renege, and their "L'il Angels" went out on schedule. But suddenly Jimmy and Fred Swackhammer found themselves long about 300,000 golf balls, with no place to send them.

Undaunted, Jimmy plunged further. A more commercial version of the "personalized" golf ball is the "premium" ball, upon which large concerns have their names or trademarks printed, for their salesmen to hand out to customers. Fred Swackhammer hit the road that winter and came back with fat premium ball orders from Seagrams, Schenley, General Electric, and five major insurance companies. All these concerns bought thousands of dozens of balls specially branded and packaged, mostly of top quality and some with special refinements.

Schenley, for instance, thought it would be cute to inject whiskey into their liquid cores instead of glycol, and hang a ball on each bottle. Jimmy and Fred happily complied, and laid in a supply of vintage bourbon for the purpose. They shared Schenley's chagrin when the Government ruled this gimmick out of interstate commerce.

Ever since his desert experiments, Jim had been seeking a tough synthetic substitute for natural balata, the price of which was zooming. Monsanto, duPont, Phillips and other petro-chemical companies knew this and were constantly sending to Lambertville samples of experimental elastomers for trial in the Bartsch ball covers. DuPont came up with a urethane which made covers tough as nails, but it was prohibitively expensive and (as others were to find out) it broke out in horrid blisters if not cured just right.

Quietly on the side—for the golf-ball industry, he had found, is laced with whispering galleries— Jimmy was also searching for a "hot" new core for his ball, a solid one that would obviate the glycol needling. When Phillips sent him one more "interesting new material" Jim followed his usual procedure. Instead of forming it at once into cores, with their finically small diameters, he first shoved the stuff into some of his cover molds and turned out full-sized balls. Tests of these predicted that the new stuff, which Phillips described as *cispolybutadiene,* would not only make the "hottest" of centers, but that it also, with a bit of tinkering to increase its toughness and damp its resilience, just might be formed into that age-old inventors' dream, a solid, one-piece golf ball—no core, no winding, no cover.

Tinkering synthetic rubber molecules is about as simple a business as firing rockets at the moon. A half-dozen categories of ingredients must be brought together, with hundreds of compounds possible in each category. The number of combinations to be tested and compared becomes astronomical, and still must be multiplied during the curing stages by factors of time, temperature, and pressure.

In the late spring of 1962, when his experiments with cispolybutadiene began to look promising, Jim went scouting for a production manager with a flair for mathematics. An ad in the Trenton *Times* brought him Chetwood B. Lee, Jr., a Rutgers '51 graduate who, after a hitch in the Navy, had been quality control chief for Thiokol, the solid-fuel makers.

The Bartsch rubber formulas involving mers, elastomers, monomers, polymers, initiators, accelerators, cross-linkage, fillers and whatnot were pure Greek to Chet Lee, at first. But he caught on fast, and the main line of Jim's research was plainly understandable. It paralleled the line taken for years by chemists seeking new synthetic fibres and plastics. By grouping basic building-block molecules and splicing them together, they have evolved nylon, dacron, orlon and other "miracles."

Jim Bartsch's goal was to rebuild the cis-polybutadiene molecule. He surprisingly discovered that by reacting it with a certain new chemical (methacrylate) which he obtained from Rohm & Haas, a novel material was formed consisting of a complex, three-dimensional network with just the right kind of long, flexible chains to provide the strength, resilience and "click" needed in a golf ball.

In order to get optimum properties in this new material, Jim had to test many different conditions of heat, pressure, and time. Chet Lee's job was to tabulate results obtained and from them extract guidance for further experiments.

Another man might have referred this task to a computer, but Chet sweated it out using only his own brain and plentiful stationery, working nights and weekends. He adopted the "fractional factorial design" method of elimination, whereby whole series of steps can be bypassed on a probability basis. Soon he reduced Jim's necessary number of trials and errors from millions to mere thousands; and as results improved, to a few hundreds.

When you use the fractional factorial method, you perform a certain number of trials with the expectation that they will be errors, just to check them out and make sure your system is working. Jim had a shop foreman whose job it was to mix the test formulations exactly as they were handed to him on paper. This man became smart enough to recognize mixes that were not going to work, but without understanding the rightness of their wrongness. Time and again, without telling anyone, he would alter his proportions and even switch ingredients to suit his own notions of what would avert failure and perhaps bring sudden success.

This well-meant ad-libbing cost Jimmy and Chet much time and confusion. But before the leaves fell that autumn they brought out of the old ice plant, for testing by the U.S.G.A. as to rules conformity, by expert players for performance and feel, and by the scientists for exact description, a solid-molded golf ball which they believed was unique in all major respects. Every test confirmed them in this opinion.

Besides having regulation bounce to the ounce (initial velocity not exceeding 255 ft. per sec. at 70° F on the official testing machine), it was so tough you couldn't cut it with a cold chisel or hand axe. In the standard "guillotine" test for covers, the heavy drop-knife simply bounced off the Bartsch ball, leaving no mark at all.

You could squeeze it in a vise to half its diameter and leave it so for long minutes. Unlike a rubber core it would not explode, or even crack, and within a few seconds would return to its original roundness.

Being physically homogeneous and chemically stable it was impervious to internal damage (by impact) or deterioration (by heat, cold or aging).

Due to its hardness, it wasted far less of the energy imparted by a clubhead than do rubber-wound balls, which "flap" (pulsate) many times after being hit.

Moreover this hardness, by reducing the area of the clubhead's impact and thus its friction, reduced also the vertical spin of a squarely hit shot. Wound balls make 4,000 to 8,000 r.p.m. at takeoff. The Bartsch balls made only fractions of that.

This reduction of spin brought one adverse criticism from Arnold Palmer, who said that the ball did not "hang" to suit him on far, high approach shots. Golfing savants at the Forrestal Testing Laboratories in Princeton where Jim submitted his ball for scrutiny theorized that this loss in "hang" was a negative manifestation of the Beernoulli Effect, well-known in aerodynamics, wherein airflow over a moving curved surface creates a vacuum which causes the surface (a plane's wing) to rise.

But this one possible drawback was acceptable because the same negative effect was noted in Bartsch balls hit obliquely. The clubface imparted less *lateral* spin, too, giving the ball less hook or slice.

Satisfied that he had experienced what the statutes describe as a "Flash of Genius," a new "Basic Insight," and had created if not yet perfected something novel and sophisticated, Jim Bartsch applied for patents domestic and foreign; and he set about introducing his work to the golf-ball industry. Having sweated out a long apprenticeship with cores, winding, and covers, he knew just

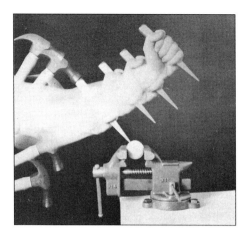

COLD CHISEL BOUNCES OFF BARTSCH BALL . . . *leaving no mark.*
(Jerry Focht)

WHAT ARNOLD PALMER MEANS. *Dotted "65" line shows Dunlop ball "hanging" on approach as Palmer would prefer. Lower dotted trajectory is that of a harder ball with less Bernoulli Effect.*
(Dunlop Rubber Co.)

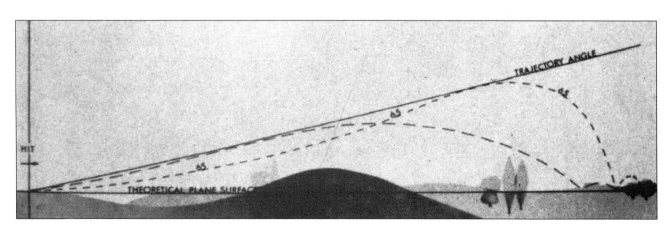

how attractive his new material and process were from a purely manufacturing viewpoint.

Instead of the 80-odd steps required to make a top-quality conventional ball, he could produce a ball as good or better in less than a dozen steps, including painting and packaging. His cost sheets showed the following contrasts:

PER DOZEN FOR 1,000,000 BALLS

Bartsch Solid Ball		Top-Grade Rubber Core
$0.60	materials	$2.00
0.60	labor	1.25
0.80	plant overhead	1.00
$2.00		$4.25

Before painting and packaging, actual ball-making time was cut from three days to two hours, and the critical stages requiring quality control were reduced from eight to four, as follows:

Bartsch	Rubber Core
Mixing	Core-forming
Extruding	Core-filling
Slug-forming	Thread-making
Heat-molding	Thread-winding
	Cover-stock-mixing
	Cap-making
	Cover-pressing
	Vulcanizing

Moreover, by virtue of its material's immunity to heat, the Bartsch ball could take a paint formulated to dry in 30 seconds per coat (at 300° F) as against 24 hours per coat.

Because of the Bartsch ball's homogeneity, its tests for compression and concentricity were vastly simplified. Each batch of mixed material, before being extruded into rods and then segmented and heat-molded into balls, could be sampled and pre-tested for consistency. The formed balls needed no X-raying to check their centers of gravity. All you had to do was float them on a pool of mercury. They remained motionless, hence must be perfectly balanced.

By the time Jim Bartsch was ready to march on the industry, he had sunk well into six figures of his and Judy's money on research, and several friends had also invested in the Bartsch Co. All now agreed that the best way to exploit the invention was to place it in strong, experienced hands on a royalty basis. Where this decision led them is a cautionary tale for young inventors and their friends, albeit with a happy ending.

CHAPTER 11

How the Bartsch Ball Bounced

When ballmakers meet to talk shop or swing deals, they are prone to pick a men's grill with a tile floor. Even before cocktails arrive, somebody will fish out some balls, hold them in pairs at arm's length, and let them drop to show how a new model outbounces an old. Sometimes this leads to apologetic scrambling under neighboring tables to retrieve errant balls, but it is standard practice at golf-ball gatherings. When next you see it happen, be advised that it is a serious business, not just grown-ups playing jacks.

Beginning in the summer of 1962 and on through until the spring of 1965, Jimmy Bartsch had many a meal of that sort, and many a meeting in other people's offices. For his was a long row to hoe before he found where his new solid golf ball belonged.

Among the first concerns to whom he offered an interest was Faultless Rubber, whose young president, Bill Miller, Jr., had revived his late father's solid-ball project. But Bill wasn't quite ready to move away from conventional cores, in which he did a big business.

Jimmy next approached his friends at Easthampton Rubber Thread, but they demurred at his prices. Then he made a presentation to A.G. Spalding & Brothers, deans of the industry. They were impressed but did not buy, having some solid secrets of their own in the oven.

These unproductive negotiations extended into mid-summer of 1963. By that time the general nature if not the precise chemistry of the Bartsch invention was common knowledge throughout the trade. And there was plenty of talk to the effect that the Bartsch formulas—as rumored or revealed—might not prove novel enough for a patent. After all, Phillips was offering its cis-polybutadiene to all comers, and several of them were trying to polymerize it in various ways, even as Bartsch had done.

So Bartsch and his friends took two prudent steps. They engaged Princeton Chemical Research, a sharp technical firm specializing in basic polymer research for blue-chip chemical and petroleum companies, to confirm and precisely define Jim's work and claims. And they hired a top-flight specialist—Patent Attorney Arnold Sprung of Manhattan—to strengthen their patent applications in the light of P.C.R.'s findings, and of patent searches in Washington, Toronto, London, Canberra, and Tokyo.

A Wall Street investment banking house was asked to explore the field for a suitable buyer of the Bartsch patent(s)—if and when issued—on an exclusive manufacturing basis.

Now began a long series of conversations and negotiations through 1963-64 which it is best to summarize, not detail, since all resulted negatively, and a number of nice people missed the Bartsch boat. Suffice it to say that the investment bankers did their job thoroughly. They brought Jim Bartsch into touch and talks with such logical leading companies as A.M.F. (Ben Hogan), Rubbermaid, Shakespeare, Sheaffer Pen, Acushnet, Carlisle Rubber, Lever Bros., Firestone, General Tire, and several more.

One factor that deterred progress was Bartsch's quite natural stipulation of a secrecy agreement before revelation. Other negative factors were Bartsch's lack (so far) of any patent, and of proof that his novel ball might take the golfing world by storm. People not already in golf balls hesitated to pioneer. People making conventional balls were reluctant to risk rendering their present expensive equipment obsolete. People already exploring polymerics stuck to their own efforts and hoped for the best.

Nevertheless, certain persons and events conspired now to brighten the Bartsch ball's future, though at the time they seemed fatal. This interlude might be epitomized by saying "Technology marches on, one way or another."

Just when the Carlisle Rubber Co. was about to purchase an exclusive Bartsch license, up turned a solid ball which was to all intents, purposes—and analyses—identical with an early Bartsch version. It was prone to shatter, and to shed its paint—two faults which Jimmy had long since eliminated from his own ball—but it was gaining acceptance by duffers and driving ranges for its unquestionably high resistance to cutting and its attractively low price.

Carlisle quite naturally backed away from any deal with Bartsch, exclusive or otherwise. Jimmy, with equal reason, set out to discover the source(s) of his competition, and how they had outflanked him with an ersatz product. In this he was not soon successful, and by the spring of 1965, Jim Bartsch was in a mood to wash golf, golf balls, and the whole foozling industry right out of his prematurely thinning hair. He offered his Lambertville plant for sale—lock, stock, and icehouse.

The response was surprising. Into Golf Ball Plaza flowed a stream of inquiries and visitors from companies great and small, including Dunlop, Plymouth, Zippo, Arnold Palmer, even A.G. Spalding and U.S. Rubber (UniRoyal). All expressed greater interest in Jim's polymeric secrets than in his modest equipment. So now began a new round of negotiations and confidential revelations.

In the midst of this activity, up called Bill Miller of Faultless. His technicians had never remitted their efforts to perfect a solid ball of their own, nor had they yet improved on the Bartsch invention. The moment now seemed ripe for Faultless to make the Bartsch ball to Jim's specifications for its own account, if Jim was still willing.

Jim consented, and so it came to pass that Faultless became Bartsch licensee No. 1 on a non-exclusive "prior disclosure" basis, binding for seven and a half years whether or not a patent should ever issue.

Bill Miller set about greatly expanding his Ashland plant's capacity. He started advertising, retaining his own Faultless brand (which had been his father's) and adding a "Golf Flash" and "Blue Flash." with no mention of Bartsch. He signed up several proprietary customers, including Zippo and Shakespeare. He priced his new products so that they would retail at $12 per dozen or less.

INVENTOR JAMES R.
BARTSCH. After eight hard
years, a seat on Cloud Nine.

So the day of the polymeric ball had really dawned, and the sun at last shone bright on the little farmstead at Stanton, N.J., with Jim Bartsch in the cat-bird's seat on Cloud Nine. But soon, over the horizon loomed other clouds.

Most obvious was a bottleneck in molds—the hollow metal hemispheres in which all golf balls, spun or solid, must be pressed to make them round and imprint their markings. Only one machine-tool concern in the whole U.S.A. — Atti of Union City, N.J.—made these, for *all* the ballmakers. With demand for golf balls bounding ever higher, Atti was far behind on its orders.

If Faultless and subsequent licensees were soon to get out Bartsch balls and pay him royalties, it behooved Jim to break this bottleneck. Characteristically he said, "Can do," and proceeded not only to remedy the shortage but to innovate the entire process of mold-making—right in his own back yard.

He leased a building behind the Stanton crossroads store and there assembled, with his own nimble hands and two helpers', the latest in furnaces, presses, and sophisticated automatic controls. He created a little mold foundry quite as novel in its way as the Bartsch ball, capable of supplying all comers as well as Faultless.

Subsequent clouds were less easily dispelled. At both ends of New Jersey, on Long Island, in Pennsylvania, and out in Michigan there sprouted new little companies making approximations of the Bartsch process solid golf ball. With no patent yet issued to him, there was not much Jim Bartsch could do, yet he owed some protection to his invention and to Faultless, its first bona fide licensee. So he engaged investigators, analyzed products, and marked time.

On April 19, 1966, Canada issued to James Richard Bartsch the first of his patents, which of course described his lengthy research in full detail. In July he sold his patent rights to Princeton Chemical Research Inc., for cash, royalties, and 20 per cent equity in a management and production company which P.C.R. would form to administer the Bartsch patents and to make golf balls in a plant of its own, with Jim Bartsch as consultant.

Later in 1966, London issued to Bartsch his patent for the United Kingdom. Now a queue of British ballmakers started to form—and some from Australia and Japan—seeking options and licenses. The Princeton people marked time, awaiting issuance of the American patent which would be essential for global operations.

When this document finally came through it was dated—by the wildest coincidence—April 11, 1967, the 68th anniversary of the Haskell rubber-core patent!

Now the sky was clear. Spectroscopic analyses and judicial review would soon determine just who were or were not infringing upon the Bartsch patents and could be brought to terms, in or out of court.

Hitherto the golf-ball industry had tended to take lightly the young inventor with the rural New Jersey address. Now it became apparent that he and his new corporate colleagues meant business, in every sense of that word. News soon got around that P.C.R. had armed itself with new Wall Street capital in seven figures, not merely to make pirates walk the plank but to equip a model ball factory near it laboratories, with initial capacity of 100,000 dozens a year easily expandable to a million dozens. Here "the Cadillac, the Rolls-Royce" of golf balls would be produced, under quality controls available to all Bartsch licensees.

Actually P.C.R.'s aims in buying control of the Bartsch patents had been fourfold:

To arrange and supervise their further licensing.

To advance the golf-ball art beyond the high point to which Jim Bartsch had carried it.

To acquire for P.C.R. a promising consumer product.

To develop other, unrelated products from Bartsch's versatile new material.

Founded in 1960, P.C.R. was well-geared for such a program. Starting with a modest volume of contract research it had boot-strapped itself into much profitable proprietary research, conducted by a constellation of Ph.D.'s, and was now ready to phase into major manufacturing ventures. Masterminding the new golf ball would be two scientists in their mid-forties. Both were non-golfers, but far from ivory-tower types.

Slender, slow-spoken Calvin N. Wolf, Ph.D., Chem., Iowa '49, founder-president of Princeton Chemical Research, Inc., is a polymer specialist who was with the Ethyl Corp., later a director of research for Food Machinery Corp.

Hefty, hearty Tom Zawadzki, B.S., M.S. Princeton '47, is a plastics engineer. He worked in research and sales for some years with the Borden Company, then was organizer and executive secretary of the Plastics institute of America.

Before snow fell in 1967, these two had their ball factory near Princeton blue-printed and the Bartsch patents' course clearly mapped. Breaking trail for them to the golfing public were the Faultless Company and its customers. Control of Faultless had been bought, partly on the strength of its Bartsch license, by Abbott laboratories of Waukegan, Ill. Unlike that huge combine, P.C.R. had never before handled a consumer product. In doing so now, it proposed to put quality before quantity, to re-examine and refine Jim Bartsch's formulas and processes to the nth degree.

Ten percent of the domestic demand (about a million dozen golf balls) seemed a reasonable goal for Princeton to shoot at after the first year. Meantime, P.C.R. had certain lab work to do. The Haskell Ball had taken something like 35 years to perfect. Modern technology should be able to perfect the much simpler Bartsch Ball in a small fraction of that time.

To gain acceptance first by average golfers and the driving ranges, leaving the P.G.A. trade till later, Faultless had kept its and its customers' ball compressions below 75, stressing their durability (Shakespeare went so far as to advertise: "After 365 holes and 2,850 strokes . . . still as good as new!") But low compression costs big hitters a little distance, so no Bartsch-patent balls were yet being played in major tournaments (wherein Haskells were played almost at once when they first came out.)

There was no physical or chemical reason why Bartsch compressions should not be stepped up at once, for added yardage even beyond the longest conventional balls. But a deterrent here was the possible new ruling, under discussion by the U.S.G.A., whereby a distance limitation linked with initial velocity might be imposed, determined by a new testing machine which the Association was having built in Chicago. Wolf and Zawadzki watched that machine closely, and awaited developments before gearing up for really mass Bartsch production.

Meantime, interest overseas intensified. First foreign purchaser of a Bartsch license was Berwick, a new little English company (subsidiary of giant Mineral Separations Ltd.), which sought at once to realize a fat capital gain by offering to sell its United Kingdom franchise instead of operating it. With the solid-state plastic balls—genuine Bartsch and otherwise—capturing 10% of the huge U.S. market almost overnight, to the tune of more than a million dozens, this offer occasioned grave brow-knitting at large Dunlop and Penfold upon whom—though it now does on the British Empire—the sun never sets. An educated guess was that one of the two would buy out Berwick and sublicense the other one.

Well content with his eight years of hard work, and desirous of indulging in some of that Leisure Time he had heard so much about, Jim Bartsch proceeded to sell his Stanton home and remove himself, his bride, and their brood (now five) to restful Nantucket, where he bought the historic house at No. 5 Orange Street. With him he took, in a couple of trucks, his new little mold foundry and its sharp young superintendent, Phil Osley.

It seemed not unlikely that, while millions enjoyed the new plaything he had given them, Jim Bartsch would presently come up with other inventions, including what he quizzically calls "something useful."

Nostalgia and Curiosa

When, in starting this book, the author indulged in nostalgia about bygone balls, he sought to share the fun by sending a questionnaire to oldtimers of his acquaintance with such queries as, "What was the first ball you remember playing?" "What new brands, as they came out, became your favorites, and why?"

All the answers contain fond echoes of a golden past. All are far out of our present world of standardized balls, between which there is as little to choose as between one or another of a gnat's eyelashes. Reading these reminiscences reminds us that, in the old days, every golf ball had a character all its own, or we thought it did.

WILFRED ("TICH") REID, pioneer of golf in France, teacher of kings, princes and presidents, first president of the P.G.A. (1916), now eighty-three and still going strong, writes from West Palm Beach: "I served my apprenticeship in Edinburgh making clubs and later golf balls. I was sent to Rose Street, to the ball factory operated by the North British Rubber Co. There I learned to make gutta percha balls with disc molds, a press, and a basin of boiling water. I became the top, No. 1 maker—15 dozen balls a day. These we made in four sizes and weights: the large floater 26 [pennyweights], the slightly smaller 27, the 29, a little heavier, and the small 31 for against winds.

"These balls after being trimmed were then put downstairs in a cellar and air-dried for some three or four months. They would harden, and a well-seasoned gutta ball would travel a long way—230 to 250 yards . . . .

"I saw many feather balls in old Forgan's shop, and also in old Tom Morris' shop . . . . Then, we had balls with wooden centres, and also elastic, and some with centres of quicksilver, too. These were molded from the centre and covered with gutta percha and called 'Acme' . . . .

"Today they [the rubber cores] have the advantage of great length. But for and in the short game, the old gutta could run rings around the fast ball. When we played for the pin on a very small greens we knew we could command the ball from any specified distance of 180 down to 30 yards. The old ball could be *commanded!* We knew how to crush it and hold it, stop it on the second bounce and, when great finger pressure was applied, pull it back. With our weight slightly on the left leg we could really massé it . . . Jock the Hutch has never had an equal at the stop-shot game!"

JOCK HUTCHISON, now living in Evanston, Ill., says he played first at his native St. Andrews with a hand-hammered guttie in 1894. He recalls the progress toward greater accuracy made, successively, by the bramble patterns, then by Spalding's dimples, then the meshes (Spalding and Silver King). From 1914 to 1928, his best years, Jock played Spalding Dots, which he thinks drove best. He thinks Wilson balls when they appeared after 1917 pitched and putted best, and that Acushnet improved over previous brands with its consistency of compression. Invited to comment on some of the far-out innovations he was asked to try over the years, Jock protests, "Wait till you are eighty-three years old and see if you can remember! I just 'dinna.' "

The late FRANCIS OUIMET remembered playing Ocobo, Silvertown, and Vardon Flyer gutties at Brookline as early as 1900. He well recalled the arrival in 1902 of the Haskell and Kempshall rubber cores. He liked the fat, floating Glory Dimple of 1908, chiefly (he later suspected) for its patriotic marking. In 1909 he switched to the brambled Green Circle, a Wright & Ditson brand, because George Sargent used it in winning the U.S. Open that year. Francis won a school-boy championship with the Green Circle in 1909, but later adopted the heavier Black Circle (also brambled) and with it scored his historic triumph over Vardon and Ray in the U.S. Open of 1913. He also won the 1914 U.S. Amateur with a Black Circle. In winning the 1931 National Amateur he played a Spalding Dot.

Ouimet thought that brambled balls pitched best, but ones with recessed markings drove and putted best, especially the Baby Dimple, first of the 1.62 x 1.62 balls. "It seemed to have more thrust than the others." With amusement he recalled, "I was invited to try anything and everything the human mind could conceive in the way of a golf ball—balls with water cores, honey cores, white lead cores, steel cores, semiplastic cores . . . and with all kinds of mesh markings." He remembered the Goodyear pneumatics and how, on a hot day, they could explode in your bag or in your pocket.

The first ball BOB JONES remembers hitting was "the Haskell Whiz, about 1909 or 1910," when Bob was seven or eight years old. He further says: "I always played either Wright & Ditson or Spalding. I especially liked the Red Honor, about 1916, and later the Spalding Dots, dimpled or meshed, with which later I won the Grand Slam in 1930." In answering "What brands do you think drove best, pitched best, putted best?" Bob replies with characteristically terse humor and accuracy, "Depended on the player."

RICHARD TUFTS, the Squire of Pinehurst, recalls: "When I started golf in 1904, the rubber-cored ball was in use but was too expensive for a kid, and for a number of years I used the guttie except when I found a treasure in the woods. Actually there were several features of the old guttie which made it a good ball to start with.

"In the first place it was economical, as cuts could be repaired with a little heat, and with paint it would last indefinitely (or until lost). We used to paint the balls by rolling them in our palms, after application of ordinary house paint, and then dry them on the ends of three nails driven through a board.

"The guttie also encouraged one to strike it properly, as I can still recall how one's hands would tingle when it was struck off center with a slightly loose grip.

"The early balls I liked best were the Red Dot, Glory Dimple, and Baby Dimple. Except for the Silver King there was nothing to compare with them. But the only hole-in-one I ever made happened to be with a U.S. Royal in 1921."

SAM SNEAD might have been expected, in his mock-hillbilly way, to assert that he first played with unripe crabapples, which he probably did. Instead he says, "As a caddie I often found gutta percha and Haskells on a thing called the Goat Course at Hot Springs, Va." His first serious ball was the small, heavy Spalding 50 of 1919. For many years he has been a confirmed Wilson staff man—"more consistency in roundness and compression."

STUART MURRAY, who understudied Henry Cotton in the 1930s and later gained fame around Boston as an exponent of the Ernest Jones (ball-on-a-string) method of teaching, remembers best the Colonels, Star Challenger, Dunlop 29 and 31, Why Not, Silver King, and Triumph. "I always thought the most important part of the game was into the green and on it. So too lively a ball was costly. I remember once using a ball called the Clackheaton because it was so soft it didn't run too fast on fast greens.

"Maxfli marked the change in 1924, and then came the Penfold, which was brilliant for distance but a little lively on the greens."

GEORGE LANE of Brae Burn started in 1912 with the Silver King. Later he favored the Colonel Click, Bullet Honor, and Spalding Tournament. He considers today's Spalding Dot the best ball to drive and to pitch; the Titleist best to putt.

George remembers a short-lived experiment of 1930: a ball whose makers painted it yellow. It was great for practice ranges because few people were tempted to steal such a conspicuous object. But in regular play it was frustrating. You couldn't find it for the dandelions.

This brings to mind LAURIE AUCHTERLONIE'S recollection of a ball striped red, purple, green, and yellow which one day made its appearance on the first tee at St. Andrews. Some jokers had doctored it up for the benefit of a fellow-member whose habit it was to lunch largely on strong drink. While his caddie teed it for him, the bemused gentleman stepped forth gazing far down the fairway and waggling ferociously. When he looked down at his ball he had a double-take, staggered away from it and back into the club house, covering his eyes with both hands.

(More recently, one day at the Houldsworth course in Cheshire, England, whenever a golfer holed out on the third green a hairy hand came up out of the cup and, without a word, returned the ball to its owner. To one player who had knocked in a hacked-up specimen, it handed a brand-new ball still in its wrapping. The gimmick: a roomy box sunk beneath the hole and sodded over, with a man in it for Candid Camera. Some of the players' comments recorded by the camouflaged shooting truck beside the green: "I say, how unusual!" "Thanks awfully." And, "Well, let's get on with it.")

Golf balls do the darndest things. ABE MITCHELL had a dear old Aunt Polly who eked out her income, well into her sixties, by caddying at the Royal Ashdown Forest Club, often assisted by her two spaniels which were trained to find and fetch lost balls. She kept a longhand journal about her clients, which Henry Longhurst of the London *Sunday Times* was privileged to see. In it she told, and he retold,* the singular episode of the Rev. Mr. Williams of Copthorne, and the big red cow with the sharp horns.

---

* In his book *Only on Sundays* (Cassell, London, 1964).

"The reverend gentleman, having driven into the ditch at the seventh, picked out and dropped in a bad lie. He almost missed the ball and hit the cow, who was standing directly in front and swishing her tail to keep off the flies. The ball lodged under her tail.

"The poor cow, getting more angry every minute, ran off in the direction of the green. The Rev. Williams said, 'What do I do now?' I told him to drop another ball. I said, 'I don't suppose the cow will go far away, so I can get your other ball.' But the man on the mowing machine, waiting to mow the fairway, was doubled up with laughter at my predicament. And of course he was back at the golf club before I was, so they had the laugh on me."

Golf balls often "lodge" in queer places. Not long ago, at Masters' time, RED SMITH reminisced in his column about two memorable episodes of bygone years in that august event.

One player's ball ran up over the 18th green and under the skirt of a galleryite seated on the grass. When the lady arose and stepped away, the ball went with her. When it finally returned to view, a most delicate ruling had to be made.

Another player's ball bounced into another lady's bodice and stayed there. The moot question was: who should retrieve it for a free drop—the lady, the player, his caddy, or a duly constituted U.S.G.A. official?

EDGAR ALBERT GUEST, the corny "poet" of the Detroit *Free Press*, used to receive every year a gift dozen of Colonel balls from their maker, his good friend jolly JACK JOLLY. One year the present didn't arrive, but Guest made a hole-in-one—his first ever—with one of his remaining Colonels. Of this event he was not slow to notify Jolly, in a plaintively hinting vein.

Jolly replied with a postcard, congratulating Guest and declaring that, in 47 years of playing, he himself had never performed such a feat. He added that he hoped Guest was aware of the Scottish custom, on such an occasion of giving the club professional a bottle of Scotch. He hoped Guest would keep alive this old tradition.

Retorted Guest in public print: "I know now why that bird hasn't made a hole-in-one in 47 years of golf. He isn't trying, because of the tradition.

Continued the poet: "It might interest you to know that for making a hole-in-one you can get a nice certificate with your name on it; a bronze medal from a golf-ball manufacturer; your name in a sporting goods publication; and, if you should happen to be a dentist, a dental supply house will send you a set of false teeth free, or something. My dentist ought to collect a lot of stuff from that concern. Every time he goes over my teeth he makes a hole in one . . . ."

DOUGLAS GOURLAY, the renowned featherie maker of Musselburgh, one Sunday put one of his finest creations into the offering plate at church, just to tease the addicted but penurious old golfer who took up the collection. As Douglas had suspected he would, the gaffer goggled at his rare oblation, and could not resist diverting it from the Lord's to his own use.

How precious are their golf and golf balls to the Scots? Hear this:

In the crook of the dogleg 17th hole on the Old Course at St. Andrews has been built a new five-story, 80-room Queen's Hotel. For more than a century the site was occupied by a railway switchyard and a line of coal barns, known as the "Black Sheds," over which hard hitters tried to carry from the tee to cut distance to the par-4 green. The sheds' old boards were battered and dented by the ball barrages of golfing generations.

" . . . for making a hole-in-one you can get a nice certificate with your name on it; a bronze medal from a golf-ball manufacturer; your name in a sporting goods publication . . ."

Lest the Old Course lose this historic hazard, the architects have provided a long gazebo, housing refreshment and golf-watching facilities, whose silhouette exactly matches that of the "Black Sheds." The original scarred boards were used for siding, and into the windows was put glass tempered to withstand the mightiest drive.

"But what," asked St. Andreans, "if our balls lodge on the roof of this gazebo?"

The architects had a solution for that one, too. They installed roof gutters and a downspout, to return all balls to the ground.

A medium reported hearing from SANDY MC NAB, deceased, that he was not surprised to find himself in the lower regions instead of on high. It's not so bad," Sandy was quoted as saying, "except for one thing.

"I found down here a lovely golf links, with clubs for the asking and the bonniest lady caddies a man could imagine, all dressed up as you might expect for this climate, in their birthday suits.

" 'Very well,' says I to one of them, 'tee one up.'

" 'One what?' she asks me.

" 'A ball, ye ninny,' says I.

" 'Ah,' says she, 'there's none o' them down here—none at all.'

" 'There's not?' says I. 'And how's that?'

" 'Ah,' says she, 'that's the Hell of it.'"

Part 2

The Fourth Revolution to 1997

Bartsch sold his patent rights to Princeton Research Corporation.

A Two-Piece Ball Overwhelms the One-Piece Ball

T HE BARTSCH innovation marked the opening of a new chapter in the history of the golf ball (presumably the Fourth Revolution). Bartsch and Martin thought that the advent of the molded, integral one-piece ball would have an effect on the game similar to that of the solid gutta-percha ball invented by Rob Paterson in nineteenth-century Scotland, but that did not materialize. Like Paterson, Bartsch found a way to make the ball simpler, and eventually better, through technology.

Though filed in 1963 and issued in April 1966 in Canada, the Bartsch patent wasn't granted by the U.S. Patent office until April 11, 1967. The invention, as Bartsch wrote in his patent, "relates to a molded golf ball having all the desirable characteristics of the best conventionally-wound golf balls while avoiding many of the disadvantages."

Looking back from 1997, the advantages of Bartsch's molded one-piece were relatively insignificant because it lacked the qualities of the wound ball, namely distance and feel; what proved to be an even greater deterrent was its brittleness. But the innovation led to what would become the golf ball of the future.

Ever since Haskell's wound rubber core (the Third Revolution) replaced the "gutty" at the turn of the century, a smattering of visionaries have toyed with the notion of making a ball of one homogeneous substance, but because it can't be done with an ordinary elastomer such as rubber, the idea has never proved feasible. Bartsch, with Phillips Chemical Company, took the idea one step further. Through chemical polymerization, they cross-linked an elastomer (cis-butadiene) with a monomer (molecule of low weight) to produce a substance that, when molded, was thought to have the characteristics required in a golf ball.

Soon after the patent was granted, Bartsch sold the rights and his modest operation in Stanhope, New Jersey, to Princeton Chemical Research (PCR) in nearby Princeton, New York. PCR was a research group primarily involved in plastics. The Bartsch ball would be their first foray into the field

The Bartsch Ball, c. 1968. A homogeneous one-piece ball.

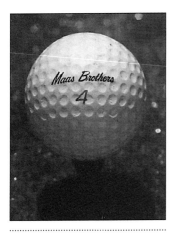

A Bartsch contract ball for Maas. Bros. department stores.

of ball manufacturing. They hired young, energetic Duncan Pollitt as Executive Vice President to set up and operate a separate plant to produce and market golf balls, about a million dozen a year, providing he could do so with improved durability. In their biggest year they produced 345,000 dozen, about 1.5 percent of the U.S. total.

Labeled simply "PCR"/Bartsch and without any promotional blitz, the truly innovative one-piece ball scarcely rippled the market. Explained John Toedtman, who was President of PCR in those early days: "The company just didn't have the funds to do the necessary PR, nor did they have the name or tradition of ball makers like Acushnet or Spalding." Consequently, "PCRs" did not sell well, nor were many made. But as the first identifiable one-piece balls (with the exception of the "White Streak" by licensee Faultless) marketed under the Bartsch patent, they are prized collectibles today.

For PCR, it was back to the lab in an attempt to make the ball more acceptable to the golfing public. They fiddled with the chemical recipe, trying to find a mix that would liven the ball. To some degree they succeeded, improving it enough to get a new ball, the PCR II, on the USGA's list of conforming golf balls. Technically, the ball (Bartsch II) was a major breakthrough, but not a commercial success, according to Duncan Pollitt (who was Mr. One-Piece).

PCR hit upon a marketing strategy that carved a niche for their one-piece ball. They contracted to supply private label brands to retail chains such as Sears & Roebuck, Maas Bros., Woolworth's and Herman's Sporting Goods. They passed on their low manufacturing costs, enabling the retail outlets to offer the one-piece balls for about 50 cents each—half of what a Top-Flite or Titleist sold for. This was a good deal for the consumer, especially the beginner or high-handicap golfer to whom high trajectory, feel and extra distance off the tee doesn't mean much. PCR also contracted with a smorgasbord of corporations, organizations and companies to supply balls with their own company logo or insignia on the cover. This enabled PCR to grab a three to four percent share of the market for a limited time.

In the 1970s, PCR would go the way of the rest of the golf world, producing two-piece balls (a successful off-shoot of one-piece technology), but they never stopped their research towards developing a superior one-piece ball. This switch failed to breathe enough life into the project to keep it alive. PCR shut down about 1977.

When the U.S. patent had been granted in 1967, Bartsch's innovation was no shock to many manufacturers. He had begun working on the solid core in the late '50s and was testing it in 1963. His rivals had had their feelers out for a long time and knew, though perhaps not exactly, what Bartsch was working on. Many were doing their own experimentation, and it has been suggested that the reason the patent took so long to be granted was that the discovery was so widely known that it was questionable whether or not it was an original idea. Duncan Pollitt reported that the real cause was a change of chemistry suggested by Arnold Sprung, PCR's patent lawyer.

Most of PCR's early licensees were smaller companies like Plymouth Division of Shakespeare of Kalamazoo, Michigan, who introduced the Black Watch and Chemold, followed by the Fireball. Others produced were Faultless, Dunlop, and Worthington/Victor Comptometer Company. One of the true solid-core golf ball pioneers was the Faultless Rubber Co. As early as 1923, Faultless President William Miller had been issued a patent for a solid-core ball, an idea several decades before its time. Forty-plus years later, Miller's son, Bill Jr., seized the opportunity to follow his father's dream.

Knowing of the elder Miller's 1923 patent, Bartsch approached long-time friend Bill Jr. with his idea well before any patents were granted. Miller agreed to work with Bartsch and market a one-piece ball, believed to be the first since the gutty. Around 1966, Faultless came out with the one-piece White Streak which reportedly infringed the findings of James Bartsch. It was, however, flawed. Faultless touted the new ball as one that "wouldn't crack or smile," but it was very brittle and was prone to chip and break up. The White Streak also lacked the distance off the tee of the standard three-piece ball, and consequently made little dent in the market.

Undeterred, Faultless as well as Plymouth altered the ball's chemical make-up using many of the ideas incorporated by Bartsch. By 1967, Faultless had two new offerings, the Blue Flash and the Gold Flash, both of which had new and improved solid cores. They were indeed an improvement. They were tougher, as Faultless demonstrated with the hand-ax test, and sold quite well that first year (about a half million). But the rock-like quality was a turn-off to people who had grown accustomed to the lively, wound rubber cores which, by the late '60s, had been improved to near perfection.

While the Blue and Gold Flash sold modestly, they would soon be overshadowed by a new development in golf ball manufacturing. Yet the impact of the Bartsch "solid core" innovation can never be discounted. Some might describe it as one important ingredient in the Fourth Revolution of the ever-evolving golf ball; we might not have had the two-piece ball, as we know it, without James Bartsch.

▰ THE TWO-PIECE BALL—1967

Spalding Worldwide Sports, headquartered in Chicopee, Massachusetts, had been pursuing the notion of a solid-core golf ball since the late 1950s. As one of the giants in the industry, they could not afford to risk their reputa-

On the left, a Faultless Blue Flash one-piece ball c. 1967. On the right, a later example of a Blue Flash one piece

First U.S. ball with dimples: licensed by Spalding from Taylor in 1909 and so named.

The Executive by Spalding. The first performance two-piece ball since the feather/leather ball.

tion on unproven one-piece technology that looked destined to fail. Other industry leaders—Acushnet (now Titleist), Wilson, Dunlop and Worthington—were distancing themselves from the solid core, though keeping a watchful eye on its progress. But Spalding had always been on the cutting edge of new technology since 1907 when they introduced Taylor's invention of a ball with dimples and not surprisingly named it "Dimple." They also knew something Bartsch didn't. Realizing that the one-piece lacked feel and had a penchant for chipping, Spalding took the process one step further. They enclosed a solid core, similar to Bartsch's, with a coat of polyurethane plastic. This became the first two-piece ball since the featherie. Spalding called it the Executive, today another attractive collectible.

When released in 1967, the two-piece Executive was so far superior to the one-piece that companies like PCR and Faultless started producing their own two-piece balls. The bell was tolling for the one piece, at least as a viable alternative to the wound rubber core. Said William Mann, Spalding advertising and sales promotion manager, "The one-piece, simply put, is an oversimplification."

The two-piece ball would soon become the Fourth Revolution of the golf ball, following the featherie, the gutty, and the wound rubber core (which is still going strong), and would obliterate the one piece. However, the Spalding Executive Ball will not go down in history alongside the Haskell wound rubber core or the Paterson Composite as the breakthrough ball. Three major factors led to a successful two piece as it is known today:

1) The Bartsch research and introduction of a solid core.

2) Spalding's addition of a cover material.

3) The advent of Surlyn.

Surlyn is one of a new class of ionic crosslinking polymers as opposed to earlier systems to produce plastics and synthetic rubber—as in the Bartsch ball. It was developed by DuPont Chemical Company in the mid-1960s, and on August 2, 1966, DuPont scientist Dr. Richard Watkin Rees received patent number 3,264,272 for a substance that would be used to cover most golf balls. What Rees did, in effect, was combine apples and oranges by a new method of cross-linking two completely different chemicals, with the addition of sodium salt. The result is what is commonly referred to as a modified thermoplastic resin which DuPont named Surlyn—the generic name is an isomer.

Surlyn finally proved to be perfect for the golf ball cover, but that was not the reason Dr. Rees invented it. Initially, DuPont was hoping this substance could be used to make soda pop bottles, but they discovered that it cracked. Over the years, Surlyn has been used in a variety of products including auto parts, sneaker soles, toys, ski boots and lacrosse sticks, but the name has become synonymous with golf balls, thanks largely to the insight and efforts of a ball manufacturing plant called Ram.

In the early '60s, according to Will Rogers, DuPont's expert on Surlyn balls, DuPont was trying hard to peddle its new unnamed chemical marvel, but people found it hard to work with because of its high processing temperature. It stuck to the equipment and to everything else in sight.

DuPont's invention piqued the interest of Terry Pocklington, a promising young chemical engineer who worked for the Campbell Ball Co. of Canada—

Dr. Richard W. Rees, a DuPont scientist, developed a method of crosslinking polymers and hit a giant jackpot in 1961. Later given the name Surlyn, the substance was offered to the market by 1964, for commercial use. Ram Golf Company was the first to use it.

a golf ball manufacturer, but on a smaller scale than larger companies like Spalding, Acushnet and Dunlop. Pocklington was struck by the toughness of this then unnamed substance (Surlyn). Innovators had long been thinking of ways to improve the golf ball, for despite the level of perfection the wound rubber core had reached in terms of performance feel, spin and distance, it lacked durability. The balata cover would split when mis-hit. Could it be possible, thought Pocklington, that this chemical maverick was the answer?

By 1965, with some assistance from DuPont engineers, he felt confident enough to approach management with the idea of using Surlyn as a cover material instead of balata. On the grounds that they didn't have the capital to see the project through, Campbell higher-ups denied Pocklington's request.

Subsequently Pocklington left Campbell, but he carried with him the belief that DuPont's thermoplastic breakthrough was a winner and would revolutionize the golf ball. He found work at Sportsman Golf Company in suburban Chicago, which would later become Ram Golf Corporation. Once again he pitched the idea of a new cover, and Sportsman agreed to back the development cost.

Pocklington and DuPont trouble shooters set about to tame the cantankerous substance. By late 1967 such problems as chewing-gum-like stickiness, the high-temperature degradation of thread windings, and the failure of the paint to adhere to the finished cover had been surmounted.

While all this was transpiring, a small outfit in California, the Metropolitan Ball Company, was also trying to find a formula for successfully using the DuPont substance. Ram beat them to the punch and produced a better product to boot—but neither Pocklington nor Ram did their work with patent protection. "We did it on purpose," explained Pocklington, now President of Hansberger Precision Golf, manufacturer of Ram balls. By foregoing the patent route, innovators didn't have to disclose the specific technology to tempt others to get into the act. Issuance of a patent is often like opening a Pandora's box. One sage years ago said, "A patent is only worth the money you have to defend it from competitors." Pocklington said that it was the big companies with deeper pockets who benefit from patents.

A Ramlon Ball. The first golf ball using DuPont's new cover material, now known as Surlyn.

Terry Pocklington, now President of Hansberger Precision Golf Co., makers of the Ram golf ball, was developer and producer of the first golf ball to use this yet unnamed material. The Ram Golf Ball Company named it Ramlon.

In 1968, about the time Bartsch came out with his one piece and Spalding countered with its Executive, Ram introduced a ground-breaking new ball of its own, the Golden Ram. It was a *three-piece* wound rubber core, but instead of balata, the cover was made of DuPont's durable new discovery, which Ram dubbed Ramlon. Later, the world would come to know it as Surlyn. The Golden Ram marked the first step toward the ball of today, which is durable enough to be used by the high handicapper or beginner, yet performs well enough for the distance demanded by some professionals.

While the Golden Ram didn't match other high performance three-piece balls off the tee, it was extremely tough. In fact, Ram set out on the promotional trail touting their Ramlon Golden Ram as the toughest ball in the land. Crisscrossing the country from conferences to state fairs, the Ram salesmen showed people how the Golden Ram survived the infamous guillotine test while other balls "split." The razor-sharp blade would be dropped from four feet onto different makes of balls, one of them being the Golden Ram. While the blade would sever the balata-covered brands through to the thread windings, it would bounce off the Ram ball without administering a scratch. If that wasn't enough to convince the skeptics, Ram supposedly conducted tests wherein they fired a .38-caliber bullet from seven feet away at a three-quarter-inch slab of Surlyn, without denting it.

Guillotine and handgun tests didn't help the Golden Ram off the tee, since it fell considerably short of the standard balata-covered ball in distance and performance characteristics. Despite this, Ram found a good-sized market.

Admittedly, the Surlyn cover did absorb some of the lively bounce supplied by those super-charged thread windings. First of all, its bounce to the ounce was hampered by the sheer thickness of the Surlyn cover. The normal balata ball cover was around .03-inches thick. The Golden Ram cover was .09 inches—equal to attack by machete, perhaps, but far too much for a golf ball. But even if there were only .03 inches of Surlyn surrounding the threads, the touring pro still feels that a balata-covered, wound ball gives him or her more spin, greater directional control and better trajectory—for the rest, the Golden Ram does a super job. 🌰

Surlyn's Stamina: Dupont's Chemical Magic

eading into the '70s, the golf world was swirling with new technology. Just years prior, the only type of golf ball available was the wound rubber core with balata cover, but now there were choices. In the coming years, as the golf ball industry became highly specialized, these choices would proliferate and become very confusing to the average golfer. At the start of the decade, however, the jury was still out on things like the one piece, the two-piece solid core with polyurethane and Surlyn covers, and the three piece with balata and Surlyn covers. These were all out there, but did they have a real role?

▬ SYNTHETIC BALATA

This extremely productive era also spawned another idea ahead of its time, at least in the United States: The Polymeric Corporation of Canada developed a synthetic balata material as a substitute golf ball cover, to replace natural balata. A relative of rubber, made from the sap of the Bully Gum tree in tropical America, it tended to vary in quantity and quality. The new synthetic was a petroleum derivative known as isoprene, also an elastomer related to rubber. For whatever reasons, North American manufacturers didn't embrace the new idea, but the Japanese did. Only around 1980 did balata in the form of isoprene return to the United States, when Titleist and other balata users started to mix increasing amounts of synthetic into their materials—until a complete conversion was made. The isoprene variety is still referred to as balata, being essentially the same product, but with greatly improved uniformity and cost.

Dupont's Surlyn covers introduced by Spalding's Top-Flite ball in 1971.

SURLYN SOARS

In America in the early 1970s, ball companies focused their energies on Surlyn because of its durability. Most were experimenting with it, and six had actually introduced Surlyn-covered balls by 1971. Leading the charge, of course, was Ram, where since 1965 Terry Pocklington had been modifying the Golden Ram to produce a ball good enough to be used by the pros. In fact, 1971 was a breakthrough year for Ram and Surlyn, because it was the year PGA pro Tom Shaw won the Bing Crosby Pro-Am using the Golden Ram—the first Surlyn ball to win a professional tournament. Other companies to release Surlyn-covered balls by 1971 were First Flight, Plymouth, Shakespeare, and U.S. Royal.

Here again was secretive Spalding, a company rich in tradition, fiddling around with this new and as-yet-unproven technology behind locked doors. This company, founded by Hall-of-Fame baseball pitcher A.G. Spalding in Chicago in 1876 to make baseballs, predates the sport of golf in America. By the late 1800s, Spalding tapped into the golf craze by first importing and then producing golf balls and clubs at its new plant in Chicopee, Massachusetts. It has been there ever since.

Much as with Bartsch's solid core, larger, established companies stayed away from Surlyn at the outset—but Spalding got on the wagon when Terry Pocklington and Ram showed the way. While Ram, First Flight, Shakespeare, Plymouth and U.S. Royal had introduced wound rubber cores with Surlyn covers, Spalding was the first to come out with a solid-core ball with a Surlyn cover in 1971, dawn of the Fourth Revolution. It was christened Top-Flite, and turned out to be the ball of the future—a ball for the masses, not the classes. The developments of the last decade or so all came together in the two-piece Top-Flite, which had the simplicity and magic of the solid-core, plus the durability of Surlyn.

The man behind Top-Flite was Spalding engineer Robert Molitor. Molitor understood that the solid-core concept could work with a strong cover material. At first Spalding failed, using a coat of polyurethane, but when Surlyn came along, the marriage was a natural. Molitor found a way to make Surlyn softer by combining two forms—zinc Surlyn and sodium Surlyn. Because Top-Flite's core was much harder than the three-piece Golden Ram, it could afford to have a softer cover and still be the most durable ball on the market.

Spalding hit the jackpot with Top-Flite. Ever since cross-state rival Acushnet of New Bedford, Massachusetts, perfected the Titleist in the mid-1940s, Spalding had taken a back seat. But Top-Flite would vault the company to new heights as it became Spalding's "bread and butter" for the next twenty years. In fact, the Top-Flite became so successful that Spalding turned its back on three-piece balls, at least until now, but has been breathing hard ever since trying to get the Top-Flite to satisfy the tour pros.

Top-Flite is best described as a Chevy in an industry in which everyone aspires to drive a Mercedes. It is durable, dependable, and less expensive to make. In 1972 it was the

Spalding's all-new ball introduced in 1971 with solid core and Surlyn cover.

jeans-wearing, beer-drinking weekend golfers' choice—that of those who were out there having fun, not worrying about their handicaps.

In effect, Spalding bucked the "trickle-down" theory of golf ball economics when it came to Top-Flite. Most ball manufacturers planned their budgets to include paying professionals to use their balls, reasoning that if John Q. Public's favorite golfer Joe Sandshot uses a particular brand, John will be inclined to buy it. But Spalding took a different tack. The Top-Flite offered durability and more distance, which is basically what every ordinary golfer needs. Larry in Keane Valley, New York doesn't necessarily need the high trajectory or high spin that a professional like Fred Couples does. Most average players can't make the ball do spins and "drop deads" anyway. Although most pros scoffed at the Top-Flite and few if any of them used it in those early days, Spalding found that the professional seal of approval was not necessary at first to sell the Top-Flite. There was a huge market out there just waiting to be tapped, and it was only a matter of years before Top-Flite was the best-selling ball in the world.

Not only did the Surlyn ball prove to be more durable than the brittle Bartsch ball, but it had a little more bounce to the ounce. While the two-piece Top-Flite could not compete with the balata-wound rubber core in all-around performance, it surpassed the standard-bearer, Titleist, in combined distance of driver and iron shots. In fact, when Spalding ads called Top-Flite the longest ball, the claim was based on the combined driver/iron distance, while all other makers used only the driver distance. The Federal Trade Commission "suggested" that the ads be accompanied by an explanation in the future, but did not fine Spalding for misleading advertising.

The success of the Golden Ram and Top-Flite opened the floodgates, and nearly every company, small and large, came out with Surlyn balls. Many of these were following in Spalding's footsteps and turning out the sensational new two-piece balls, proven effective by Top-Flite's success. By the mid-70s, Dunlop, Hogan, Wilson and even Acushnet all offered Surlyn balls. Hogan did this with its three-piece Hogan Leader in 1976, as did Dunlop with the Black Max-Fli XLT-15.

By 1979 Spalding followed up the Top-Flite with the two-piece Molitor, named after the man who had adapted Surlyn for the company. This ball also had a softer Surlyn cover designed to play more like balata, without the loss of durability. Whereas "old" Surlyn balls were dubbed "cut-proof," these new offerings were scaled down a notch and called "cut-resistant." The goal of these manufacturers was to find that perfect combination of distance, performance and durability—to equal Titleist's balata-cover-wound construction. Today they are getting closer.

Indeed, the company that held out the longest on Surlyn was Acushnet, the industry leader. Since 1949 their Titleist has been considered the best ball on the market. It is the overwhelming choice among professionals—who didn't show much interest in a two-piece Surlyn ball. Acushnet's view was that the balata-wound rubber core was the best type of ball. But in an effort to offer balls to all levels of players, Acushnet came out in 1974 with the Surlyn-covered Titleist DT—a three-piece wound ball (DT stands for durable Titleist).

Twenty-five plus years from rags to riches for a deserving golfer: Lee Trevino, or "The Happy Mex."

Just eight years after their introduction, Surlyn-covered golf balls had claimed a 65-percent share of the market. There were thirty different makes of Surlyn-wound rubber cores, and nine different Surlyn two-piece balls. Among them were two from Faultless: the Omega and the Lee Trevino Sombrero; four from Spalding: Top-Flite, Molitor, Era-1 and Flying Lady; the Rawlings; the Red Wing; the U.S. Royal Master; and the Confidence. By comparison, there were just twelve different types of balata-wound balls in production in 1976, just eight years after practically everything on the market was made of balata.

While the golfing public at large was gobbling up these low-cost, long-lasting balls made of Surlyn, the professionals on the PGA Tour played almost exclusively with balata-wound rubber cores during the 1970s. But there were some who played Surlyn, and even a few who used the two piece. Whether they did so because they thought they were using a better ball, or because they were getting six-digit bucks from the maker to use it is another question. Whatever the reason, players went on to win some pretty big tournaments playing Surlyn—like the aforementioned Tom Shaw, and like Billy Casper, who won an event with the Wilson Pro-Staff, a Surlyn three-piece ball.

Lee Trevino was an early proponent of Surlyn; the Merry Mex was the first professional to win a tournament using a two-piece ball. In 1974 he won the World Series of Golf playing the two-piece Faultless Omega. Hall-of-Famer Trevino had a special interest in Faultless because he had an endorsement contract with the company and even had his own name on one of the balls—the Lee Trevino Sombrero. After Faultless discontinued making balls in 1974, Trevino signed on with Spalding. Later he used Titleist balatas; once again he returned to Spalding. Since he has won twenty-seven tournaments and over three million dollars, Trevino's choice of balls didn't hurt him. This seems to confirm the opinion that performance depends on how the pro is playing that day rather than upon the ball he is using. One old-timer confided that he could use almost any type of ball equally well when he was playing well. Perhaps all of us mid- and high-handicappers should pay more attention to the pros advice than to what ball, club, glove, and shoes we use.

In spite of this swing to Surlyn solid-core balls, Jim Russell, the innovative President of Fulflex—which supplies 90 percent of the rubber thread for wound balls—said he was supplying just as much as ever. He claims the ball business is growing so rapidly that the two-piece ball has merely picked up the increased demand.

Currently Surlyn covers over 90 percent of the balls made, mostly with solid cores. The basic patent expired in 1983. Since then there have been a bevy of new patents—modifications of the original formula, or various combinations of over twenty kinds of Surlyn formulas.

Pimples to Dimples: The Ball Flies Farther

AERODYNAMIC MAGIC

Perhaps the first to discover the advantage of doctoring the surface of the golf ball were nineteenth-century Scottish golfers. In 1848, a young Scottish divinity student named Robert Paterson had invented the solid golf ball, which was molded from a Far Eastern gum called gutta percha. The material was durable and rubber-like, which made it travel farther than the formerly-used "featherie." However, the smooth-surfaced ball flew very low and erratically. Like a bottle rocket, it moved pretty fast, but you weren't sure which way it would turn.

It didn't take long before golfers realized that a slightly-used gutta-percha golf ball was better than a new one because the relatively soft gutta material, prone to cuts and nicks, was easily indented by mis-hits with the club. With indentations the used gutta flew better because it gave the ball some traction and lift as it shot through the air. Soon, ball makers were hammering dents into the new guttas before selling them; in fact, people were hired for just that purpose.

Later, some balls were given grooved markings by being heated in a pattern mold. As crude as

Rev. Dr. Robert Paterson moved to Binghamton, New York in later years.

115

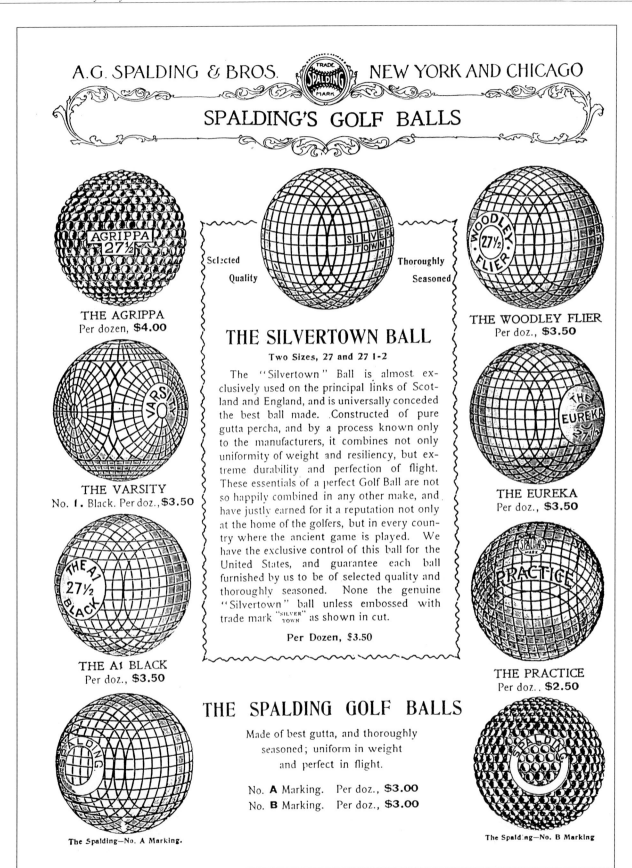

A.G. SPALDING & BROS.   NEW YORK AND CHICAGO

SPALDING'S GOLF BALLS

THE AGRIPPA
Per dozen, $4.00

THE VARSITY
No. 1. Black. Per doz., $3.50

THE A1 BLACK
Per doz., $3.50

Selected Quality   Thoroughly Seasoned

THE SILVERTOWN BALL

Two Sizes, 27 and 27 1-2

The "Silvertown" Ball is almost exclusively used on the principal links of Scotland and England, and is universally conceded the best ball made. Constructed of pure gutta percha, and by a process known only to the manufacturers, it combines not only uniformity of weight and resiliency, but extreme durability and perfection of flight. These essentials of a perfect Golf Ball are not so happily combined in any other make, and have justly earned for it a reputation not only at the home of the golfers, but in every country where the ancient game is played. We have the exclusive control of this ball for the United States, and guarantee each ball furnished by us to be of selected quality and thoroughly seasoned. None the genuine "Silvertown" ball unless embossed with trade mark "SILVER TOWN" as shown in cut.

Per Dozen, $3.50

THE WOODLEY FLIER
Per doz., $3.50

THE EUREKA
Per doz., $3.50

THE PRACTICE
Per doz., $2.50

THE SPALDING GOLF BALLS

Made of best gutta, and thoroughly seasoned; uniform in weight and perfect in flight.

No. **A** Marking. Per doz., $3.00
No. **B** Marking. Per doz., $3.00

The Spalding—No. A Marking.

The Spalding—No. B Marking

A grouping of nine Spalding gutta percha balls molded in two designs:
A–circle, B–bramble (also referred to as pimple) designs.

Like-new smooth gutta-percha ball invented by Robert Patterson c. 1845. A rare ball in this condition.

Hand-hammered gutta-percha ball—to improve the flight by roughening the surface, c. 1860.

The Spalding Agrippa Ball in bramble pattern c. 1898. Value today is perhaps 200 times the dozen price for <u>one</u> ball.

Atti Pattern for dimple balls from early 1900s to 1971. (Colored cross is for design emphasis).

***Mesh-pattern ball invented by Albert Penfold in 1912 (indented
squares instead of circles). Used into the 1930s.***

these measures may have been, they were the start of aerodynamic inventions. The hammered indentations had a profound effect upon the way the ball flew, because the turbulence caused the ball to spin more rapidly; the faster it spun, the higher it flew.

Today, ball-makers strive for balls with high spin rates and high trajectory because these two properties give the golfer the most control over the ball, allowing him to direct the ball to drop "dead" on the green, for example, with much greater accuracy. Today a 150-yard shot by a tour member may drop within two feet of the pin and roll a few inches.

Surprisingly, in an industry that seems today to be constantly moving forward technologically, most of the twentieth century saw stagnation rather than progress. Up until 1908, Brambles, balls with bumps rather than dents (more like pimples than dimples—convex, not concave) were in vogue—that is, until 1908, when Englishman William Taylor received a patent for a ball with indentations, or dimples, which flew better than one with pimples. Spalding bought the rights to the Taylor patent and came out that same year with the first dimpled ball, "Glory," featuring "Taylor Dimples."

For the next 60-plus years, most balls looked exactly the same—on the outside, anyway. Except for balls patterned after experiments by Albert E. Penfold with mesh and lattice designs in 1912 and used until the 1930s, nearly every ball had 336 round Taylor dimples on the exterior. It seems that companies were too focused on supercharged cores with compressed air, glycerine, or steel balls, to worry about simple aerodynamics that steered the ball.

In the 1970s the United States Golf Association set regulations to control the distance the ball can travel; these are covered in detail elsewhere in the book. Temporarily derailed in their drive to make the longest golf ball, manufacturers discovered a way to tiptoe around these USGA regulations. By shifting their focus to aerodynamics, ball makers learned that they could improve the ball's distance and performance without altering the size, weight or construction of the ball. By redesigning the way the dimples are laid out, they found a way to get maximum distance while staying within the parameters of the initial velocity ruling.

Until 1971, the only dimple pattern was the "Atti Pattern," named after Ralph Atti, owner of a tool-and-die shop in Union, New Jersey. The Atti pattern was an octahedron pattern, split up into eight concentric rows of straight lines of dimples around the ball. Mr. Atti had a near-monopoly on dimple pattern molds and supplied his one pattern to practically the whole trade. This pattern covered 66 percent of the ball surface with dimples.

But in 1971, Atti would run up against some competition—lots of it as the decade wore on. This was the year that the "dimple war" officially began, and it has been going strong ever since. A company named Uniroyal fired the first shot in 1971 when they introduced the Royal "Plus Six." The name derived from the company's claim that their ball would carry six yards farther than any other ball off the tee. Perhaps it was no coincidence that the Plus Six featured hexagon-shaped dimples. Developed in consultation with Dr. John Nicolaides, an aerospace engineer at the University of Notre Dame, who used their wind-tunnel for trials, this new six-sided dimple breakthrough was credited by Uniroyal with the extra distance: They claimed that the 252 randomly-spaced, hexagon-shaped dimples created more "lift" than conventional dimples arranged in straight rows. Whether it was any better than the Atti pattern

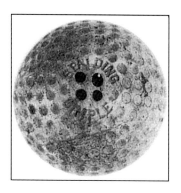

After Taylor invented the Dimple ball in England, Spalding, under license, produced the first U.S. ball called Dimple. (Photo courtesy the Olmans).

Uniroyal Hexagon Dimples. One of balls featuring various-shaped indentation patterns in addition to a range of dimple diameters and depths.

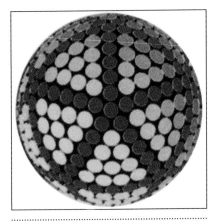

The Titleist icosahedron pattern in 1971, which improved the Atti pattern by covering more of the surface.

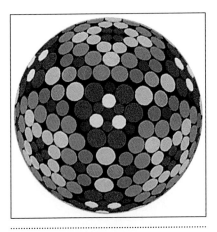

Titleist HVC (high velocity core), covering 78% of the surface with new cubocahedron pattern giving more lift and less drag. Five different size dimples—each size shown in different color for emphasis. Invented by Dr. William Gobush.

is questionable, because very few, if any, companies obtained rights to utilize this pattern for their balls. But what Uniroyal did with the Royal Plus Six was to open other manufacturers' eyes to the seemingly endless possibilities that exist with regard to dimple science, and the profound effect they can have on the ball's flight.

In 1973, just two years after the Plus Six, Acushnet introduced a new dimple design that shook up the industry and prompted manufacturers to dive head first into dimple technology. Unveiled on the new Titleist Regular and Titleist 100, this break-through ball featured the icosahedron dimple pattern—a configuration that divides the ball's surface into twenty triangular regions. This very complicated and scientific-sounding design created a more consistent spacing pattern between dimples, boasted Acushnet. Acushnet's tall, pipe-smoking research director John Jepson said that this new kind of "spatial relationship" reduced drag and improved flight consistency because the air flow remains essentially the same regardless of the ball's orientation. Basically, it helped the ball fly straighter and higher.

The Titleist had fewer dimples than the conventional ball—336—but they were larger (by fifteen percent) and shallower (by ten percent), and, importantly, they covered more of the ball's surface. Dimple size, dimple depth, dimple coverage . . . all can have very different effects on the flight of the golf ball, as ball makers were learning. Balls with larger, shallower dimples had a tendency to fly higher, or had a "higher trajectory" (the path in which a ball flies). Larger, shallower dimples reduced the force of drag, allowing the ball to almost float—higher—through the air. Conversely, balls with smaller, deeper dimples tended to fly at a lower trajectory because the deeper pockets on the ball gave it better "traction" through the air—such a ball flies in a more boringly direct manner.

With the advent of Surlyn and these new aerodynamic dimple discoveries, suddenly the discerning golfer had a smorgasbord of choices. Did he or she want to hit towering drives that stop on a dime, or low shots that run for many yards? Maybe something in between? No problem. In the past all balls had the same dimple pattern, and all ball covers were made of balata, which meant that all balls generally performed similarly. Some were more souped-up on the inside, which set them apart—but in terms of the exterior, there was little difference. Beginning in the 1970s, however, suddenly it was both Mr. Inside and Mr. Outside who decided how the ball would travel in the air.

For example, in 1972, the first year USGA published a list of balls that conformed to the rules and were approved for tournaments, Spalding had three balls on the list—the Dot 90, Dot 100, and Top-Flite. Twenty years later it had 80 on the list. Acushnet/Titleist had gone from two listings (Titleist K and Titleist K100) in 1972 to 72 listings. In the Spring 1996 edition each company had about 180. This may be progress, but how much diversification is worthwhile?

POLE/SEAM MARKINGS	COLOR	COMPRESSION	CONSTRUCTION	COVER	DIMPLES	COLOR	COMPRESSION	CONSTRUCTION	COVER	DIMPLES
Titleist *PTS 90*	yellow	90	WS	S	392	white		WS	S	420
Titleist *PTS 100*	white	100	WL	B	392	white		2P	S	420
Titleist *PTS 90*	white	90	WL	B	392					
Titleist *Tour Distance*	white		2P	S	392	white		2P	O	410
Titleist *WLS 100*	white	100	WS	S	392	white		2P	S	422
Titleist *WLS 90*	white	90	WS	S	392					
Titleist ▲ HVC ▲	white		2P	S	440	white	100	2P	S	432
Titleist ▲ HVC ▲	yellow		2P	S	440					
Titleist ▲Eclipse▲	white		Oth	S	456					
Titleist ▲Project X▲	white		Oth	S	456	white	100	2P	O	422
Titleist ◄DT 100►	white	100	WS	S	392	white	90	2P	O	422
Titleist ◄DT 90►	white	90	WS	S	392	white	90	2P	O	422
Titleist ◄Tour 100►	white	100	WL	B	392					
Titleist ◄Tour 90►	white	90	WL	B	392					
Titleist Beta.One	white		Oth	S	456	white		2P	S	492
Titleist Beta▲One	white		Oth	S	456					
Titleist DT ▲ 100	white	100	WS	S	392	white	90	2P	S	432
Titleist DT ▲ 2-Piece	white	80	WS	S	392	orange yellow	90	2P	S	432
Titleist DT ▲ 80	white	80	WS	S	392	white	90	2P	S	432

Typical page from USGA Conforming Ball List 1996, page 3.
WS=wound; 2P=two-piece; S=Surlyn; O=other

Balls made with balata were softer by nature, which meant they could be made to spin faster, fly higher, and drop more steeply. On the other hand, Surlyn is tougher and heavier than balata: it spins less upon impact, flies at a lower trajectory and a little farther.

Now manufacturers could make a super high-flying ball by making it out of balata with larger dimples, like a Titleist balata, or a virtual worm-burner, by going with Surlyn and smaller dimples. Combinations and permutations were unlimited.

Dunlop was one of the first to experiment in this manner, releasing two different balls in 1979 that had similar flight characteristics. The Max-Fli XLT-15 was of three-piece construction with a soft synthetic balata cover and smaller deeper dimples, while the Silver Max-Fli was a two-piece model with Surlyn cover that had wider, shallower dimples to promote higher flight. Both had the standard 336 dimples, and both had elements to mitigate against either extreme distance, height, or spin.

Spalding also came out with a new ball in 1979, the Top-Flite XL, a companion to the best-selling Top-Flite. In coming out with the new Top-Flite XL, Spalding attempted to incorporate some of the qualities that the Top-Flite lacked, like high trajectory. The Top-Flite, famous for its durability, low trajectory and distance with the irons, was still not a favorite among the pros, who generally preferred the higher-flying balls because they gave them the ability to better control their shots. (Presently more tour pros use Titleist than all other makes combined). To court that group, Spalding made the XL with 330 wider, shallower dimples.

Moving in an opposite direction, the other industry giant, Acushnet Titleist, was in the process of expanding the mass market as they already had the class market, with Titleist. Acushnet came out in 1979 with the Titleist "Low Traj" (marked LT)—a synthetic balata-covered three-piece with smaller, deeper dimples to keep the ball at a low trajectory.

Dr. William Gobush, brilliant Titleist mathematician and inventor who led the way to covering 79% of ball surface with dimples.

After Uniroyal and Acushnet, the third company to deviate from the norm was Wilson in 1976. The new Wilson Pro-Staff had 300 flat-bottomed dimples, with the sides of each one tapered and straight, creating a truncated "cone" dimple. These truncated cone dimples were twenty percent larger, and shallower than the regular dimple, producing a higher trajectory in this three-piece ball made with a cover of soft-blended Surlyn formula. Wilson said that the cone-shaped dimple gave the ball more carry without excessive height, and let it land at a steep angle, minimizing roll and maximizing control.

The innovations with regard to dimple science by Acushnet, Dunlop, Wilson, and Royal were only the tip of the iceberg. In the 1980s and into the 1990s, dimples became the focus of ball manufacturers. Instead of covering more of the ball's surface with the large, shallow dimples, ball makers found it more effective to use smaller or various-sized dimples which covered a greater percent of the ball's surface. Not only did an increased number of dimples reduce drag, but it created a cushioning effect that made the ball softer when struck. In the early 1980s, dimple counts increased to 384, 392, and 400, and by the end of the decade there were balls with more than 500 dimples—even one with more than 800. In 1991, William Gobush, Titleist's renowned mathematician magician, received Patent #5,060,954 for a breakthrough design that covers 78 percent of the area, with superior performance: about a twenty percent improvement.

Today men and women pros can choose from more than 1,000 different conforming balls that fit their style or playing conditions—a difference of light years from 1930, when all balls were balata-covered three-piece wound balls all having the same number of dimples: what might be called a level playing-field, a test of skill. Perhaps what goes around may come around again so that some day there may be a standard ball for pros, also one each for low, medium and high handicappers—to compensate partially for the increasing complexity of golf courses, make golf more fun for all golfers, and possibly take the place of handicaps.

The box contains St. Mungo's Colonel balls: 1.55 oz. and 1.68-inch balloon balls. The display shows some of proliferating trade names and design from 1900 to c. 1930.

Harnessing The Lively Ball: Rules and Regulations

The trend to standardization of the golf ball has been going on for over one hundred years. In the nineteenth century in Britain there was none. Guttie golf balls were merely classified by measuring in pennyweight and ranged from a low of 26 or 27 dwt. to the heavies of 32 to 33 dwt. (about 1.4 to 1.6 ounces).

BALL SIZE AND WEIGHT

Until the 1920s, there were no set regulations in the United States on the size or weight of balls, so makers produced a wide variety based mostly on whim and demand. There was the "small heavy," which flew like a bullet,

Lack of standards in ball size in the 19th century.

Three diameters: Wilson 1.62, Penfold 1.65 (experimental), and MacGregor 1.68 (but with a 1.55 weight, played only one year and known as the "Balloon Ball.")

then there was the "floater," which was so light that it floated on water. (This was popular among those golfers with the unwanted knack for finding any existing water). Realizing that this unregulated situation was seriously threatening the integrity of the game, the British R & A and the USGA went to the table in 1920 to agree on a standardized ball. But each had very different ideas of what the answer should be.

The Royal and Ancient wanted a heavier ball, primarily because of the geographic/atmospheric conditions in Britain. In Britain, most of the golf courses were laid out in traditional links fashion; that is, the holes were linked together like sausages, nine holes in one direction and nine holes in the other, mostly along the seaside, where heavy winds, rain and fog predominated. Hence the heavy ball.

But in America, weather wasn't as much of a concern. The biggest concern of the USGA was the innovative and creative genius of American ball makers, evidenced by the turn-of-the-century discovery of the Haskell three-piece wound ball. Almost annually, another company would introduce a new ball composition, size, weight, or design—each supposedly longer than the last. From 1900 to 1920 the average distance of tee shots had increased about twenty-five yards, as a result of the Haskell wound ball's having replaced the gutties. The goal of the USGA was to draw rein on some of these wild-eyed mavericks with a limit on length of carry. A lighter ball was favored than what the R & A proposed, because the lighter the ball the shorter the flight, and distance was already a problem (as it still is today).

As a result of the 1920 conference, the two sides agreed (after long and heated discussions) on a standardized ball measuring not under 1.62 inches in diameter and weighing not over 1.62 ounces. The new rule went into effect in 1921. From then on any ball used in a tournament, local or national, had to be what was termed a 1.62 x 1.62 ball.

While the R & A was quite satisfied with this new standard, the USGA still thought the standard ball was too small, too heavy, and too powerful for American golf courses. After fending off a lot of static from all sources until the mid-1920s, the USGA tried to convince the R & A to rethink the agreed-on standard, but there was no enthusiasm for the American idea. As a result of this stand-off, the USGA began a serious series of tests, concluding that the ball had to be lighter, regardless of British opposition.

In 1931 the USGA broke away from the R & A to institute a new standard-sized ball in America, one measuring not less than 1.68 inches in diameter and weighing not over 1.55 oz. This ill-fated creation became known as the "balloon ball," and lasted only one year before it became a memory (and a worthwhile collectible). The USGA shelved it because it was too light, and the rest of the public disapproved because it did not go far enough. So in 1932 the USGA found a suitable compromise. They left the size at 1.68 inches or more, but upped the weight back to at least 1.62 oz. Now there were two standards: the 1.62 x 1.62 in the United Kingdom and the 1.68 x 1.62 in the United States.

For more than 35 years it remained that way, until 1968, when the R & A made the larger American ball mandatory for all British PGA events. The British had come to the stark and painful realization that the 1.68 x 1.62 ball was better suited to the modern game. First, newer, inland courses like those typically built in the United States and Canada were popping up all across Great Britain. No longer was the dense British ball an advantage.

Second, and perhaps more significant, the R & A had realized that American professionals were dominating the international circuit. Whether or not this was due to the superior performance of the United States professionals is questionable; at any rate, in the next few years after the R & A adopted the American standard, British pros saw a marked improvement in their own performance against Americans.

The R & A had only adopted the American standard for British PGA events, not the British Open or British Amateur events. But there was a loud minority within the R & A which did not at all want to adopt the larger ball. Perhaps it was the "Ugly American" syndrome. It may go back to 1900 and Haskell's "bounding billy." Or perhaps it was out of a desire to come up with a ball that everyone could accept. Whatever the reason, a compromise ball was proposed within the R & A.

The compromise called for a ball measuring at least 1.66 inches in diameter and weighing 1.62 ounces or less. After kicking this proposal around for a few years, both the USGA and the R & A decided against it, and the "compromise ball" was never heard from again. It is not clear if any of these were ever made, or, if so, how many. In 1974 the last bastion of British opposition, the British Open, made the American standard theirs. Now after more than 50 years of vacillation, the world was playing with the same size ball, specifically a ball not less than 1.68 inches in diameter and not more than 1.62 ounces in weight.

The USGA Rules for Tournament Play are shown in the accompanying illustration. They cover not only size and weight, but also velocity and distance and further very important characteristics.

Appendix III
THE BALL

a. Weight

The weight of the ball shall not be greater than 1.620 ounces avoirdupois (45.93 gm).

b. Size

The diameter of the ball shall be not less than 1.680 inches (42.67 mm). This specification will be satisfied if, under its own weight, a ball falls through a 1.680 inches diameter ring gauge in fewer than 25 out of 100 randomly selected positions, the test being carried out at a temperature of 23±1°C.

c. Spherical Symmetry

The ball must not be designed, manufactured or intentionally modified to have properties which differ from those of a spherically symmetrical ball.

d. Initial Velocity

The velocity of the ball shall not be greater than 250 feet (76.2 m) per second when measured on apparatus approved by the United States Golf Association. A maximum tolerance of 2% will be allowed. The temperature of the ball when tested shall be 23±1°C.

e. Overall Distance Standard

A brand of golf ball, when tested on apparatus approved by the USGA on the outdoor range at the USGA Headquarters under the conditions set forth in the Overall Distance Standard for golf balls on file with the USGA, shall not cover an average distance in carry and roll exceeding 280 yards (256 m) plus a tolerance of 6%.

Note: The 6% tolerance will be reduced to a minimum of 4% as test techniques are improved.

From the 1996 USGA Rules of Golf, page 118.

■ BALL DISTANCE

The changes in the late 1960s and early '70s put the USGA in another tight place. Their goal has always been to preserve and protect the integrity of the game—"to over-regulate it," some ball manufacturers would say. Imagine the game of golf without some benevolent despot—yes, chaos. In 1941, the Association took a major step in corralling the potential power of science's impact on the golf ball. This was done by instituting the present initial velocity test.

The regulation mandated that a ball would not conform to USGA standards if the velocity of the ball upon impact with the club was more than 255 feet per second (which includes the two percent allowance for variation). This is equivalent to a speed of about 173 miles per hour, somewhat less than that needed to qualify for the Indianapolis 500. The USGA Testing Lab, under the direction of capable Frank Thomas, uses a mechanical device called the Armour machine to deliver highly standardized impact. (This ball velocity should not be confused with the club-head speed attained by the golfer—the speed of the ball is always greater than the club-head speed). But storm clouds were ahead.

The scientific analysis of the design of the cover in the 1970s, and the resulting aerodynamic breakthroughs, enabled the ball makers to increase ball performance and distance without violating the words of the velocity rule—but perhaps the spirit of the rule suffered. Actually, the initial velocity test did not limit the distance the ball traveled. The improved balls flew through the air with less resistance, and therefore went longer distances.

While the initial velocity test still was extremely useful, it had to be supplemented. This was done by adopting the Overall Distance Standard in 1976.

The Overall Distance Standard dictates that any ball traveling farther than 280 yards (plus six percent allowance, totalling 296 yards), including the carry and the resulting roll, is not approved for tournament use. The USGA uses a standard testing machine called the Tru Temper at their outdoor range, and adjusts for variations in weather and other variables. For this test the machine is set for a club-head speed of about 106 miles per hour, greater than a majority of golfers can generate. In effect, the test warned the manufacturers that whatever they do to the ball is their business as long as it does not go farther than 296 yards under standard conditions.

John Daly in 1995 had the highest average for driving for the PGA Tour: 280 feet.

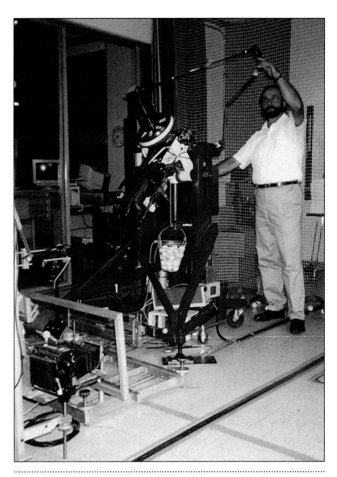

Initial Velocity Test. To test for initial velocity, balls are placed on a tee and hit with a metal striker. The ball speed is measured and recorded. The speed of a top-grade ball is approximately 173 miles per hour.

USGA "Iron Byron" driving machine, which monitors maximum distance.

Indoor Test Range. The Indoor Test Range (ITR) is the first of its kind and was developed by the USGA.

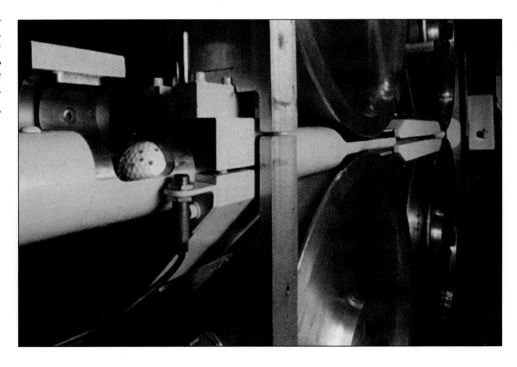

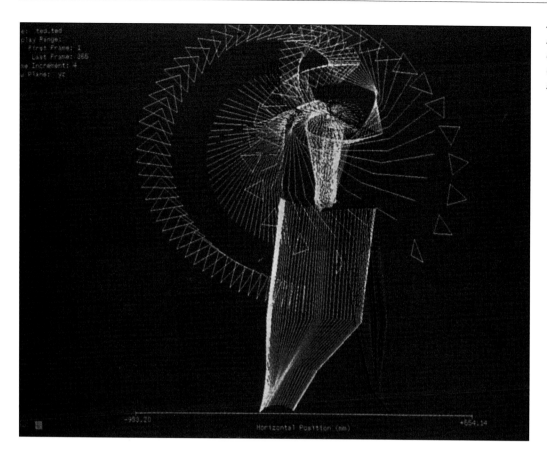

An electronically-described and computer-analyzed swing of any golfer.

Driving records are set with the wind, not driving against.

In 1992 tournaments and contests this limit has been exceeded by John Daly. As winner of the 1991 PGA Championship he averaged 288.9 yards per drive. Monte Scheinblaum, 25, of La Quinta, California, won the Chrysler Long Driving Championship in the finals with one blast of a whopping 329 yards, one foot, and one inch. Many others have done better than 296 yards under varying conditions. This does not mean that these two and other heavy hitters like Freddie Couples are violating the rules. The answer is the difference in the conditions under which the drive is made. In short, the word is "variables": variation from standard in club-head speed, the temperature, the elevation, the direction and the velocity of the wind, the condition of the fairway, the placement of the tee (perhaps much higher than the green) and numerous less important ways. *The Guinness Book of Golf* shows drives of over 400 yards and a freak of 747 yards, perhaps from Pike's Peak with a 100-mile tail wind.

BALL VARIATION

Earlier in the twentieth century the inability of manufacturers to maintain a high degree of uniformity in golf balls was due to many factors. For example, balata, used on three-piece wound Titleist balls, preferred by pros, is a natural gum produced from a Bully Gum tree under varying weather conditions. Varying trees, gathering and processing resulted in variations of the finished ball. In the early days, when scratch golfers or pros like Walter Hagen bought a dozen balls, they would go to the range and drive each one. From a dozen they might only select as few as four to play in competition. That uniformity problem, or related quality problem, is in the past. No problem. U.S. balls stack are equal to and in most cases superior to those from Japan. Every one in the dozen can be used. However, ball selection still exists.

During the 1970s and '80s, with the explosive jumps in choice of types of U.S. balls from 25 in 1972 to 58 in 1980 to 132 in 1985 to a more than double 300 in 1992, a different kind of ball selection developed. The pros began to use as many as four different types of balls in one eighteen-hole round of big tournaments. By experience they matched the ball (length, spin and trajectory) to the existing conditions on any one hole—based on the weather, fairway design and condition, or other subtle differences. The Test Center at USGA is now testing 20,000 balls a year.

The days of specialization had arrived. But not without adverse comment. Up to 40 percent of the pros were using this refinement, which maneuvering cancelled out some of the advantages the more skilful players had acquired. Pros who had a six-figure contract to promote a Top-Flite had better not be caught using a Titleist around the green because it "dropped dead" better. Naturally, they were also against this switch and match practice. The USGA resolved these differences among the players by ruling in 1979 that only one type of specifically listed, approved ball could be used throughout any tournament event. This ended ball switching—but not the proliferation of balls. Again the question—why not one standard ball such as other sports have?

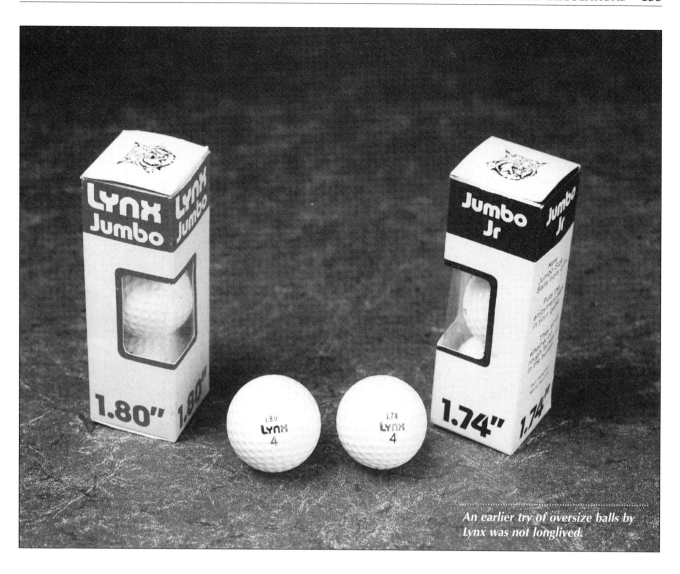

An earlier try of oversize balls by Lynx was not longlived.

A 1993 re-introduction of an oversize ball—1.72 inches— by Spalding. Similar to other Lynx balls.

■ SYMMETRY RULE

It took only one ball in 1975 to promulgate the newest ball restrictions. It was the Polara ball, designed and patented by David Napala and Dr. Fred Holmstrom, that triggered the ruling. The story of this ball and how it reduced slices and hooks by simple aerodynamic changes is more fully told in Chapter 17, The Polara Ball. While the ball was quickly disapproved by USGA it took until 1981 to issue the new Symmetry Rule. This rule provides that every conforming ball approved by USGA must perform exactly the same in flight, no matter how it is oriented when placed on the tee. This made the Polara—which had to have its row of dimples lined up in the direction of flight—illegal. The rule was phrased differently: ". . . a ball must in general be spherical in shape and designed to have equal aerodynamic properties and equal moments of inertia about any axis through its center."

Scottie is happy to use USGA's new ESP (Equitable Stroke Procedure). With his handicap in the 10 to 19 range, the highest score he has to record is a 7 for any hole.

The decision on a ball is made by taking a submitted sample of forty balls and passing them through a ring gauge with a maximum diameter of 1.68 inches. If twenty-six of the balls pass through the ring, the ball is approved on this particular test. At the 1993 PGA Show in Orlando, Spalding introduced a new ball called the Top-Flite Magna, measuring 1.72 inches in diameter, 0.04 inch more. This does not violate the present USGA standard of not less than 1.68 inches, but it does mean Frank Thomas had to make a new ring gauge. Lynx did not succeed earlier. Perhaps Spalding's marketing power and copywriter mesmerism will.

HANDICAPS

A major simplification of the nineteen-year-old system for applying handicaps became effective January 1st, 1993. Dean Knuth, Director of USGA Handicapping, said that after all these years of using the old system, less than twenty-five percent of players knew how to use it. Jeanne Myers, a member of Women's Handicapping Procedure, came up with a "maximum number idea," a drastic change after years of confusion. Golfers now only have to remember one number that is based on their handicap, as shown in the table below. That number is the maximum score you record on any of the eighteen holes.

USGA 1993 EQUITABLE STROKE PROCEDURE

18 Hole Course Handicap	Maximum Number Posted on Any Hole
9 or less	6
10 through 19	7
20 through 29	8
30 through 39	9
40 through 49	10
50 and above	11

Arnold Palmer might have won the 1961 Los Angeles Open if this rule had been in effect. He would have entered only a six for the 508-yard, par 5, ninth hole, instead of an unheard-of 12 that he actually took to finish the hole—except handicaps don't count on the Pro Tours.

*Revised Polara Ball with shallow dimples added at
the poles (instead of none) to improve performance.*

The Polara Ball: Hit the Courts, Not the Greens

Alastair J. Johnston, golf bibliophile par excellence, Arnold Palmer associate, concludes from his research and experience that various improvements in the golf ball have been more important than all the gains in players' skill, golf course design/maintenance, club materials design and accessories combined. When one scans the results of the U.S. Open for the last fifty years it appears that the winning scores have improved about two strokes for eighteen holes. From 1900 to about 1940 it appears to have been about six strokes, mostly due to the change from the gutta percha to the three-piece Haskell ball.

Some of the improvement is certainly due to greater uniformity. At one time pros tried every ball in a new box of a dozen, and might select three or four for tournament use. Today that practice is no longer necessary. All companies making balls today have given quality top priority. For example, Titleist inspects every golf ball for a number of physical and visual defects.

But in 1975, along came a ball which dramatically threatened to change the game, maybe not immediately, but certainly down the road. And it took USGA by surprise. The ball was produced by PGA/Victor, the interim name for the veteran Worthington Ball Company, who had also shocked the industry some years before by selling a ball that contained radium (and so was named The Radium Ball). This latest product was called the Polara, touted as a hookless and sliceless ball. You can just visualize how the high-handicappers dreamed of lowering their scores by five to ten strokes.

Now there have been balls in the past for which this very same claim was made: in particular, a ball released in the 1800s. However, the Polara dream bubble burst because what the ball gained in staying on the fairway was more than lost by its poor performance in distance off the tee.

Nevertheless, the Polara was purely and simply genius. Through applying simple aerodynamic principles, a couple of California inventors devised a ball that would fly straight without violating anything in the USGA rule book. David Nepala, a Saratoga, California chemist working for IBM, and Dr. Fred Holmstrom, a physicist at San Jose University, developed a three-piece wound ball that was smooth at the poles and had a band of dimples around its equator. The fact that the bald portions lacked any indentations gave the ball the gyroscopic effect of holding a straight flight line. When struck, as touring pro John Lots would attest after sampling the ball, the Polara ball righted itself in flight, because the smooth poles practically eliminated any sidespin effects. This makes such obvious sense that one wonders why, with the millions spent yearly in research, this idea lay dormant until the late 1970s.

The fact that the original Polara test ball went a thirty-to-forty yard shorter distance off the tee was a real downer, but for high-handicappers, keeping the ball in the fairway was more important. The distance deficiency could and would be remedied in the coming years. USGA, however, was deeply worried about the dire effects the ball was having on the game.

It was America's bicentennial year, 1976, when PGA/Victor submitted the Polara ball to the USGA for approval as a conforming ball for tournament play. The inventors saw no problem in getting an OK, and why should they, since their balls met all USGA standards? But on testing the ball that year, USGA found that this ball would drastically change the way the game of golf was played. They reacted accordingly, refusing to approve the Polara while they began to draft a law to ban the Polara and all similar balls. The USGA ruled, "It [the Polara] would reduce the skill required to play golf and threaten the integrity of the game." Until tests were completed and a rule adopted that would ban the Polara, the USGA mandated that no ball designed to correct a hook or slice in flight would be placed on the approved list.

The USGA staff was working assiduously on a rule requiring a ball to perform similarly no matter how it was oriented on the tee. More specifically, ". . . a ball must in general be spherical in shape and designed to have equal aerodynamic properties and equal moments of inertia about any axis through its center," the USGA stated. This became known as the symmetry rule, but it would not go into effect until 1981. Polara cried foul.

Conforming or not, PGA/Victor went ahead and put the Polara on the market in 1977. Remember, just because a ball is not approved for conforming to USGA rules doesn't mean golfers can't use it in their own games. Conforming balls, however, are the only ones that can be used for sponsored tournaments.

Nepala and Holmstrom modified the hookless/sliceless ball a bit before putting it on the market. Instead of smooth or bald poles the modified Polara had added six rows of dimples in addition to a band of eight dimples at the equator. The Surlyn-covered Polara had the standard .014-inch-deep dimples around the middle and only .0085-inch dimples around the poles. Claimed Polara, "The [air] overflow over the ball is modified by the dimpling pattern. We're sure the ball rights itself in flight." The above-described configuration was asserted to reduce curved shots by 50 percent. Then came the Polara Plus, a companion introduced with the Polara. With even shallower dimples around the poles, measuring .0055 inches deep, the Polara Plus was said to reduce curved shots by 75 percent.

The balls sold well the first year, for about twenty dollars a dozen. Since they were produced in limited numbers, distributors couldn't keep up with the demand and were forced to back-order.

Nepala and Holmstrom were the first to admit that their ball would help golfers improve their game. After all, that is why they developed it—and they saw nothing wrong in that. They claimed history was on their side. The inventors argued that improvements in equipment, specifically in the ball, have more than anything else made the game easier for centuries. The Polara was just the next step in the evolution, or revolution. Look at what Haskell's wound-rubber-core ball did for the game, or what Taylor's dimples did for flight control. "We're not out to ruin the game of golf," said Nepala. "It's in everybody's best interest to keep the game essentially as it is, but I do think there has to be a recognition of evolution." (In an earlier book, John Stuart Martin had characterized it as a series of revolutions).

Themselves frustrated golfers, Nepala and Holmstrom said they made the ball to take some of that frustration out of the game for the average, recreational golfer. It was never intended for the pro or low-handicapper. Given its awkward flight and shorter distance, the folks at Titleist or Spalding did not see it as a threat. And Polara was well-received by the average golfer, who didn't care so much about clubbing it a country mile but just wanted it to stay in the fairway—at a time when many felt that the game was becoming too professional and too demanding for the average player. With "water, water everywhere, and not a drop to drink" on both sides of the tunnel-wide fairways in front, and impenetrable rough surrounding the greens the game was really getting difficult.

Was the USGA over-reacting about the little Polara, as many seemed to suggest? No. Equipment has, of course, made the game easier to a certain degree. The question is—where do you draw the line? What if five years from now Polara, or Titleist, or Spalding introduces a ball that goes farther than any other on the market, has the spin and feel of balata, the durability of Surlyn, rights itself in flight and meets all USGA regulations? It would dominate the market. Everyone would start to produce these balls. The face of the game would change forever, scores would drop, courses would have to be redesigned, and almost everyone would be qualifying as a pro.

Has this happened in the past? Sure. USGA Open winners in the early 1900s scored about 78/79 for eighteen holes. Today the winning scores are at least ten strokes less on courses that have had to be lengthened. So where do you draw the line? The USGA says right here.

After a relatively successful year on the market, the Polara was still waiting for action from the USGA. By 1978 this inactivity was beginning to affect the ball's sales, and Nepala was losing his patience. Later that year Polara Enterprises brought the first-ever lawsuit against the USGA and also against the Golf Ball Manufacturers' Association. The multi-million-dollar suit alleged that the two organizations conspired to keep the Polara and the Polara Plus off the market and to throttle sales. The suit claimed that the USGA's rejection of the ball was discriminatory, claiming that other companies had made claims of reducing hooks and slices without having to undergo this harassment. Polara officials claimed golf shops were discouraged from selling the balls and Polara users were being stigmatized as cheaters.

The main point of contention for the courts to figure out appeared to be semantics. The USGA contended that the Polara corrected the ball in mid-flight, while the Polara people said it merely reduced the amount of curve in flight.

In January 1981, U.S. District Court Judge Robert Schnake in San Francisco ruled in favor of the defendants. Schnake claimed that the plaintiffs, Polara Enterprises, failed to prove any conspiracy. End of the story? Hardly. Polara immediately appealed the judge's decision, and early in 1982 the Appellate Division decided to reverse Schnake's grant of summary judgment, giving Polara the right to a trial. By this time (in fact, the previous year), the USGA had adopted the symmetry rule.

Polara got its trial in 1984, and it was worth the wait. A six-member jury in the U.S. District Court for the Northern District of California found against USGA and GBMA and awarded damages and costs to Polara of close to five million dollars.

However, later that year Schanke ruled that the jury erred in their decision. He overturned the verdict, granting the USGA's motion for "judgment notwithstanding the verdict." Schanke found that there was not a conspiracy against Polara; rather, he said that the USGA had acted solely within their responsibility to the game of golf. Rebuffed, Polara appealed the Schanke decision once again in January 1985. Just before the two parties were scheduled to appear in the Appellate Court, a settlement was reached. The USGA agreed to pay Polara $1,375,000 and Polara was never heard from again. The reader has to decide whether anyone other than the lawyers won. Many feel that the USGA established the right to regulate the game of golf. ✐

The Cayman Ball: A Short Ball, A Short Life

Way back in the 1930s, golf course architect William H. Diddel had a vision, but the man best known for designing the Northwood Country Club in Dallas would not realize this vision until later in life. In the late 1970s Diddel and Robert H. Wells of Ormond Beach, Florida developed a polyurethane ball that went about one-third as far as the average ball—on purpose. They commissioned architect Bill Amick of Daytona Beach to design a course for this "short ball," which he did, a nine-hole course called the Oceans Golf Club in Daytona Beach. The ball, aside from the fact that it didn't go far, didn't bounce or perform correctly either, and the first ever short course experiment ended a few years later without much fanfare.

Whether or not the renowned Jack Nicklaus knew anything about Diddel's little operation is unknown, but one thing is clear: Nicklaus had his own vision for the game he loves, a game which he thinks is getting out of control. Far away in the tropical paradise of the Cayman Islands, Nicklaus created a whole new ballgame.

Through the ages, manufacturers have spent millions to develop a ball that achieves great lengths, because, as one observer so accurately put it, the four most important things the consumer looks for in a golf ball are 1) distance; 2) distance; 3) distance; 4) feel. Which is why it's so significant that Nicklaus, at that time part owner of the MacGregor Sporting Goods Company, commissioned Troy Puckett, a twenty-five year veteran ball designer for Wilson and MacGregor, to create a new ball. After three years of rigorous development he and Larry C. Cadorniga, a Filipino chemical engineer, were granted Patents #4,836,552 and 4,839,116 in January and June 1989, on a ball that goes about half as far as the standard ball. Can you imagine crushing a ball 130 yards? Or what about a mis-hit—it probably wouldn't travel much farther than your shadow. Named after the islands themselves, this new ball was called the Cayman. In terms of chemistry and production it was unique to ballmaking. Some called it revolutionary, saying it would change the game, even save the game that is becoming too long for its own good. Others said it was doomed to fail.

Jack Nicklaus. Proponent of the short ball/short course.

Troy Puckett, President of Cayman Ball Company, inventor and developer of the short ball and many others.

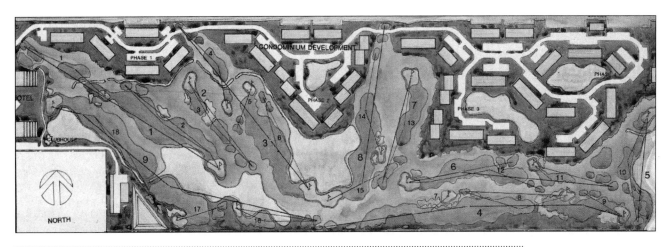

Britannia Golf Course, Cayman Islands. Conceived, designed and paid for by Jack Nicklaus. Brittania, the home of the Cayman Ball, is a multiple course carved out of the woods and scrublands of Grand Cayman Island in the Caribbean. The larger numbers identify the 9-hole, par-35 course for the conventional ball; the smaller numbers connote the 18-hole, par-72 course for the short ball. An 18-hole executive course has also been designed over the same property.

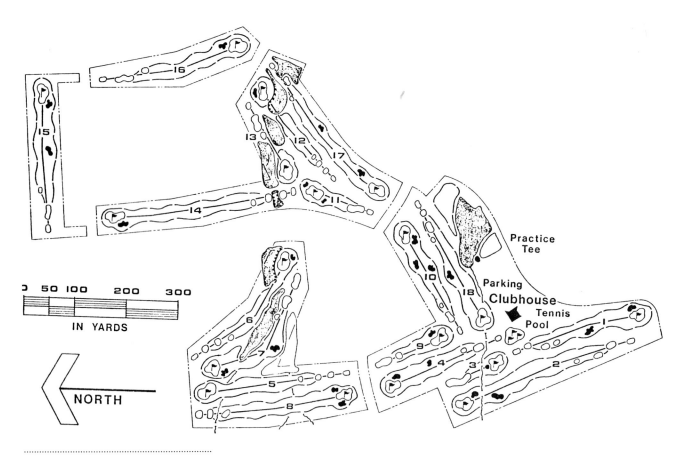

*Eagle Landing Golf Club,
Hanahan, South Carolina.*

Jack Nicklaus-conceived ball, invented by Troy Puckett to go half as far on half-size courses. Also being used as a practice and range ball. Note pimpled cover rather than dimpled.

In the late '70s Nicklaus conceptualized the development of a ball with normal performance characteristics that would go half as far as the regular ball. Measuring 1.68 inches in diameter and weighing about .88 ounces (about half of the 1.62 ounces of a regular ball), the ball conforms to the USGA's standards. What he had in mind for this "short ball" was a short course he was developing on Grand Cayman Island. On about 40 acres, Nicklaus built Britannia, a combination of three courses in one. *One* was an eighteen-hole, 3,338-yard short, par-72 course—a small fraction of the acreage of a regular eighteen-hole layout—designed for his short ball. *Two* was a 3,108-yard par-35 nine-hole course with a separate set of superimposed greens, and *three* was an eighteen-hole, par-60 executive and course—with the latter layouts designed for the normal ball. Included on all of 88 acres, Britannia included a clubhouse, a 240-room hotel and marina, plus villas and condominiums.

Why did Nicklaus do this? When you think about it, it's pure genius, and as with most genius, a fine line separates it from folly. Coming from such a preeminent golfer, the idea immediately had credibility, and got exposure in newspapers and magazines across the country, including *Golf Digest* and *USA Today* (with a feature article). Diddel lived to see a variation of his dream fulfilled before passing away at age 97 in 1992.

On the plus side, short golf would need only about one-third of the land and cost to build as regular golf, and much less to maintain; yet it would accommodate more golfers, including older players. Imagine eighteen holes in less than two hours, with half the clubs and with just as much challenge. Not

only would it be less expensive to play, it would be cheaper to develop—and because just one-quarter the acreage is required, golf courses could be constructed in urban areas. This new idea would open the game up to more people who don't now have the resources to play at a country club in the suburbs. The Cayman ball is designed to play like any other ball in your bag, except that it's lighter, doesn't go as far, and floats.

Now for the downside—distance. When it all comes down to basic motivation, who wants to hit the ball 125 yards?

But consider this—"A 150-acre municipal course that would normally accommodate 200 people in one day [and where the wait for a tee time may be longer than playing time], could handle up to 1,600 if it were designed for the short ball," says Nicklaus. One could envision short ball in cities, or in golf-mad Japan where land is equivalent to acres of diamonds. "The possibilities are endless," says Nicklaus. "I'm not trying to revolutionize anything; I'm just trying to reach people we haven't reached before—to bring new people into golf who can play the game in less time and less expensively."

The intriguing Britannia complex is the first golf course on Grand Cayman, an island no bigger than 118 square miles, with a population of just 18,000. Located in the West Indies, some 480 miles south of Miami, the island course's holes resemble the regular holes you'd see on a par-3 course in size. (In fact, the average par-3 hole would constitute a par-4 with the short ball). The three-in-one golf course at Britannia cost three million dollars to build; the new Cayman ball cost $100,000 to research.

According to Puckett's patent, the Cayman is a solid one-piece ball consisting of a heated mixture of microscopic glass bubbles and Surlyn. All patents mention a truly one-piece ball which has features of a two-piece. The ball is of variable density, softer in the middle and harder on the outside. It is light, but plays like a golf ball.

Nicklaus hits the short ball around 135 yards with a driver, 100 yards with a three-iron, and fifty with a wedge. Putts ten feet and shorter react roughly the same as a normal ball while longer putts have to be hit a little harder.

Short golf had an initial appeal, attracting schools interested in using the Cayman ball for instruction, par-3 courses looking to convert, driving ranges

Six samples of Cayman half-weight experimental balls made during development stages. Some (lower left) carried the MacGregor name.

and country clubs. "Land and how it relates to how much is needed for a golf course is dictated by a little $2 golf ball," said Nicklaus, adding that it's "a lot cheaper to design a golf ball to fit the land."

Remember Bill Amick, golf course architect, who designed the original short course in Daytona Beach? Well, he became the founding member of the American Short Golf Association in Daytona. The ASGA planned a series of short golf tournaments in Florida even before Nicklaus' Britannia made its debut in 1985. Speaking of short golf, "It's a fun game," says Amick, likening the short golf/regulation golf relationship to how softball compares with baseball, being easier for the beginner to play.

A conversation with Bill Amick between trips to Italy, where he was supervising the installation of his combination short course eighteen-hole and regulation nine-hole course, revealed that he felt this to be the trend at the present time. Land cost is running at about one-third of the regulation eighteen-hole course, as is the construction. Operation and maintenance are about one-half. Amick had another on stream in 1993 in Montegallo, France. A new one near Milwaukee has been named the Missing Links. . . . This seems to make sense. For example, during the first four days of the week a course could be played as an eighteen-hole short course—two days set aside for all seniors, men and women, and two days for beginners. Friday, Saturday, and Sunday the course would be a nine-hole—home only for the heavy hitters.

Some specifics on the Cayman ball: it floats, unlike regular balls; it weighs around .8 ounce; and it comes in white, yellow, and orange. Whereas there is a ten to twelve-yard difference between irons with a standard ball, the difference is roughly five to six yards with the Cayman. Nicklaus says a full set of clubs is not necessary. However, he recommends a driver, a three-iron, an eight-iron, a sandwedge and a putter.

Is Cayman Golf the golf ball's next revolution after the Haskell and the Bartsch were overwhelmed by the concurrent Surlyn Fourth revolution? Or is it just another curious oddity in the fascinating game of golf? At this stage it would be more accurately categorized as a very innovative possibility for some future date.

The USGA's Frank Thomas called it a "neat idea" but doubted its ability to catch on. "There may be a group of people who'll play and enjoy Golf II, the shortened game, but it'll never replace Golf I." Others feel differently. While the short course and ball may not be popular now, the demand may be more evident in time to come. Furthermore, this innovative process of molding a complete playable ball at one time may with more research be the way all golf balls are made twenty-five years from now. The twenty-first century Fifth Revolution?

The accompanying illustration of experimental balls will give collectors some idea of the variation of models of the Cayman ball that have been marketed, including some with special logos and the MacGregor name. 🌙

On Into The '90s: Two Giants Wrestle

In the 1990s as in the 1970s and '80s, Spalding's never-ending struggle to improve the two-piece solid core with durable Surlyn-type cover continued at an accelerated pace, attempting to equal the overall performance that Titleist had built into the 1900 invention of the Haskell three-piece wound ball. Dissatisfied with being the Avis of the golf ball industry, they aped their slogan of "We Try Harder." Their Avis-like status had certainly held since 1949, when more pros used Titleist balls than any other make. In fact, at the present time, more Titleist balls are being used in tournaments than all other makes combined.

By this decade Spalding was coming much closer due to inventions by Michael Sullivan and other scientists on the staff. In 1991, Sullivan added another blend of Surlyn-type ionomers in another patent which was called Zynlin—this was supposed to inch closer to the softer balata cover used in the Titleist while at the same time being more rugged.

Acushnet Titleist, now named Titleist/Foot Joy Worldwide, had two strings to their bow—Titleist, the three-piece ball, beamed at and enjoyed by the less-than-one-half of one percent of the 25 million golfers (the touring pros), and Pinnacle, the two-piece solid core with Surlyn cover (like Spalding's Top-Flite), which suited most of the other $99^1/_2$ percent of the players. No, as the Hertz of the ball business they had not been coasting. Their most dramatic move came when they crowned an improved and high-velocity two-piece solid core with a Lithium Surlyn cover by naming it Titleist HVC (high velocity core)—also in 1991. This was the very first time any Titleist was other than a three-piece with balata cover.

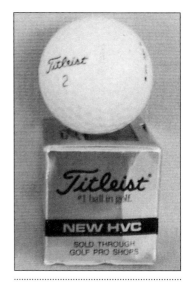

First two-piece ball with the Titleist name. All Titleist-named balls prior to 1991 were three-piece wound balls with a core (HVC-high velocity core, 1991).

Acushnet/Titleist's first two-piece ball 1981.

This was a very smart, although confusing, move on the part of Titleist. Since the two-piece ball was approaching the excellence for pros that had been the cherished boast of the Titleist family, they merely adopted and improved the Pinnacle two-piece ball and dubbed the cousin "Titleist HVC" instead of Pinnacle. So, you say—a big deal? Yes, you are right. Now as some of the pros were recognizing that two-piece balls were, under some conditions, worthy opponents of the three-piece Titleist in tournaments, they could just as well use the Titleist HVC instead of an almost identical Pinnacle Gold or the new 1991 Spalding Tour Edition, and not change brands or lose family membership.

In looking behind the scenes another possibility for this dramatic move might have been the most important part of the drama. Consider this scenario. It was the best insurance policy Titleist could buy to keep wearing the 1949 numero uno crown in the golf ball kingdom. This is what many astute investors call hedging your options. Now it made no difference if the pros used two- or three-piece balls, as long as they used a Titleist. No matter which ball becomes predominant in the future, Titleist is very unlikely to be dethroned. This move was undoubtedly an important factor in their selling more golf balls in 1991 or 1992 than Spalding or any other maker (according to the most reliable report available). The Titleist ball was not just the ball of the touring pros; now with the "trickle-down" effect being very in, and with two types with the same name, they had the perfect choice for the $99^1/_2$ percent masses.

This intense rivalry between Spalding's Top-Flite and Titleist, an American Brands subsidiary, not only took place on the playing field but, one could almost say, also in the industrial bedroom, where new materials and ways of making golf balls are conceived. A nine-year rassle in the "bedroom" took place between 1981 and 1990. As told elsewhere, Spalding's Molitor mixed two patented types of DuPont Surlyn, maybe with some other flavoring, called it Zynthane, submitted it for and was granted a patent to keep out the competition. Titleist was far from dumb and were probably trying similar combinations of some twenty-one varieties of Surlyn available from DuPont, and got too close to Spalding's preserve. Spalding hollered foul and took Titleist to court. In 1985 Titleist pulled the balls in question off the market to limit their possible liability. After another six years of lawyer's profits and

Modern Wilson Ultra. Full line of two- and three-piece balls (left), Slazenger's new 1991 trade dress (right).

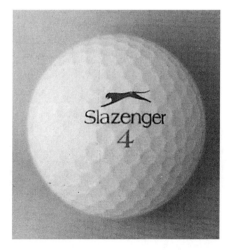

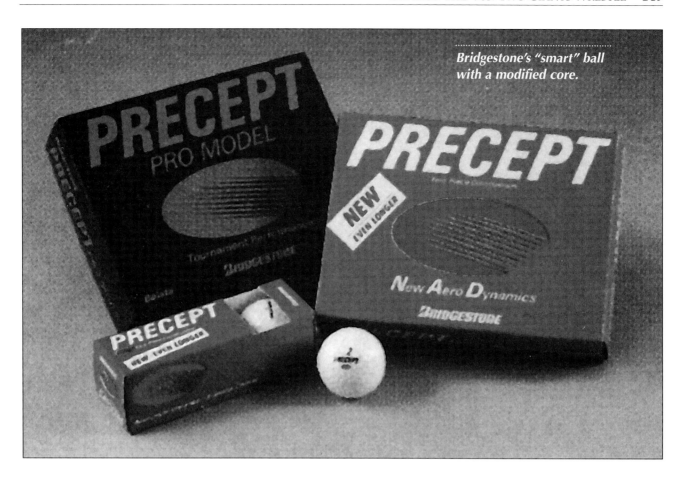

Bridgestone's "smart" ball with a modified core.

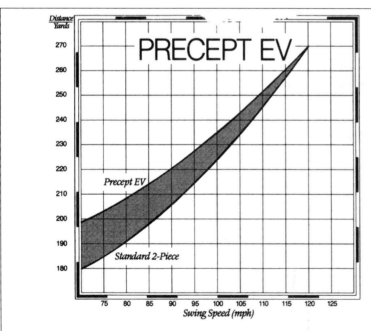

With an ordinary two-piece ball, as swing speed drops, there's a corresponding loss of distance. The EV compensates for swing speeds below 120 mph, maximizing distance by reducing deterioration of velocity.

Note the varying density of the core.

With an ordinary two-piece ball, as swing speed drops, there's a corresponding loss of distance. The EV compensates for swing speeds below 120 mph, maximizing distance by reducing deterioration of velocity.

Spalding's new 1993 double cover, for better performance.

court delay, linger and wait, they both sat down at the table and agreed to a settlement some say amounted to around twenty million dollars.

With all the ball family playing in a small field of organic chemistry and aerodynamic physics, not only the big boys were fighting. Some of the smaller ones were, too. Wilson, third in the ball volume hierarchy, blanketed both Dunlop and Slazenger with a lawsuit for infringing the patents covering their innovative 1985 ball, the Ultra. Dunlop went one way, Slazenger went the other. Dunlop pulled its ball off the market, made a few changes and got back in the game. Slazenger took a six-year hiatus and in 1991 came growling back with the logo form of a preying, pouncing panther, plus pictures and diagrams claiming superiority in golf balls—any kind. Dunlop, on the other hand, implied their superiority but set the suggested retail price at $51 a dozen, $4.25 each, double many other balls and four times the quite adequate balls that can be purchased by average players at one buck in discount stores.

Moving down the volume ladder, Bridgestone, whose Japanese sales are proportional to those of Spalding or Acushnet in the United States, has been cutting a bigger and bigger piece of the pie since they introduced their Precept EV in 1991, aptly termed the "Smart Ball." The ball is supposed to be all things for all handicaps, big or scratch—a graduated density of the core from softer at the cover to more resistant toward the center supposedly allows both Seniors and Tour Pros to obtain full use of their different club-head speeds, ranging from 125 miles per hour for heavy-hitting pros to little more than half that for some seniors and women.

An analysis of the USGA Conforming Ball List reveals the start of a new trend in the construction of the cores. In the early '90s all cores were listed as either two- or three-piece construction with a maverick one-piece for an Asian producer. Each year there were more and more listings for "Other" instead of one- or two-piece core. Instead of a trend toward one-piece, an about-face has happened. Spalding's Strata is a good example, as is Titleist's four-piece wound introduction. The smaller ballmakers followed the leaders with similar changes in core and cover combinations at the famous January Orlando PGA Show.

Odd Balls: Hot and Cold, Long and Short, High and Low

The golf ball world is occupied by two giants, Spalding and Titleist, and some 40 or more smaller but essential novel entrepreneurs. To get a truer picture of the whims of the golfers and the creativity of the producers both in designing and (especially) in marketing, some of the following odd balls are discussed.

HOT AND COLD BALLS

The balls that exceed the distance tests made by USGA for use in tournaments are known in the game as "Hot Balls," some say illegal. Yes, but only for tournaments. The non-conformist Troy Puckett, inventor of the Cayman short ball (cold ball), tells the story that in working with the Short Ball, the most common complaint he heard from the average to below-average golfer was that to enjoy the game, "I need more distance, not less." So, without taking a deep breath, Puckett leapt to the other extreme and brought forth the Renegade 410, truly so, as the first ball to cross the 400-dimple barrier and to disregard USGA standards for length. It was made smaller and heavier than the USGA standards. Puckett soon after, in 1990, bought all rights to the Cayman ball and issued two high-powered balls, the Pirate and the Gorilla, names signalling that they both are rough and unruly competitors.

Ever since the early 1980s when they introduced the Robinhood ball which gave to the poor what the rich already had—distance—the National Golf Center, a division of Bost Enterprises, operated from the ethical fringe. The purveyor of supercharged, non-conforming balls that outdistance all others, the company prospered by selling hype through the mail, using claims and promises that border on the unbelievable.

For example, in the late '80s, National Golf Center featured ads for a still "hotter" ball, code-named, in ads, "S" for secret. This turns out to be the

Three current examples of long balls that exceed USGA's distance standard of 298.6 yards. These balls cannot be used in tournaments. Otherwise there is no limit. (Made by Cayman Ball Co.)

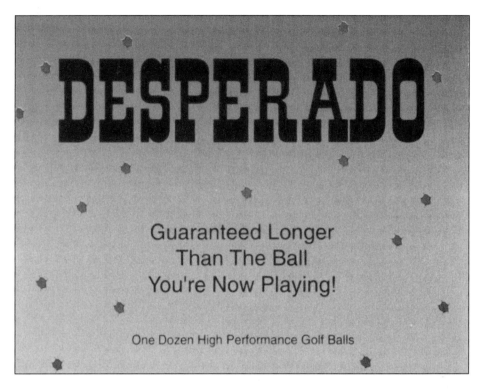

Condor, not on the USGA List, for sure. The company says, "Condor Gold flies like a U-2, putts with a steady roll of a cue ball, and bites the green on approach shots like a dropped cat." Not to mention another claim that it can be driven 400 yards. It sure can if the wind behind it is strong enough and the tee is several hundred feet higher than the green.

National Golf in 1992 had another new ball being offered called the Miracle Flite in trade and newspaper ads designed to appear as a news item complete with by-line: "by Mike Hensen." This one "sails like a glider. If you would like an eagle or two, here's your best chance yet." Further on the company guarantees a golfer a prompt refund if the new ball "doesn't cut five to ten strokes off his or her average score. . . . simply return the balls—new or used—to the address below." "No one else dares do that," boasted the company's director—probably a true statement.

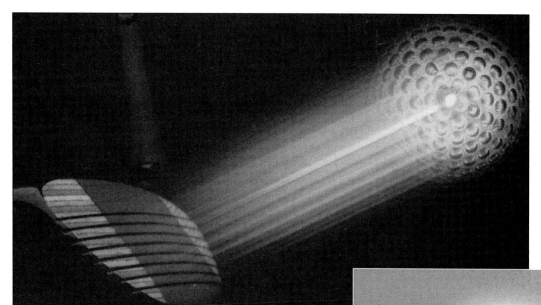

The Nite-Lite ball by C.N. Isbelieving Co.

A new special Nite-Lite "Twilight" ball for extending daytime playing.

DAY AND NIGHT BALLS

If you thought July in Alaska was the only way to play golf at night—think again. The go-go '90s, when more people than ever took up golf, heralded the beginning of night golf, thanks to an energizing President Nelson F. Newcomb and staff of Pick Point Enterprises up in the New Hampshire woods. So if your partner calls you next Friday and says he's got an 11:30 PM starting time, don't laugh; it's night golf.

The ball is called Nite-Lite™ and looks like a regular ball that is semi-translucent and has a thin hole drilled through it for the "Lite Stick" which energizes to give a fluorescent glow to the ball. The complete package includes the balls, glow-in-the-dark tees, similarly illuminated flag pins and cups to guide your shots. Lighted 150-yard markers complete the kit except for a lighted putter. A miner's cap lamp is not included but might be useful in the rough. You can play golf Pick Point-style moon or no moon. Pick Point's (now C.N. Isbelieving Co.) punchline motto is "Night Golf: the second most fun you can have in the dark."

An alternative for playing night golf, by neu-glo Company.

Since it began in 1986, Pick Point/C.N. Isbelieving claims to have supplied more than 21,000 events and tournaments in the United States and 32 other countries. "Moonlight on the Links" has become an annual event at the Camelback Country Club in Scottsdale, Arizona and Highland Hills Country Club in Southern Pines, North Carolina—just two examples.

By 1996 the Nite-Lite system of balls and accessories was being distributed by C.N. Isbelieving of Wolfeboro Falls, New Hampshire, with impressive statistics on the growth of special events each year, for a grand total of 90,000 events, according to Vice President Corky Newcomb.

▨ More Light on Night Golf

It did not take long. By late 1992 Pick Point found that they no longer had a monopoly on golf after dark. In October, "neu-glo" in Lakeland, Florida, with Streator Fenton as National Sales Manager, announced that after years of research a new coating on a standard ninety-compression ball might make the Nite-Lite ball obsolete; they have patented a complete system for night golf. Essentially the balls are coated with a special fluorescent coating that when energized by light will glow in the dark in the same manner that similarly-coated watches and hands do. The balls are kept in a glo-pak illuminator that can carry eight balls. When removed, they will glow brightly for up to fifteen minutes. Some hackers need more time than that to find theirs.

Auxiliary equipment that is solar operated, such as illuminators for tee markers, greens flags and 150-yard markers, are all available to make night golf a practical and fun reality. For more information or orders call 1-800-394-8688 or write to neu-glo, Night Golf Supplies. The balls are presently priced at $5 each, or 3 for $13.95, plus $1.35 for postage and handling. The balls can be energized by any standard light source. The Grenelefe Resort in Orlando may still be regularly scheduling weekly events.

Except for the above special night balls, golf is a daytime sport, private or public. Other night golf is mostly miniature golf, and never the twain shall meet. Never say never. Already driving ranges in many places are on day and night schedules, with area lighting. So are the double-tiered courses in Japan, where reservations are necessary a week in advance.

A January 1993 ad for nuclear-enhanced balls. This service has been discontinued.

CURRENT ONE-PIECE BALLS

In the 1992 USGA Conforming Ball List there were two one-piece balls listed out of 181 primary names: the Miracle and the Spirit. These were made by the Yardley Ball. You might consider them grandnephews of the Bartsch Ball invented in 1967, since their grandfather, owner of the Yardley Ball Company, was Duncan Pollitt, who set up the factory to first mass-produce the Bartsch and who has been continually trying to improve its acceptance. Yardley is no longer producing golf balls.

In the 1996 USGA list only two one-piece balls are listed, none of them made in the United States. Bridgestone of Japan listed one of them out of 300 primary names: the Eagle, with a red symbol. Dunlop's (Japanese company) ball's name is Flash, with the name in purple.

The stampede to various multiple cores and covers has rough-ridden over the few remaining one-piece cousins. This merely means "gone but not forgotten." A recent talk with insiders in the laboratories verifies that the search is still considered worthwhile.

"NUKED" BALLS

Want a hot, hot ball—yea, atomic hot? Then Nuked Balls are for you, and were available in 1994 from E-Beam Sports Company. You could order a dozen of your own favorite brand sent to you for thirty-six dollars, plus three-dollars shipping/handling charge. These dozen balls were accompanied by a certification that they had been "enhanced." More specifically, Paul Minibole, president and owner of E-Beam says that this enhancement was accomplished in an accelerator that he purchased from the A.E.C.L. Ltd. of Canada (Canada's NASA).

The accelerators of all sizes, up to miles in circumference, bombard various materials with electrons to change their characteristics. The Canadian group found that by doing this to golf balls they could increase their performance. Minibole says that one can expect from ten to fifty yards more from the ball, along with a dropped spin. He also added that the cover could be made softer or harder.

Duncan Pollitt, considered one of the country's authorities on golf balls, said that the accelerator will change the characteristics of the ball, but he is not convinced whether it will always be for the best, or to what degree. He suggests that perhaps putting them in a home microwave might accomplish about the same results. Dr. Harry Szmant, former head of the Chemistry Department at Wayne State University in Detroit, and author of a definitive book on chemistry, also agrees that bombardment will change the ball, but is not convinced that it will be for the better.

A recent call to the E-Beam Sports Co. reveals that this service has been discontinued. The only tangible collectible evidence of a nuked ball will be a dozen box with the certificate stamped on it.

Performance: Longer, Longer, and Longer Balls

Bobby Jones

Bobby Jones edited an anthology published by *Golf Digest* in which he remarked, "I think I can say without contradiction that the most significant change made in golf equipment since the inception of the game was the development of the wound ball, the steel shaft notwithstanding." (This does not take into consideration the development of the one- and two-piece balls later on, or the great strides in chemistry and aerodynamics from the 1970s on). Elsewhere some actual examples were cited on performance in the U.S. Open since its inception in 1895: The conclusion was that tournament scores for eighteen holes had decreased in this century from around 84 to around 68.

The golf ball cannot take all the credit for that, and Jones was not implying that it should. The game of golf is full of variables. Probably one of the biggest ones is the players, pro or high-handicaps. A sea of twenty-five million golfers will spawn more talent than the puddle of a few thousand at the turn of the century. Today's sophisticated club, with metal head and exotic materials in the shafts, the weather, ground and grass conditions (spongy to concrete-like), every course's different challenges (sea level or sky top)—all play a part. Alastair Johnston, associate of Arnold Palmer and one of two great golf bibliophiles (another being Joe Murdoch) feels that the golf ball alone has contributed more than any other of the above-named variables.

Trying to single out just one variable in the ball itself—length of drives—the following table has been arrived at by anything but scientific method. It is a combination of verbal hand-me-downs, records and reports over at least two hundred years.

APPROXIMATE IMPROVEMENT IN BALL DISTANCE

DATE	TYPE OF BALL	LENGTH OF DRIVES
1600-1845	Feather Ball	120-160 yds
1845-1903	Gutta-Percha Ball	175-200 yds
1903-1950	Haskell 3-Piece Ball	200-240+ yds
1950-1997	Hi-Tech 2-, 3- and 4-Piece Ball	240-285 yds
1976-1997	New USGA Max. Distance	296 yds.

There seems to be magic in distance. Distance overrides all other niceties of play, such as accuracy on the fairway, approach, or putting. A missed three-foot putt counts just the same as a 250-yard drive into the lake. One is spectacular and the other is an "oh-damn!" The thrill of distance is basic in both players and spectators but may encourage the silent majority to try too hard on today's over-extended courses.

In 1896 the Shinnecock Hills course on Long Island was 4,400 yards long for the U.S. Open. By 1986 the Shinnecock course had been extended to 6,600 for the U.S. Open. Today the trend is toward courses over 7,000 yards, mostly due to the longer ball. The longer the distance, the more difficult it is for the high-handicapper to make the same score—but not the pros. Jack Nicklaus has been vehement for years in his opposition to this long-ball trend, and in the 1980s put his money with his idea and commissioned the shorter Cayman Ball and designed the Cayman course to fit it. (See Chapter 18, A Short Life, A Short Ball)

Less dramatic changes in the ball since 1950 have been beneficial in more important ways. The word "feel" is a pro term for just that—how the ball actually feels to him. The silent majority—no. Most players swing speed is too slow to extract all the performance built into today's ball. Fifty years ago all players had very little choice in ball selection. Now there are over 150 choices in both the Titleist/Pinnacle stable and Spalding's Top-Flite/Molitor group.

Spin, plus trajectory, helps the balls drop dead on the green. Pros' spin rate has increased from 5,000 per minute to over 10,000 by juggling the chemistry and aerodynamics of the ball. Today a touring pro can control his ball in a way not dissimilar to the way a first violinist in the Boston Pops can control his violin. The ball has become a controllable instrument—for some.

Improved durability is more related to economy than it is to play. On scorching hot days a great player like Harry Vardon, the twentieth-century British wonder, would keep his gutty balls in a pail of ice water. Otherwise when he belted the ball it would be flat-sided. In play before 1920, a slight mishap might result in a ball with a toothless smile—putting it out of play. Spalding came out with the Kro-Flite in the '20s—a major improvement, but not comparable to DuPont's 1967 Surlyn cover, which almost qualifies for the title indestructible. A ball that used to be good for perhaps eighteen holes is now good until it is lost, if treated with some care and respect. Today, retrieved from a pond, washed and inspected, it is ready to behave just as well as before at a price less than half of original cost—that's the economics.

Should the "silent majority" portion of twenty-five million golfers be as concerned with the distance the ball travels as is the pro? The answer could be both yes and no. If the thrill of seeing the ball outdistancing those of the other three players in the foursome on a few holes exceeds the desire to make an optimum score for the round, the answer is yes—a longer ball is more necessary as the courses get longer.

It seems that golfers shooting under 85 fairly consistently are in a better position to use an extra ten yards. That is the distance that Frank Thomas at USGA in 1986 found between a variety of 72 balls he tested on the "Iron Byron," USGA's standard testing machine. Furthermore, the golfers will be getting additional benefits from their ability to control the ball's spin, trajectory and direction, principally due to higher club speeds than their partners with higher handicaps. Even the longest off the

Corey Pavin, winner of 1995 USGA Open at Shinnecock Hills on Long Island, NY, with a score of 280.

tee, like Daly and Tiger Woods, may not be winning more tournaments or money than lighter swatters who may intentionally choose a shorter ball in order to better control the flight condition. The following comparison is an example of that.

The number one money winner in 1991 was Corey Pavin, with a total of $979,430, but with a driving average of only 252 yards, but a very high driving accuracy of .740. Freddie Couples was number three with earnings of $791,749, a driving average of 280 yards and accuracy rating of .659. Daly, the boomer, earned $574,783, pushed the ball to 289 yards, but was all over the course with accuracy of only .547. Perhaps this says that the macho boys are a delight to watch, but their counterparts with the ball under control put more bacon on the table. And if more of the silent majority bought a copy of *Harvey Pennick's Little Red Book* they would take more strokes off their score than by listening to the wild claims made by most ball and club producers.

For those readers interested in more facts on performance of golf balls and other aspects of the game of golf, the book *Science and Golf*, edited by A.J. Cochran, published by Chapman and Hall, London and New York in 1990, is suggested reading. This book has reprints of papers presented at the First World Scientific Congress of Golf at the University of St. Andrews, Scotland, July 9th-13th, 1990. Here is scientific reality as opposed to many copywriters' fantasies. Reproduced on the next page is an example is an analysis from page 157.

Dr. Lucius J. Riccio, distinguished scientist and author on golf facts about performance. His latest contribution is a new book **Golf, The Scientific Way.**

Statistical Analysis of The Average Golfer

L.J. Riccio, PhD, Golf Analyzer, New York

ABSTRACT:

"Although much is known about the statistical profile of professional golfers, little has been published on the play of other golfers. This paper presents an analysis using data from over 100 golfers ranging in ability from Jack Nicklaus to 35 handicappers. The analysis was designed to determine which aspects of play separate the average players from the top amateurs, and to determine the statistical profile of the average golfer of all scoring images."

4.1 PROFILES OF THE AVERAGE GOLFER

The equations provide a way of estimating the average golfer's performance in each of the key statistical categories. Not all of the equations are as strong predictors as others. The following table provides the profile of the average golfer in each scoring range for several of the key statistical categories:

AVERAGE SCORE

CATEGORY	71	75	79	81	85	89	91	95	99	
Greens in Reg	12	10	8	7	5	3	2	0	0	Strg
% Fairways	81	71	61	56	46	36	31	21	11	Weak
Iron Accuracy	80	68	53	47	33	20	13	0	0	Good
Not Well Hit	2.8	5.6	8.5	10.0	12.8	15.6	17.0	20.0	22.8	Good
Putts per Round	29.0	30.3	31.7	32.3	33.7	35.0	35.7	37.0	38.3	Weak
Penalty Strokes	0	0	.4	.6	1.2	1.7	1.9	2.4	2.9	Fair
Birdies	3.2	2.4	1.8	1.5	.8	.1	0	0	0	Strg
Pars	11.8	10.3	8.8	8.1	5.1	4.3	2.8	1.3	1.3	Strg

Each GIR (Greens in Regulation) is equal to two strokes off the average score. Obviously one green does not save 2 strokes by itself, but by improving your tee-to-green games to increase GIRs by one, on holes you missed the green your ball is much closer to the green after the regulation number of shots. The rule relating greens hit to the key scoring breaks points is "3 Greens break 90, 8 Greens break 80, and 13 Greens break 70."

5. CONCLUSION

Everyone remembers Sam Snead's famous phrase "drive for show and putt for dough." Based on this analysis a phrase more appropriate to describe where emphasis should be placed is "hit hard for thrills and hit greens for bills—dollar bills, that is." Cochran and Stobbs found that long iron accuracy was the key to success for touring pros. This study found thta tee-to-green accuracy was the key for all golfers.

Chick Evans used to say goodbye to his friends by wishing them "a long walk with a putter," indicating to those who used a caddie that they had hit the green with their iron shot. He must have known that that was not only an extremely satisfying situation, it was also the one that won matches.

THE BALL FOR YOU

With confusion abounding in the minds of the "silent majority" as to what is the best ball for them, we are indebted to *Golf Shop Operation Magazine,* a subsidiary of *Golf Digest* magazine, for permission to include the table on the following pages from its November 1996 edition. This should help remove a little of the haze and assist each golfer to make a more informed selection. The information in the tables is based on reliable testing procedures and backed up by the judgment of experts. It is not based on listening to Joe Blow, whose handicap is 27, tell how he made a hole-in-one with a Titleist HVC and therefore knows that this is the best ball for all golfers to use under all conditions. Play a ball that the chart says is right for you, and **by keeping your eye on the ball** you will do better than using one because Tiger Woods does. The short explanation of each category of balls below is from *Golf Shop Operation Magazine.*

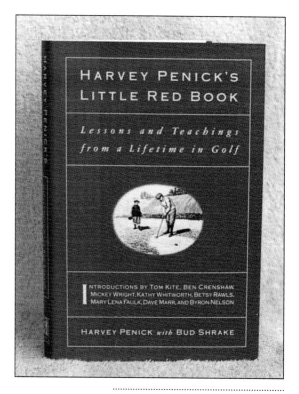

Harvey Penick's Little Red Book

BALL CATEGORIES

Ultimate Control-Maneuverability: Have a relatively soft cover and the highest rate of spin (which requires high club head speeds). These are mostly used by pros and low-handicappers. Their performance is so similar that 99 percent of golfers could not distinguish one from the other in a no-name test—and a lot of the pros could not either. The difference in driving distance might be five percent but probably less.

Ultimate Distance-Durability: Have less back spin and therefore get more roll where you want it on the fairways and don't want it on the greens. Generally speaking there are more choices in this group and probably less difference among them.

Distance-Control Blends: In between the above two classes. They are compromise balls that take a little off the spin to get a little more distance with roll and a tougher cover. This may be a group to appeal to the large group of mid-handicappers.

Here's a chance to compare your performance with that of one of the most famous golfers in the history of golf. In 1964 Bobby Jones and O.B. Keeler were shooting the seventh episode in the famous series "How I Play Golf." They were discussing how long the ball stayed in the air on full shot swings with different clubs, so they ran a test. The answer was six seconds flat on all shots on all woods and the high irons. Have someone with a stop watch or a watch with a second-sweep hand or, less accurately, counting "thousand and one, thousand and two. . . ." check—and see how you compare on flight time with the master.

COMPANY	MODEL	CONSTRUCTION	NUMBER OF DIMPLES	COMPRESSION(S)	COVER MATERIAL	PRICE PER DOZEN
SPALDING	Top-Flite Hot XL	2-piece	492		Zylin	$27 (15)
	Top-Flite XL	2-piece	422		Zylin	25 (18)
	Top-FLite XL W	2-piece	422		Zylin	25 (18)
	Flying Lady	2-piece	410		Iotek	19 (15)
	Molitor	2-piece	422		Iotek	17 (15)
SQUARE TWO	S2 LPGA	2-piece	398	80	Lithium Surlyn	24
STRIKER	Superball	2-piece	384	90	Surlyn	30
SUNSET	Platinum +	2-piece	432	90, 100	Surlyn blend	24
TITLEIST	*DT 2-Piece	2-piece	392		Litium/Sodium Surlyn	32
	HP2 Distance	2-piece	440		Lithium Surlyn	36
	HP2 Distance	2-piece	392		Lithium Surlyn	36
	Pinnacle Distance Extreme	2-piece	392		Lithium/Sodium Surlyn	25 (15)
	Pinnacle Power Icon	2-piece	332		VLMI/Lithium Surlyn	20 (15)
	Pinnacle Gold	2-piece	392		Lithium/Sodium Surly	19 (15)
WILSON	*Staff Titanium Distance	2-piece	500	90, 100	Magnesium Surlyn	35
	Ultra 500 Distance	2-piece	500	90, 100	Surlyn	36
	Original Ultra DPS	2-piece	432	90, 100	Surlyn	29 (15)
	TC2 Tour	2-piece	432	90	Surlyn	25 (15)
	TC2 Distance	2-piece	432	90	Surlyn	25 (15)
	ProStaff Distance	2-piece	432	90	Surlyn	20 (18)
	ProStaff Distance Women	2-piece	432	90	Surlyn	20 (18)
	ProStaf Distance Senior	2-piece	432	90	Surlyn	20 (18)

ULTIMATE CONTROL-MANEUVERABILITY

COMPANY	MODEL	CONSTRUCTION	NUMBER OF DIMPLES	COMPRESSION(S)	COVER MATERIAL	PRICE PER DOZEN
BEN HOGAN	428 Balata	3-piece	428	90, 100	Balata	$42
BRIDGESTONE	*Precept Tour Double Cover	4-piece	396		Surlyn	54
HANSBERGER	Ram Tour Pro Balata	2-piece	442	90, 100	Balata	40
	Ram Tour Balata LB	2-piece	442	90, 100	Lithium Balata	35
MACGREGOR	VIP	2-piece	432	90, 100	Balata	36
MAXFLI	*RM	3-piece	432	90, 100	Balata	56
	HT	3-piece	432	90, 100	Balata	48
	XF	3-piece	432	90, 100	Synthetic Balata	42
NITRO	Balata LD +10	2-piece	440	95	Balata blend	30
SLAZENGER	420 Interlok	3-piece	420	90, 100	Balata	44
SPALDING	*Top-Flite Strata Tour	3-piece	422	90, 100	ZS-Balata	52
	Top-Flite Z-Balata	2-piece	422	90, 100	Z-Balata	40
SUNSET	Lollipop	2-piece	432	90	Surlyn blend	21
	Floater	2-piece	432	90	Surlyn blend	18
TITLEIST	Professional	3-piece	392	90, 100	Elastomer	50
	Tour Balta	3-piece	440	90, 100	Balata	43
	HP2 Tour	3-piece	440		VLMI/Lithium Surlyn	36
	HVC Spin	2-piece	440	90, 100	Lithium Surlyn	36
WILSON	*Staff Titanium Balata	2-piece	500	90, 100	Balata	43
	Ultra 500 Tour Balata	3-piece	500	90, 100	Balata	42
	Classic Wound Ultra DPS	3-piece	432	90	Surlyn	29 (15)
	ProStaff Control	3-piece	432	90	Surlyn	20 (18)

DISTANCE-CONTROL BLEND

Brand	Model	Construction	Dimples	Material	Compression	Price
BEN HOGAN	428 Hi-Spin	2-piece	428	Lithium Surlyn, Zinc		$35
BRIDGESTONE	EV Extra Spin	2-piece	392	Surlyn		38
DUNLOP	*DDH Explosive Spin	2-piece	360	Surlyn		20 (15)
	*DDH Explosive Control	2-piece	360	Surlyn		20 (15)
	*Pin Attacking Spin	2-piece		Surlyn		28.25 (15)
FEAR & LOATHING	Death Stick	2-piece	450	Lithium Surlyn	96, 106	25
HANSBERGER	*Ram Tour Acra	2-piece	442	Lithium Surlyn	100	30 (15)
	*Ram Tour Lite	2-piece	380	Surlyn	85	30 (15)
KARSTEN	Karsten	2-piece	374	Polymer blend	100	36
	Pink	3-piece	392	Surlyn	100	32
	Eye2	3-piece	392	Surlyn	100	32
MAXFLI	XS	2-piece	432	Ionomer blend	90, 100	36
NITRO	Plus 8	2-piece	440	Surlyn	90, 100	28
PLAYERS	Players	2-piece	518	Lithium Surlyn	80, 90, 100	25 (15)
SLAZENGER	420t Touch-spin	2-piece	420	Surlyn	90	34
SPALDING	*Top-Flite XL Performance	2-piece	422	Zylin	90, 100	27 (15)
	Top-Flite Tour SD	2-piece	422	Zylin S	90, 100	34
	Top Flite Magna EX	2-piece	422	Zylin		29
	Top-Flite Magna EX-W	2-piece	422	Zylin		29
	Top-Flite Magna	2-piece	422	Zylin		29 (15)
STRIKER	Big Strike Mid-size	2-piece	432	Lithium Surlyn	95	36
SUNSET	Platinum Tour	2-piece	432	Surlyn	100	24
SUTHERLAND	*Sabre	2-piece	402	Trilion	95	32
	SS402	2-piece	402	Trilion	95	28
TITLEIST	*DT Wound	3-piece	392	Lithium/Sodium Surlyn	80, 90, 100	36
	HVC Distance	2-piece	440	Lithium Surlyn	90, 100	32
	Pinnacle Distance Oversize	2-piece	3902	Lithium/Sodium Surlyn		25 (15)
	Pinnacle For Women	2-piece	332	VLMI/Lithium Surlyn		19 (15)
	Pinnacle Equalizer	2-piece	392	VLMI/Lithium Surlyn		19 (15)
WILSON	*Staff Titanium Spin	2-piece	500	Magnesium Surlyn	90, 100	37
	Ultra 500 Competition	2-piece	500	Surlyn	90, 100	36
	Tour Spin Ultra DPS	2-piece	432	Surlyn	90, 100	29 (15)
	P.S. Performance/Spin	2-piece	432	Surlyn	90	20 (18)
	ProStaff Tour Trajectory	2-piece	432	Surlyn	90	20 (18)

BALL LEGEND. GENERAL FEATURES: *=New for 1997. (15)=15-ball pack. (16)=16-ball pack. (18)=18-ball pack.

G.S.O. '97 Buyer's Guide. Section I.

ULTIMATE DISTANCE-DURABILITY

COMPANY	MODEL	CONSTRUCTION	COMPRESSION(S)	NUMBER OF DIMPLES	COVER MATERIAL	PRICE PER DOZEN
BEN HOGAN	428 Distance	2-piece		428	Lithium Surlyn	$35
BRIDGESTONE	*Precept Dynawing DC	3-piece		392	Surlyn	46
	EV Extra Distance	2-piece		432	Surlyn	38
	EV Senior	2-piece		432	Surlyn	38
	EV Lady	2-piece		432	Surlyn	32
BULLET	Lady Bullet	2-piece	85	450	Lithium Surlyn	35 (16)
	.444	2-piece	90, 100	444	Lithium Surlyn	32 (16)
DUNLOP	*DDH Explosive 110	2-piece	110	360	Surlyn	20 (15)
	*DDH women distance	2-piece		360	Surlyn	20 (15)
	Yardage Eating Distance	2-piece			Surlyn	28.25 (15)
DYNACRAFT	Dynacraft	2-piece	90	432	Lithium Surlyn	24
HANSBERGER	Ram Tour XDC	2-piece	90, 100	442	Lithium Surlyn	26 (15)
	Golden Girl	2-piece	80	442	Surlyn	26 (15)
KENNETH SMITH	442KT	2-piece	100	442	Lithium Surlyn	34
MACGREGOR	Tourney	2-piece	90	432	Surlyn	16
MAXFLI	XD	2-piece	90, 100	432	Surlyn/Ioner blend	34
	MD 80, 90, 100	2-piece		432	Surlyn	24 (15)
NITRO	440	2-piece	90, 100	440	Surlyn	24
SLAZENGER	420p Power-spin	2-piece	95	420	Surlyn	34
	420i Raw-distance	2-piece	100	420	Surlyn	34

BALL LEGEND. GENERAL FEATURES: *=New for 1997. (15)=15-ball pack. (16)=16-ball pack. (18)=18-ball pack.

G.S.O. '97 Buyer's Guide. Section II.

Best Balls at the Best Price: Take Your Pick

At this point, some of the readers may be confused over the variations they have encountered in the prices for balls. In Chapter 21 the tables listing some 100 choices of balls, classified by how they perform, also listed their prices per dozen, from a high of $54 ($4.50 each) for Spalding's new four-piece Striata down to $20 for eighteen ($1.11 each) for the Wilson Pro Staff. In other parts of the book the price of one dollar a ball has been mentioned over the period of 100 years. The reason for this apparent discrepancy is that the high prices are the suggested retail price. As every shopper today knows, such prices are widely discounted (otherwise known as a multi-tiered price structure).

The Pro Shops usually have the highest prices but many of them charge less than the prices given in the Performance Tables. To exist today, places like the Pro Shops and old-line department stores have had to lower their prices to compete with discount chains like K-Mart and Wal-Mart. A fair generalization would be that most golf balls are sold today at prices ranging from one to two dollars. More specific information is organized for the reader's convenience in the Table of Golf Ball Prices that follows these comments.

$8 Sale
Top-Flite X-out golf balls
One dozen golf balls available in choice of white, yellow or orange colors.

K-Mart ad for Spalding Top-Flite X-Outs at 67¢/ea.

165

The table includes three major types of prices—those for new, unused golf balls, for reconditioned or recycled balls, and for X-Outs. Prices for new balls need no further explanation. The recycled/reconditioned balls will be fully discussed in Chapter 23, Reclaiming Balls. X-Outs need more explanation, as follows.

X-Outs

As is the case with many other products, X-Out golf balls today are essentially the same as new balls, but sold at lower prices. They are easily identified because a row of black Xs has partially obliterated the original ball name. Some say that these are second quality balls not worthy of the brand name, unreliable, and without warranty. Therefore, they are sold for less, usually around half the retail price. The experts say very emphatically that these balls meet all the performance specifications, but that there may be some small blemishes from the painting operation. Normally these are not noticeable to the player. These balls are sold at most "Off Course" stores, sporting goods shops, and all discount chains.

The unofficial story is that X-Outs are produced to sell additional balls to satisfy a definite demand for lower-priced balls. The least expensive way of meeting this demand is to use the same ball and mark overstruck with a row of Xs, implying that it is a second, or less desirable ball. With all the fixed costs of the ball already absorbed by the brand-name balls, the X-Outs can be sold at a fraction of those brand names, and with a profit that may equal or exceed that made on the brand-name balls.

One old-timer, a maker maker of golf balls for over thirty years, explained X-Outs this way: "While the highly-automated ball line is running, you merely insert an additional X-Out marking stamp in the progressive die and produce the number

GOLF BALL PRICES

Prices and descriptions in the golf ball price hierarchy follow:

	Price Range (in Dollars)
1. **Pros Shops ("Green Grass Shops")**	
New—top-grade pro balls in cartons	$2.00 - 4.00 ea.
May have a box or bin or recycled balls	1.00-1.50 ea.
2. **Golf & Sporting Goods Shops ("Cement Shops")**	
New—top-grade pro balls as in #1	1.50 - 3.00 ea.
New—some in cartons of 15 or 18	1.00 - 2.00 ea.
XXX-Outs—Pro balls in plain cartons*	.70 - .80 ea.
Used—loose, mixed names, like new	.60 - .70 ea.
Used—loose, mixed names, good	.50 - .60 ea.
3. **Discount Stores—K-Mart, Wal-Mart, etc.**	
New top brand pro balls, in doz.	1.00 - 1.25 ea.
May carry unfamiliar names	.90 - 1.00 ea.
XXX-Outs—undecorated boxes—Pro quality	.70 - .80 ea.
4. **Reclaimers & Shops Selling Recycled Balls Only**	
Top grades—all same make & name, Pro-grade	.95 - 1.00 ea.
Top grades—packed by name in zipper bags	.60 - .70 ea.
All grades & names mixed in bins—U-choose	.40 - .60 ea.
Same in quantities of 4 or 6 dozen**	.40 - .50 ea.
Lowest grade for ranges & water holes	.15 - .25 ea.
Balls used on cruise ships	.05 ea.
5. **Black Labrador Retriever Balls**	
Ed Deems in Quogue, New York has trained his dog to mouth them out of poison ivy and water. Ed figures the cost of dog biscuits for Moses equates to	.0168 ea.

* See previous pages for description
** Can be ordered by mail. See Chapter 23, Reclaiming Balls: Some Have Nine Lives.

Ed Deems emerging from poison ivy unscathed with a bag of balls retrieved by Moses, his faithful Labrador. The photographer, twenty feet in the clear, got dosed.

Allan Robinson, renowned feather ball maker and expert golfer c. 1830.

Twentieth century: The 1,305th Feather Ball made by Phil Mason in 1992— playable replicas of 1600-1850 balls.

that K-Mart wants—balls identical in all respects to the brand-names balls—and pack them in a plain inexpensive X-Out carton."

When Allan Robinson, one of the most skillful and productive artisans in the early part of the nineteenth century, was making feather golf balls, now called "featheries," the best he could "stuff and stitch" in a day were four or five, according to John Martin. While prices varied with quality and reputation, they averaged about the equivalent of 70 cents. Imagine, with the cost of labor today, what one would cost. Imagine no longer.

Today you can buy a new featherie, fashioned by the same tedious "stuff and sew" process, as playable as any made 170 years ago, made in Phillip Mason's garage in Kentucky. Phil is a dedicated and meticulous craftsman as well as an outstanding golf ball collector. Is his price just about what it was in 1820—70 cents? No! Seven times 70, for about 50 dollars even.

An unusually rare ball with Paterson's name and new composition of gutta percha. (Courtesy of John Olman)

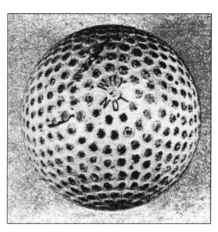

A Henley "Why Not" c. 1905. Bramble-pattern, three-piece wound ball. (Courtesy of John Olman.)

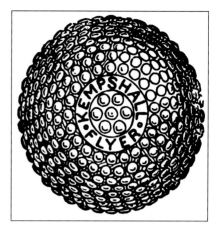

An early rubber core by Spalding, c. 1903—one of the few distinguished from earlier gutta-percha balls by the added rubber core at the center.

Kempshall, the prolific inventor of a flood of patents before 1911. (See Appendix).

In 1845, when Rob Paterson invented the gutta-percha ball, all he had to do is warm this tree gum, knead, and roll in his hand into a sphere now called a "guttie." What a marvelous simplification and superior product. Obviously the innovation of gutties reduced the cost of balls to about one-third the cost of a featherie. At least it did until the resulting stampede rammed the price at one time to several dollars. Today a good signed Paterson smooth guttie is valued in the four- to five-digit figures.

When Haskell—actually Goodrich, to whom his patent was assigned—started marketing the new three-piece balls at the turn of the century, the guttie was quickly wiped out of play because of far superior distance and durability at a modestly higher price.

When Henley, a guttie-ball maker, changed from guttie balls to the new wound ball, he did so resignedly by calling the new ball "Why Not" for only 85 cents. Eleazer Kempshall was the first in the United States to take out a license for the Haskell and issued balls with more names than you'd find in the family Bible—and just as odd. They topped the market with an unheard-of price of two dollars each, today's equivalent of twenty dollars. They had no problem in selling all they could make.

By 1904, Spalding had capitulated to Haskell balls with the appropriate name of "Wizard," at no increase in the 50-cent price of former balls. In 1906 they offered to recondition used Wizards for only four dollars a dozen. By 1920, Spalding produced a watershed ball, called "Kro-Flite," which quickly dominated all other makes and sold at the previous price of 75 cents each. This put Spalding in the embarrassing position of being unable to meet the demand. The Kro-Flite had a much tougher cover—made by vulcanizing the gutta-percha cover in a patented process by Dr. William Geer, a breakthrough similar to Goodyear's discovering the vulcanization of rubber by accidentally adding sulphur.

Can you believe that for over twenty years Spalding and other ball makers held the prices in the 75 cent range, principally due to the Great Depression and World War II? By 1955 most balls were selling at around one dollar each. In graduated steps this price climbed in the 1960s to a suggested retail price of two dollars.

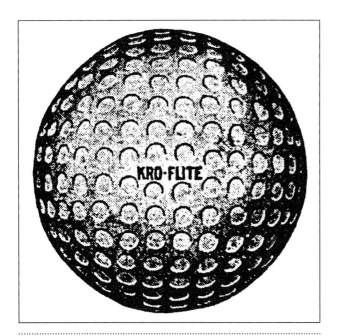

1928 Kro-Flite. Dimple and mesh pattern balls dominated the market.

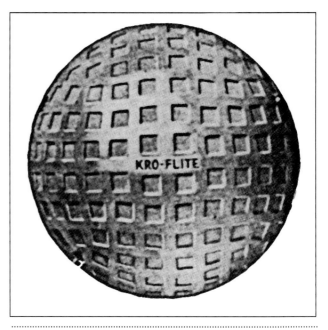

The mesh pattern design varies more than the dimple, and faded away in the 1930s because the dimpled balls performed better.

From that time until the present a basic change was taking place, to what many call the "Two-Tier Market." Actually, as any astute buyer knows, it is a many-tiered market, as the table on page 167 illustrates. Of course this 5 to 1 diversity of prices is not limited to golf balls. Razors are another example in which there are no used blades for sale, but you can buy a fancy Gillette razor for twenty-five dollars on up, or you can buy a dozen bag of disposables for twenty cents each that will still give five to twenty-five shaves each before they are pitched. In golf this many-tiered pricing has helped the explosion of numbers of players from a few thousand 90 years ago to twenty-five million today.

In the summer of 1924 when Jack Osborn got home from college, finding a job was no snap, so he signed up for pick-and-shovel work on the mountain-goat course to be known as the Conesus Lake course in upstate New York. His wage for the summer was 35 cents per hour. At that time there were no "deducts" in the pay envelope, but still not enough money to pay for playing golf. He would have had to work over two hours to buy one of the recently-introduced Kro-Flite balls, selling for 75 cents.

This past summer his great-grandson, Mark, got an equally prestigious job massaging the sand traps with a rake and driving a power mower instead of horses, mowing fairways. He was paid five dollars an hour, and after the "deducts" he wound up with slightly over four bucks. Most of the time he found enough balls to play with. If not he would have had to buy one of the "experienced" ones from the bucket in the Pro Shop, for a buck. This equates to fifteen minutes of his worktime, or one-eighth the time his great-grandfather took to earn a 75-cent Kro-Flite. 🏌

Reclaiming Balls: Some Have Nine Lives

Most people who play the game of golf are familiar with the club-pounding aggravation of plunking a brand new ball into the drink on the first water hole. That new Titleist, gone forever. After a pause to figure out what went wrong, victims of seemingly magnetic water hazards and deep areas of poison ivy shrug their shoulders and pull out another new ball from the bag, praying for a fairway landing.

Well, it should be of some consolation to know that the new two-dollar Titleist will probably find a second chance to behave better. Retrieving lost

Jim Reid, founder of Second Chance Ball Company, buried in balls ready for their second (maybe third) chance.

Some water lends itself to cross-water dragging by winches, followed by stripping the rolling disks.

Emerging from a special cleaning process, the balls are loaded into carts for sorting and inspection

balls has become an exploding, profitable business as new companies pop up all over the nation to make millions of dollars from golfers' mistakes. The venture is called golf ball reclamation, or recycling. There are a few big companies which pay up to a total of $500,000 a year to maybe as many as 100 country clubs they service for the exclusive rights to retrieve the thousands of balls that wind up each day lost in the woods or at the bottom of the pond.

The Second Chance Ball Company uses teams of divers to recover balls, for ten cents apiece. In some of the larger ponds and lakes they dredge with a device somewhat resembling an oversize disc harrow or driving range ball retriever. The balls come back to the processing plant where they are mechanically scrubbed in a special cleaning solution and then sorted into six or eight grades based on their appearance and the make of the ball. These are sold over the counter at their sales office, in dozens and in bulk. They are also sold by mail to both retail and wholesale customers. When cleaned and sorted, the balls look as bright and perfect as any new balls.

The so-called Pro-line balls, like Titleist, Maxfli, Staff by Wilson, and Spalding Tour Edition are packed by name in dozens. These sell for about one dollar apiece with further discounts for larger quantities. Others almost equally good but not sorted by ball name are sold for 75 cents to 90 cents. As some slight blemishes start to appear in some balls the prices drop again. Many processors and some retail chain golf stores have

Inspection, sorting, grading and packaging. Work stations are upper left and right and lower right, where as many as 10 or 12 choices are instantly made and deposited into the proper tube.

Storage and shipping room.

large bulk containers from which golfers can select their own balls by name and quality. Prices and different grades of these lesser names and quality balls may sell for as low as 40 to 50 cents. One Walgreen drug store in Fort Myers, Florida has a bulk lot, mixed in quality, with balls priced three for a dollar. Many Pro shops will have smaller bulk displays of first-rate balls on the floor for about one dollar apiece, which is at least half of what the new balls sell for above the counter.

Sorting to six or more grades does not account for all the balls recovered. Some of the leftovers are stained and scuffed, and maybe even have cutmarks. Some high-handicappers will buy these for water holes; others will use them

Note the handy see-through handled containers, both sides of which could be adapted to wall racks or frames to display your collectibles on front and back.

for practice balls. A goodly number of recovered balls wind up, perhaps after even a third or fourth trip round, as range balls that have had some colored stripping added by the reclaimer to identify them as such. However, not all range balls are reclaimed balls. Many large distributors like Wittek and Austeads sell brand new decorated range balls to their clients.

The large majority of the reclamation companies operate in the southern and southwestern states. The Raven Ball Company of Fort Myers, Florida, (see photo on page 172), owned by Jack Caswell, operates most of the year, using some of the most sophisticated equipment in the business. Caswell also operates in the Mount Clemens, Michigan area in the summer. A large operation correctly called Second Chance is located in Orlando, Florida; this and Birdie Ball in Margate are other examples of the growing activity in recovering golf balls. Some of this blossoming growth is due to the almost impenetrable ball covers of DuPont Surlyn and the improved, automobile-like acrylic finishes.

Jim Reid, who sold Second Chance Company, started out diving for gold from shipwrecks off the coast of Florida, and decided that diving for golf balls, which he terms "white gold," was a better bet. The company now has contracts with about 100 golf courses from which he retrieves some ten million balls a year. He, like most of the others, has an exclusive contract to retrieve all balls from those courses. The terms of these contracts vary. Some have a flat yearly fee; others guarantee the pro a certain number of balls ready for resale at a less than market price.

There are no reliable figures as to how many balls are recovered by all retrievers. Five million dozen seems to be an unofficial consensus. The grand total of new balls is about 50 million dozen a year, which means about one out of every ten balls used is a reclaimed ball. As a comparison, in 1917 the total production of golf balls was five hundred thousand dozen, according to John Martin.

A great many of the balls are recovered by individuals like Dottie Savage, who each evening used to take her beautifully-marcelled spaniel for a walk

Alligators also back on shore in the sun, waiting for the divers' return.

around the adjacent Westhampton Golf Club, where she may have spotted one or several balls. She saved these throughout the year to donate to the annual church fair. The church sold the balls for 50 cents each. Others make a hard-driving business of poaching. In that case the contract-owner may take some legal action.

What Jim Reid did not realize when he changed to hunting for the white gold golf balls instead of the yellow gold from an assortment of shipwrecks off the coast of Florida, was that the manmade ponds in the local golf courses were already occupied. They have been an ideal habitat for prehistoric creatures up to fourteen feet long—alligators. After many years and some bites later, with no recorded fatalities, the divers and the alligators have found room to operate in the same pond at the same time. One diver the author knows wears two wet suits. He found after a few uncovered meetings that the alligators' teeth are only long enough to penetrate one thickness—two suits are too much to draw blood. The advice a denizen of the murky waters gives to his neophyte companions is to make motions while in the water. Alligators are normally not aggressive and will scatter. (Just be sure to consider as No-Man's-Land an alligator's nest with youngsters in it). The truce is partly possible because of the fact that the alligators get fatter from the unattended dogs who get too near the water.

When an alligator has attacked a person it is usually destroyed by a licensed hunter who acquires the meat and expensive skin as his pay. Otherwise, if desirable, they can be removed by trained handlers to an isolated location.

More and more experienced mid- and high-handicap golfers have concluded that experienced reconditioned balls should be given a second chance, since they get exactly the same performance from this 50 cent-to-a-dollar ball as they did from the two- to-three dollar newly-manufactured ball. Based on one laboratory's tests, today's Surlyn balls have a shelf life of five years.

Lynette Pintauro

A 21st-century golfer at age 8, Eldrick (Tiger) Woods

From Now On: Playing Golf in the Twenty-First Century

█ AN OFFICIAL BALL

When Richard Frank, in his 1658 book *Northern Memoirs*, said, "Necessity is the mother of invention," he was right on target. When things get to a stage where enough of the right types of people are unhappy with a situation, things change. Emancipation, civil rights, Prohibition and Repeal, smoking—the woods are full of them.

Is there any unhappiness in the game of golf which calls out for such a change? Yes. Ninety percent of golfers are unhappy because they never play a round of golf close to par. One reason is that the pros, on TV, are beginning to make par look so easy. Tournament after tournament is being won with 66, 67 or 68 averages, vs. 72 for par.

Jack Nicklaus has been the most vocal for the longest time about the fact that present-day golf balls are so long (hot) that they are ruining the game. Another VIP who thinks that some change is imminent is former PGA Commissioner Dean Beman, who has some thoughts on one "Official" ball for all tournaments. He seems rather adamant when he says: "It would be unthinkable to believe that the PGA Tour cannot make the rules under which its membership plays. We've always played under USGA rules voluntarily, out of respect and in the spirit of cooperation. It was an act of good faith, but we were never compelled to do so." Jack Nicklaus has also been a vocal supporter of the idea of an official tour ball—which he thinks should be shorter by about fifteen yards. He, among others, feels that those who have changed existing golf course designs and designed new courses to compensate (in part) for the present longer balls have taken some of the fun out of the game—they have made it too tough for the average mid- and high-handicapper, the silent majority.

Fifty or one hundred years from now, will all golfers be playing balls authorized by the USGA as conforming balls for tournament play? Today some are not. For instance, the Pirate and the Gorilla balls are made so that they exceed the maximum distance standard. There is a variety of

Jack Nicklaus—A proponent of change.

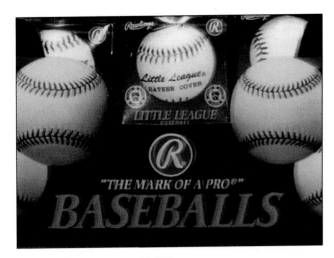 

Official baseball and official football (several makers).

others on the market. If used to cheat, these are looked down on—rightly so if used in the U.S. Open or any other sponsored events. However, pro golfers have the choice of over 200 approved balls from which to choose if they feel they can play better with one than another ball. Why should mid- and high-handicappers be ashamed of using a ball they can hit farther? The Polara, for instance, a ball that was designed to fly straighter, probably the number one challenge for the silent majority. Should these not be considered as conforming balls for anyone with a handicap of over 10? If superior and oversize attitudes and egos change as much in the next hundred years as morals and ethics have in the past hundred, golfers will be having a lot more fun playing, and more of it on the greens in regulation, rather than in the adjacent ponds or poison ivy.

Another possibility due to dedicated research for the past twenty-five or thirty years, the two-piece ball is coming very close to equality with the three piece, still preferred by pros. With recent research by DuPont, and the double-cover ball, it appears to be only a question of when. It would not be unrealistic to expect that by the year 2025 a two-piece ball would get the nod as the Official Ball.

A Better One-Piece Ball

When the two-piece ball was introduced in 1967, the one-piece ball had already been developed and marketed—but the two-piece with Surlyn cover sidelined it to fringe areas: balls for driving ranges, and a few private brands. What does the future hold for the one piece? There are two extreme opinions. Some say it has no future and will fade away, as General MacArthur said old soldiers do. Duncan Pollitt has been producing and improving on one-piece balls almost continuously since he took over from inventor Bartsch in 1967. When he was asked what he thought would be the future of the ball he said, "I am working on it." He is not about to discuss the details.

Matching ball color to tee box color used by players of varying abilities, or to white balls with only four dimples colored to indicate the class of ball.

TEE MARKERS

Another change that might emerge and lend more equality to the play of the silent majority is the placement of the red, white and blue tees, especially on holes where the green is a small island over 160 yards to the nearest landing space from the tee, a nice four-iron shot for some, but a disaster with a driver for most SMs (silent majority). Maybe there should be four, or even five, sets of tees to correspond to the four different balls, and colored to match the appropriate class.

Before anything is done along these lines some very careful analysis will be required and a formula developed to give each class of golfer an even chance of hitting the green, so that he/she would have a fair chance at having two remaining strokes for putting. Now there does not seem to be any such pattern for the placement of the tee markers. It is reported that on the Continent tees are eleven percent closer to the greens than the women's red and the "Standard" white ones. This may not be correct either. Possibly handicaps would be simplified in this case, or even eliminated. A start in this direction was taken on January 1, 1993, when the USGA mandated that the maximum score on any one hole is six strokes (see illustration on page 134, Chapter 16) for 0-9 golfers and so on up to a 9 for high-handicappers. This new arrangement is known as the Equitable Stroke Procedure.

GOLF II

When Jack Nicklaus was successful in the 1980s in establishing a short course, and a matching ball going only half as far—both named Cayman (see illustration on page 142, Chapter 18)—he said, "The possibilities are endless." Many others did not think so. Frank Thomas, Technical Director of the USGA, thought it was a neat idea, but referred to it as Golf II, an entirely different game from the present Golf I. Others said: "Who wants to drive a ball only 150 yards? Not me." Despite all the negative opinions, and the fact that it is just barely breathing at present, conditions could change to rejuvenate the short game for younger players in the inner cities (see discussion under Cayman Ball, Chapter 18). At present there are six different games of golf. Three are played on the present standard course by using the red, white and blue tee markers. There are some 15,000 of these courses. The short Cayman course, the Executive and the Par Three are the three others. There are estimated to be about 1,000 of the Executive and Par Three courses in the United States. It seems very likely that between the next twenty-five and one hundred years major changes or combinations will be made. Just look backwards one hundred years to compare the 1890 and the 1990 game of golf—different clubs, different balls, different length courses, and water, water galore.

▆ PAR GOLF

What is "par"? According to the American Heritage Dictionary the term, when applied to golf, refers to "the number of strokes considered necessary to complete a hole or course in expert play." In October 1895, at the Newport Golf Club, Newport, Rhode Island, Horace Rawlins became the leading golf expert in the States when he won the first U.S. Open Championship with a score of 173 for 36 holes, an average of over 86 for eighteen holes. Was that par? A year later, at the Shinnecock Hills Golf Club in Southampton, New York, James Foulis won the Open with a score of 152 for 36 holes—an average of 76 strokes for eighteen holes. Was that par? Hardly. The course, which is now over 6,600 yards long was only 4,400 yards. In 1913, Francis Ouimet was the first American to break the monopoly the British had on the U.S. Open. He beat the renowned Harry Vardon, the epitome of expertise, by five strokes—with a total of 304 strokes and an average of 76 per round. Was that par? YES—for that time and place you would think it would be.

While par was 72 for most golf courses then and now, the courses have been lengthened by varying amounts since that time, and eight-foot deep fox holes called bunkers and island greens have been added. Until 1900 the winning scores fluttered around the low 80s for eighteen holes. For the first twenty years of the twentieth century scores ranged from about 78 down to 74 strokes per round, with the exception of Chick Evans' victory in 1916, with a score of 288 for four rounds—72 per round.

From 1920 to 1940 many of the scores were very close to an average of 72 per round, ranging from 296 to a low score of 281 in 1937 by Ralph Guldahl at Oakland Hills South course. After World War II the scores were probably averaging below 72. An outstanding, exceptionally low score in 1945 was Ben Hogan's 276, a 69 average, at the Merion Golf Club in Ardmore, Pennsylvania.

David Love III—Champion of Tournament of Champions, 1993.

Chick Evans.

The above figures are selected examples, but indicative of today's much lower scores, due to many improvements, and also to today's twelve million core golfers rather than the 1,000 in 1900 trying to meet or beat par. A more accurate picture of the later years shows that since 1980, when Jack Nicklaus won the Open at Baltusrol with 8 under par, his average for twelve years has been 4.75 strokes under par.

Therefore, it appears that in the last 96 years, the scores of the acknowledged experts has decreased from about 8 over par to about 4 under par.

Tom Kite. Winner of 1992 U.S. Open. Career earnings about $10,000,000.

During this time par remained the same, with very minor changes at some courses. On January 10, 1993, Davis Love III won the Tournament of Champions, under extreme winter storm conditions, with a 16 under par—272; his average per eighteen holes was 68. Runner-up Tom Kite's last eighteen holes were 64, 8 under par.

The question is—does par represent "the number of strokes considered necessary to complete a hole or course in expert play?" Did it ever? It appears to have been very seldom so.

Should the definition of par be changed or the method of determining it be altered? Should par for any course be the current course record by professionals? Should it be a five or ten year average of the U.S. Open adjusted by the local course rating? Should it be calculated by the composite judgment of a team of independent experts from the USGA, as the course ratings are? Whatever way, it is rather obvious that something should be done about "par" in the next 25 to 100 years.

ALL NIGHT GOLF

How long will it be before some front runner will electrify a full-size golf course with "Stars in the Sky" hi-pole lights similar to Interstate Highway interchanges? It has already been done—30 years ago. The first fully-illuminated course was opened August 23, 1963 at Tall Pines Golf Club in Sewell, New Jersey. One hundred and one hi-poles had 1,000-watt mercury vapor lamps lighting this 3,230-yard executive course. For a decade or more it has been called the Jaworski Eagles' Nest Golf Club after Ron Jaworski of the Philadelphia Eagles football team, and operated without lights because the expense was more than the traffic generated.

With the scarcity of land and now rampant demand, Japan would appear to be a prime candidate to resuscitate the idea. As the appeal of golf broadens, night golf will attract employees tied down to 8:00-to-5:00 jobs—who now only have a choice of Saturday and Sunday, with hours of waiting to get on the tee and a wait at each tee as the game progresses, consuming over six hours in all. Perhaps an older municipal course more centrally located will be the first in the United States to start full-time golf, day and night, twenty-four hours a day. Don't laugh—remember when supermarkets were open only eight to ten hours, and never on Sunday, and there was no video golf.

Golf appears to be about the last sport without night play. Baseball added lights after a long-drawn-out struggle. The trend toward night lighting in sporting events has been powered by television audiences in the evenings. Remember that football is now being played indoors in winter daytime in Detroit. Night lighting of tournament golf should emerge, in spite of the tremendous costs, for the same reason. The only question about pole-lighted night golf would seem to be the date—2000, or dragged out to 3000?

Part 3

Collecting Golf Ball History

A logo ball personally autographed by Arnold Palmer

Collectible Golf Balls: One Dollar to Twenty Thousand

░░ CLASSIFICATION OF NAMED BALLS—BY TYPE AND RARITY

If someone offers to sell you a golf ball made of beechwood, the type that Mary, Queen of Scots used to play golf in the fifteenth century, don't buy it. It is a reproduction or fake. There are no known examples of this earliest wooden type of ball for sale. Early in the seventeenth century King James commissioned James Melville as official maker of a new ball made with feathers. A few of these per year may be offered for sale. These, when found in excellent condition, are very collectible and priced in the five-digit range.

About the middle of the nineteenth century a ball made of rubber-like gutta percha was invented by Robert Patterson; it quickly made the "featherie" obsolete. These balls are very collectible and expensive. A "gutty" in fine condition with the Patterson name on it might also command a five-digit price. These balls are found with a smooth surface, with irregular random chisel

Molds for various cover patterns from c. 1870 on. Hand-indenting was soon superseded by molding lines, squares, mesh, brambles and (1907) dimples in a press from about 1870 on to the present dimples.

From 1900-1910 hundreds of patents were issued for cover designs and construction. Today such odd designs command a large premium over the bramble pattern.

By 1910 Spalding had taken a license on Wm. Taylor's dimple patent of 1907 and named it "Dimple" (Note the flat bottomed circles. Modern balls have curved indentations).

No. KD—KRO-FLITE DIMPLE
No. KDM—Multidot Marking
Each, 75c.   Doz., $8.00

Spalding gave a big boost to Kroflite's dominance by using Dr. Geer's vulcanizing patent to make the covers cut-resistant c. 1930.

About 1910 the above Atti pattern (color added for emphasis) was used almost universally on all makes of balls, and this continued for over 50 years. The rows add up to 336 dimples.

sides that formed an inverted pyramid. This design was not a success, but the Cadwell cover was. The two patents were merged and both names were on later versions.

The mesh and similar lattice pattern gave way to what became for the next fifty years almost a universal dimple pattern. These balls all had 336 dimples molded on the ball surface in eight concentric bands on each side of the equator. From the equator each pair of rows had 32, 32, 28, 24, 20, 16, and 12 dimples, with four dimples at the poles. There were hundreds of millions of balls made with the 336 dimples in this design. However, a ball having this arrangement and number of dimples is not necessarily an old ball; it may be, but the age and value of the ball will be determined more accurately by the brand name, the trade dress, and the way they are applied to the ball. In 1993 the only 336-dimple balls made in the USA and listed as conforming balls by the USGA were two balls made by Duncan Pollitt's Yardley Ball Company— the Miracle and the Spirit. The 1996 list had no 336-dimple U.S. balls. There are a number of foreign balls that still use this 60-year-old configuration of dimples, some of which may be sold in this country.

In 1970 Spalding introduced a two-piece ball, called the Top-Flite, still predominant and still Spalding's front runner. This had a revolutionary solid one-piece core of a synthetic rubber ionomer, with a cover of DuPont's Surlyn.

Acushnet/Titleist started using the name Titleist in 1939. The hundreds of millions, or billions of Titleists which have been produced for a total of over 60 years are not collectible unless they have some other attribute than their name. However, some will emerge as scarce, rare or even unique in years to come. A unique ball, for example, could be the Titleist ball in the Patty Berg Collection in the Cypress Lake Country Club in Fort Myers, Florida which she certified was used in the first Women's Open in 1946, at the Spokane Country Club, when she beat Betty Jameson five to four.

Balls that are different design or construction for late 20th century—1970s and 1980s. Bartsch, PCR—first one-piece since the gutty; Polara—variations of ball that slices and hooks less; Cayman—ball that only goes half as far.

First two-piece ball with Surlyn cover that dominated the market c. 1970. Much scarcer are Ram's Ramlon (three-piece) with first Surlyn cover c.1967.

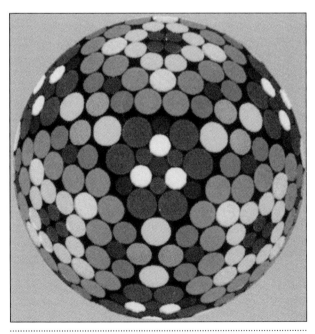

This pattern by Titleist's Gobush, called the cuboctahedron is a new high in covering the surface by using eleven different-sized dimples, repeated eight times. This gives more lift and less drag to the ball.

Scientific investigations in the 1970s and 80s revealed that the performance and distance of the ball could be greatly improved by changing the Atti 336-dimple pattern. This resulted in a seemingly endless stream of tongue-twisting names, such as cuboctahedron pattern by Titleist. Other patterns arranged from 302 to as many as 552 dimples on the ball. The size and depth of the dimples also varied from ball to ball. According to some of the more aggressive advertising each one of these designs flies farther than all other 200-brand names listed by USGA in 1992. Standardized test equipment shows that there is none over ten yards longer than all the others. With all this diversification some collectors will find areas of interest to preserve for the future. Some of the one-piece balls produced from 1965 to 1977 by Polara, Princeton Chemical Research, and Bartsch are collectible right now as historical examples of classic balls.

The other parts of this book should be studied by collectors for specific information on balls they are interested in collecting. Many illustrations show details such as trade dress, different cover patterns, and decorations that help to date the ball. Research is underway to prepare a comprehensive checklist of the names, makers and dates for all balls made during the twentieth century. The author presently has a list of all conforming balls approved by USGA since the first list in 1971 when Frank Thomas, Technical Director, inaugurated this method of approving balls for tournament play.

Sample of monogram and two sections of the annual Golf Club Society's Directory.

HOTCHKISS JOHN F.   03851   Mimi (H)813/454/6818
2509 Harbor Ct SPV   Fort Myers   FL 33908-1652   USA
6/1 - 10/1
P.O. Box 1523   Quogue NY 11959   516/653/4552
B, BA, BBL, BBS, ME

Zip Code	Name	City	State
33881-8769	Dan Duncanson	Winter Haven	FL
33903	Lloyd Curie	N Ft Myers	FL
33908-1652	John F. Hotchkiss	Fort Myers	FL
33923	Vincent A. Scola	Bonita Springs	FL
33937	Ted Myers	Marco Island	FL
33963	Charles R. Colvin	Naples	FL
33963-2811	Sydney N. Stokes	Naples	FL
33969	Mary Ann Sarazen Ilnicki	Marco Island	FL
34202	William D. Sauter	Bradenton	FL
34210-4316	Kim B. Wells	Brandenton	FL
34219	Bert Croghan	Parrish	FL

For anyone interested in collecting golf balls, or any other type of golf memorabilia, the Golf Collectors Society is the best buy. The Society-founded twenty-six years ago by Joe Murdoch and Robert Kuntz now has over two thousand members. The Society publishes *The Bulletin* four to six times a year with informative articles on collecting. An annual directory of the membership is published once a year with members' names and also with the type of golf items each member collects. A membership in this organization can automatically put you in touch with over three hundred golf ball collectors, many of whom trade their duplicate items with other members on a one-to-one basis. There are regional meetings and an annual convention, show and auction. The Annual Show and Auction is held in a different city each year and is a must for serious collectors. (See Appendix for address and further information).

Another authoritative source of information is a chapter in John and Morton Olman's book, *The Encyclopedia of Golf Collecting*, 1985. They have a more recent book, *Golf Antiques & Other Treasures of the Game*, published in 1992.

CLASSIFICATION OF LOGO BALLS.

In addition to the collectible balls mentioned above, another even faster-growing classification includes balls with additional decoration on them in the form of a symbol identifying a company, signature, product, club, team, event or organization. Shown in the accompanying illustrations are examples of balls with the well-known Pepsi-Cola logo, the name of a golf course, Desert Dunes, even the Presidential Seal with the name of a golf-playing president. In some cases, coupled with the logo is the actual date of a golfing event, such as the Baltusrol USGA Open Championship in 1993. Many other logo balls have caricatures, like the one of Iraq's Saddam, classified as a novelty ball. Many of these are given away for advertising or other promotional purposes.

Golf Antiques & Other Treasures of the Game

A common logo Organization

A golf course logo

Presidential facsimile logo then-Vice President Gerald Ford

A dated event logo

A novelty logo

Logo balls are obtained in numerous ways, such as gifts from friends. For instance, friends of ours who have contributed a logo ball to our collection receive a membership card in the Golden Retrievers Club. Golfers sometimes find logo balls while looking for their own balls on the course. Some of the best logos can be purchased from ball reclaimers or shops selling balls they have recycled. (For more information and prices see Chapter 22, Best Balls, Best Buys: Take Your Pick. Most of these balls will be in mint or excellent condition to collect or play with; sources are listed in Sources on page 261). Established collectors trade duplicates with other collectors, usually by mail. Many of the logo ball collections also include older named balls, described earlier.

COLLECTIONS

Collections range from a single special ball in a display case, perhaps one personally autographed by Arnold Palmer to from ten to one hundred balls in various types of display racks (see Appendix 17). Some of the larger collections require wall space, like that of the New England collector Ed, who has the basement recreation room of his home in Falmouth, Maine, lined with self-designed racks holding over twelve thousand balls, classified according to type or source of ball. There are about fifteen thousand golf courses in the United States, and an unknown number of them have or have had a logo ball. Ed has over two thousand of these balls displayed.

New England collector's display racks for logos. Balls supported on parallel lengths of long dowel rods—all home-made.

This custom-made cabinet holds some 4,000 balls. Each has a computer location number. The total capacity about 60,000 balls—in one room in Louisiana.

A well-known geologist is a collector in Louisiana, with a collection of about thirty-six thousand named and logo balls in custom-made cabinets—and still counting. The largest public collection was that of eighteen thousand logos in the old PGA World Golf Hall of Fame in Pinehurst, North Carolina—the golfers' Mecca. This collection, now in storage, was assembled by Ray Davis with generous gifts from the well-known collector Sam Stein, under the direction of Dick Stranahan, a former Tour pro and past curator of the collection. (Ray's own outstanding collection of balls and other memorabilia may be showcased in a West Coast museum).

In 1996 Karen Benardski, former capable curator of the USGA Golf House Museum, was appointed Curator of the new PGA Museum in the new World Golf Hall of Fame complex located off I-95 on the East Coast of Florida, where the balls and other memorabilia will be on display.

Probably the finest collection of old named balls belongs to another collector on the West Coast, whose name is being omitted for security reasons. At one time there were as many as twenty of the pre-1850 feather balls in the collection, with names such as John Gourlay (1815-1869), Allan Robertson (1815-1859), and Alexander Thomas (1803-1841). There were also a dozen or so hammered gutta-percha balls with the names of some of the above who switched careers, as well as those of Robert Forgan and Willie Dunn. There were more than a hundred molded gutta perchas, some with names, and some of the pimple guttys by the Agrippa Ball Company from the late 1800s—in all, making this a national treasure as well as a tribute to the collector's acumen in

Rendition of the New World Golf Hall of Fame, which will be at a new interchange off I-95, between Jacksonville and St. Augustine, FL.

USGA sponsors twenty-plus tournaments, a museum, library, research and technical testing center; it sets rules and standards for the game of golf, and calculates and publishes handicaps for all registered U.S. players.

assembling them when it was still possible. The ultimate destination of this collection is still under consideration—hopefully it will soon be available to the public.

The USGA, has a handsomely-displayed history of the making of the golf ball, including a silk hat full of feathers and tools used to make the featherie ball. This is only the frosting on the cake of the eighteen-room mansion in Far Hills, New Jersey known as Golf House, holding the collection, a library of ten thousand volumes on golf, and a must-see technical center where the visitor can receive a souvenir ball that has been driven by the Iron Byron testing machine. The Golf House Museum portion is under the competent direction of Andy Mutch, Curator. Librarian Nancy Stulac makes available material for research.

Former Curator Janet Seagle, a walking encyclopedia and author on the game of golf, was equally helpful. The huge library is well-used by researchers from around the world. If what you are looking for is not there, it probably does not exist. The whole complex is located about an hour northwest of New York City. As of this date it may be the only sports museum that does not charge a fee.

*Named Antique/Classic Balls by Spalding
from 1890s to 1930s:
Top row left—A gutta percha ball.
Second row left—The first Spalding Dot.
For many more see Appendices.*

George Bush Presidential facsimile signature ball.

Hillary Rodham-Clinton facsimile signature ball.

ORGANIZING A COLLECTION

Bob Leffingwell, a deceased well-known antiques collector/dealer defined a collection as three or more specimens, stating that one is only an example and that two are a pair. Three was only a starter for the New England collection of twelve thousand logo golf balls. Size isn't everything. Selecting a certain segment of logos, such as ones for each year of the U.S. Open, can be a greater challenge. Dated balls for any kind of event will become classics, as will some signature and portrait balls.

The large private and public collections usually embrace about ten general classifications of golf balls, sometimes sub-divided into thirty or forty sub-groups. Other interesting ones are confined to one small select group such as "Presidential" balls having facsimile signatures of the golfing presidents: Eisenhower, Kennedy, Nixon, and the four living ones, Ford, Reagan, Bush and Clinton. Perhaps there are earlier ones of Taft or Wilson.

A much larger, but still interesting collection consists of balls with the logos of private golf clubs with their colorful coats of arms or insignias, many with commemorative dates for fifty or more years. Pictured is a 1986 logo of the 91st U.S. Open at Shinnecock Hills Golf Club, won by Raymond Floyd. There were 5,410 entries compared to 35 in 1896 when the second U.S. Open was held there. Commemorative balls may consistently increase in value just as commemorative coins have. Further details on all of ten rather arbitrary groupings follow and are also evaluated in the two Value Guides in Chapters 27 and 28 that give an approximation of their monetary value.

MAJOR CLASSIFICATIONS OF COLLECTIBLE GOLF BALLS

Named Balls. New or old, they include all balls with the name of the maker and/or the brand name of the ball, or even just the design name such as mesh or bramble pattern. Since the majority of collectible balls are older, the condition of the balls is of utmost importance except for very rare examples such as those previously mentioned. (For valuing and more examples see Chapter 27).

USGA 1986 Open held at Shinnecock Hills Country Club. A dated event collectible.

Golf Club Logo Balls. Any balls with the name or logo of any of the fifteen thousand private or public courses in the United States and the uncounted courses in foreign countries are collectible. The importance of any one is closely associated with its national importance or history: For example, a ball from the Augusta National Golf Club, where the Masters is played annually, versus one from the small Geneseo Country Club in upstate New York. The balls from

Golf Club Logo Balls for private, semi-private and public courses.

the most famous course, St. Andrew's Royal and Ancient Golf Club, may have been reproduced in enough variations to form a collection of its own. (See Chapter 28, Reproductions, Plus and Minus: Caveat Emptor).

Personalized Golf Logo Balls. This includes balls to which names have been added by at least three methods: a) any golf ball that has been personally signed in ink by a leading golf tour pro—such as Arnold Palmer (see illustration on page 184)—or by any other VIP from President Clinton on back; b) those balls which have an original signature reproduced as a miniature facsimile on a ball. Jack Nicklaus' name probably appears in this form on more balls, and in more variations, than that of any other person (Note: a prize Type B would be one containing facsimile presidential balls for the eleven presidents of the twentieth century known to have played golf at some time); c) portrait balls—these have a small black and white photo, usually of a pro or unidentified person. Those of known golfers are much scarcer than balls with facsimile signatures.

Golfing Event Logo Balls. This category includes golf balls that have been imprinted with the name and/or logo of a golfing occasion, dated or undated. The five different Buick Open balls are examples of some with a minimum of information, while the Pebble Beach logo, with the added words U.S. Open 1972, 1982, or 1992 is an example of balls at the high end of the desirability spectrum. Events balls have the possibility to appreciate in price as the years go by, especially those that are dated.

Commemorative Golf Logo Balls. This includes all other balls which refer to some event besides golf, desirably with a location and date. The ball issued to commemorate Alan Shepard's hitting a golf ball on the moon in

Personalized Golf Logo Balls. Includes facsimile signatures, as illustrated, of touring professionals and probably the fastest-growing classes.

**Event Logo Balls
without dates.**

**Commemorative
Ball. A replica of the
"Moon Ball."**

1971 actually pictures the event. (The club he used is now on display in the USGA Museum). World's Fair balls and Olympic Games logo and dated balls are examples of desirable collectibles.

Organization Logo Balls. There is an almost inexhaustible supply of logo balls bearing the names of public and private entities, either profit or non-profit. This group includes governments, social, commercial and educational activities, and all sports other than golf. The well-known GE monogram that identifies the General Electric Company is typical; the older blue bell previously used for Bell Telephone, and the Miami Dolphin football helmets are others. Large collections are subdivided into as many as thirty or more categories, such as airlines, stores, pharmaceuticals, utilities, etc. (See large alphabetical list of categories in the Appendix 15).

Unidentified Logo Balls. These are the enigmas for collectors because they have designs that gives no clue as to what they represent—such as a color picture logo of a hula dancer in action. This could represent Hawaii, Tahiti, or other Pacific Basin island, or none of them. Some of these logos may give only a vague clue. One ball shows a bird with a golf club tucked under one wing and only the date 1923. Such collections of unknowns provide a challenge to friends viewing them. In the case of the bird-and-club golf ball, my

Allan B. Shepard, who hit a special heat-resistant moon ball over 1,600 yards due to lower gravity.

College logos are a good example of one type of organization ball.

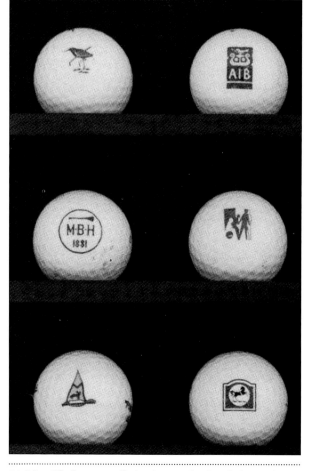

Unidentified Logo Balls having no further information. A challenge for your visitors to help you.

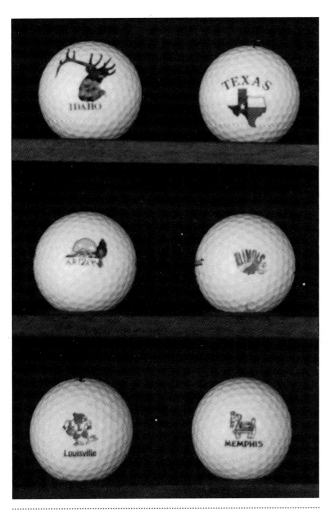

Geographic Logo Balls for countries, state, counties, towns and cities are popular.

Novelty—Greetings and sayings logo balls

wife identified the ball as that of The Creek Club on Long Island. What helped in the solution was the fact that the founding year was also shown.

Geographical Logo Balls. Many countries around the world, as well as states, counties and cities, have names and/or symbols as identifying logos. New York City is of course identified by the creative promotional slogan "I love New York," with a red heart replacing the word "love"; Hawaii has one with an hibiscus blossom with "Hawaii" underneath. Australia uses only the country name printed in conventional red letters.

Novelty Logo Balls. This refers to a wide-ranging assortment of sayings, greetings, humor, slogans, and other unusual, unconventional or bizarre decorations or designs on golf balls. For example, a small issue of balls was printed by a recycler during the Gulf War of 1992 with a portrait of Saddam Hussein and the words "Slam Saddam" printed underneath. Greetings like "Merry Christmas, Grandfather," with holly decor, abound.

Miscellaneous Balls. This might better have been called odd balls, and this category does not necessarily have logo designs. Any designs or types of balls that do not fit elsewhere have a home here until a better one is found. There

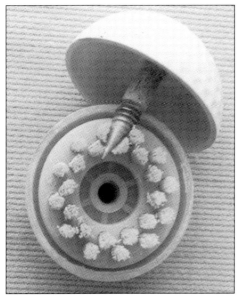

(a)

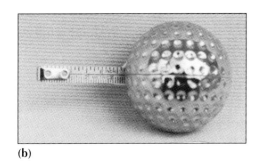

(b)

(c)

Miscellaneous Balls:
(a) A hollow dimple ball cover converted into a cleaning accessory for balls and clubs, scarce; (b) A gold dimple ball turned into a very useful tape measure. Rare for ball or tape measure collectors; (c) Trick Golf Balls: The Exploding Golf Ball and The Wiggling Golf Ball.

are many odd-colored balls and Ping bi-colored balls which might make a colorful display under this section. A conventional-looking ball made of white chocolate is another candidate, as would be the exploding ball, the off-center ball which wobbles when putted, and the golf ball with a baby's rubber nipple attached. New odd balls are announced almost on a daily basis.

In summary, if you get tired of your logo collection, you and your friends can always play golf with them or auction them to reap your reward.

A COLLECTOR'S DREAM COME TRUE

A special collection of only about 60 balls which is an outstanding example of ingenuity, persistence and artistic ability was put together by a Golf Collectors' Association member. Handsomely displayed are golf balls personally autographed by every pro who participated in the 1992 finals of the prestigious Masters Tournament held at Augusta, Georgia each year. An unusual, unique and museum-quality collection to illustrate what is possible in collecting golf balls.

*A superb collection of Silvertown 19th-century balls
and 20th-century Silver King balls. Top row, l. to r.: four
molded gutties (second ball is new and remade), and
last, one bramble; bottom row, l. to r.: a mesh ball,
three dimple balls, and a very unusual smooth 19th-
century Silvertown.*

Valuing Named Balls: Grading & Pricing with the Value Guide

O
n Friday afternoon about three o'clock, on April 26, 1991, at the Andover Country Club in Andover, Massachusetts, Kevin McGrath, Auctioneer, banged his gavel and bellowed "sold," transferring ownership of "a large size feather ball c. 1840 with most of the original paint." The price was $5,500, including a ten percent buyers' premium. A little later that same afternoon on Sanibel Island in Florida, Cyler Adams was thrashing around in the two-foot rough at the Beachview Golf Club trying to find his Titleist DT ball. No luck, but he did find a Dunlop with the Buick shield, plus the words "Buick International," worth maybe a dollar. Why the extreme difference in value? Several reasons, one being demand—the featherie is a rare ball and the "event" modern ball of as little interest at present as the featherie was in 1840, but already headed upward.

The table that follows this text is the first comprehensive attempt to record and codify the approximate value of any golf ball you may be interested in. Quite a presumptuous statement? It sure is, but having done it ten times before with some success, for ten other kinds of collectibles, gives the author—and should give golf ball collectors—confidence about the buying or selling of collectible balls.

Please remember that this is a guide and not a bible. It is opinion, based on assembling and plotting thousands of prices from auctions, mail order offerings, and lists by experienced dealers like Chuck Furjanic of Irving, Texas, and several others who form our unofficial "Board of

Ball from one of five Buick tour events. A nice collectible for Buick dealers or owners.

A random assortment of various names of balls in three-pack cartons. Individual ball markings form the trade dress to classify, date, and value the item.

This monthly catalog is the textbook, price list, guide and reference for any golf collector. Furjanic buys, sells and auctions golf memorabilia.

Experts." From the distribution pattern a price is selected—not the average or the mean. This is usually submitted to the group for comment, adjusted accordingly, and added to the following value tables as the probable range in price. This range indicates the area in which an informed seller and buyer would likely complete a sale.

The range applying to any one ball can be found by first identifying the type of ball involved. If the ball carries the manufacturers' name and other grade names like Titleist HVC*HP 90; Spalding TopFlite Tour XL 100; Dunlop Maxfli MD-100 Two-Piece 432 or some five hundred similar markings you have a "Named Ball," and should look at the table "Value Guide A to Named Golf Balls" on page 213. If the ball has further decoration or names you probably have a logo ball, which is covered in the table "Value Guide B to Logo Golf Balls" at the end of Chapter 27 on page 219. It is essential to read the entire book to use these two tables accurately, especially the first. An old adage still works: "Read the book before you buy the ball."

Over 99 percent of the balls you encounter will have the entire surface covered with small circular depressions called dimples. As an example, suppose you found one which instead of dimples had small square depressions, with the name Beckley Blue Pigeon. From the photographs in this book you have determined that this is called a mesh pattern, made in the 1920s. Considering its age it looks in excellent shape, ready to go. By referring to the Guide A and looking down the first column as far as 1910-1935, Group E, Mesh 3-PC Balls, Common Names and Designs, you will find suggested price ranges for your type of ball. You will probably decide that $40-

Example of buying mesh ball valued at $40-$80.

80 in the Excellent column is a proper choice. (More later on determining the ball's condition).

If you decide to sell it, you will probably want the highest price. Any knowledgeable buyer will, no doubt, offer much less—the lower price of $40. The final price will depend on how badly you want to sell compared to how anxious the buyer is to acquire it. Whatever you two decide on is the right price for the ball on that day and under those conditions. You are both satisfied. As the song goes, "Who could ask for anything more?"

Now, returning to the hard part of determining which of the six columns in Guide A to use for a realistic price. . . . You will notice that the range from Mint to Poor in the case of the Beckley Blue Pigeon mesh ball is one hundred to one. Some of this wide disparity is due to scarcity; more bad ones than good ones survived. As collectors grow in experience, so does their desire for perfection and willingness to pay high prices grow.

A Mint ball is one that has never been hit, one just out of the box or in its original wrapping. With the tremendous improvement in durability and finish of balls today, the distinction between Mint and Excellent has narrowed. A Good ball is a playable ball for most collectors. Therefore, a Very Good ball is a ball with slight imperfections such as a rub mark. A Good ball may have more evidence of having been played but not abused. From there on down it is just a case of how much abuse or weather the ball has been subjected to. An allowance in grading is made for older balls. A modern ball might grade Very Good but a 70-year-old Kro-Flite in the same condition is likely to grade as

A mesh pattern made concurrently as an alternate to the dimple, but which died out during the 1930s. This would probably be considered an uncommon name compared to a Kro-Flite mesh ball.

Suggested grading of older named balls according to condition. Right to left: Poor, Fair, Good, Very Good, and Excellent. A ball in a sealed wrapper would be Mint.

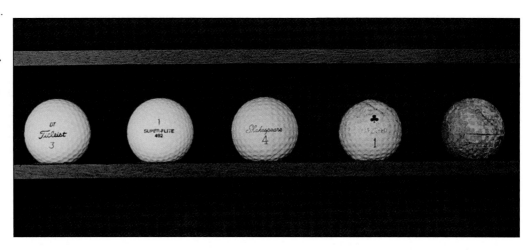

Fine collection of Mint condition wrapped balls. Discontinued in the 1930s. Presently sometimes sold in single cubed cartons, three-pack, or in boxes of a dozen or more.

Early 20th-century ball designs. Designs proliferated during the first years of the century; there were hundreds of patents with the design and construction of three-piece wound balls. These are all now scarce to very rare.

Excellent. One would not expect a featherie 150 years old to look as good as a shiny 1997 Titleist even when it might bring thousands of dollars at auction.

The nine time periods of the Value Guide (such as c. 1670-1860) are dictated more by changes in ball construction than by any other factor, and are fully covered in other parts of the book. The time periods are only approximate, since there is always an overlap while one design or construction is being superseded by the improved ball. Probably the quickest changeover came when the Haskell three-piece wound ball was replaced by the two-piece solid-core synthetic rubber core with durable Surlyn cover. Within three years the two-piece accounted for over 50 percent of all balls, but has to this day not replaced the pros' favorite three-piece wound ball with a balata-type cover, used in more tournaments than all other balls.

The description of the type of ball in the second column from the left is best understood by the many illustrations in this book of the featherie and gutty. The "smooth" and "hammered" gutties are lumped together as the price range adequately brackets both names. The gutta-percha bramble is a ball with pimples in rows rather than dimples. The invention of the superior dimple ball by Taylor, c. 1907, quickly snuffed out the universal use of the bramble pattern on the gutty and the Haskell three-piece wound ball. The "mesh" ball design ran concurrently with the new dimpled balls through the 1920s into the 30s. For example, Spalding in these years advertised the popular Kro-Flite in both designs for 75 cents per piece. By the mid-30s the dimple design had eased out the mesh designs. From about 1936 until the present day the dimple has been cock of the walk, with very few exceptions, discussed elsewhere in this book. This 60-year period has been subdivided into sections because of changes to the interior of the ball by the introduction of a one-piece ball with dimples in 1967, and the two-piece ball with a dimpled Surlyn cover in 1970.

The last six columns are headed Mint, Excellent, Very Good, Good, Fair and Poor in order to recognize the tremendous spread in values between a Mint ball and a Poor one. For example, in the table a common 1910-1935 ball in Mint condition is worth as much as a hundred times what the Poor one is worth. Exceptions, when found, could have still wider ranges. Refer to illustration on page 206 for a visual example of older balls. Please—at best these are experienced estimates or approximations. The conditions under which a sale is consummated are as variable as the odds on the Trifecta at Pimlico.

Changes in Golf Club logos help to date these balls. Top Row: Two Pebble Beach designs. Center Row: Four changes in West Hampton C.C. design—not typical, but helpful. St. Andrews has many changes. Perhaps all were not sponsored by the Club.

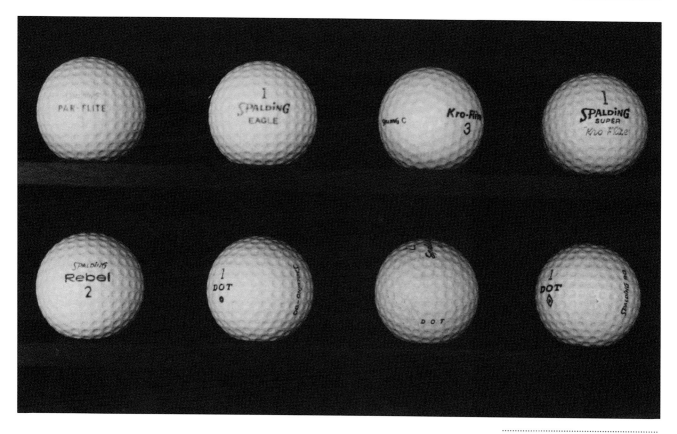

A few examples of the many variations in named balls. Design, placement of the word Spalding and ball name are helpful in estimating age and value of a ball. Titleist has been more consistent in their trade dress.

DATING GOLF BALLS

Perhaps the biggest difficulty the reader will have in using this table will be in assigning the proper date bracket in which to look for a price range. From about 1910 until 1970 mostly all of the dimples were in eight rows for a total of 336, known as the Atti pattern (see illustration on page 117 in Chapter 15), named after the tool shop that supplied most of the molds. This leaves only the names and insignia on the dimple ball as interesting collectibles from 1910 to about 1970, when the Titleist Ball sported its new dimple dress with a jaw-breaker name, "icosahedron" (see illustration on page 120 in Chapter 15). This was actually an arrangement of twenty equal triangular groups of dimples. The new pattern did two things: first, it staggered the arrangement, as visibly different; second and more importantly, it gave the player much better distance and control of the ball.

Spalding introduced the name Top-Flite in 1932 and Acushnet announced their Titleist in 1935. Both names have been used since then. In 1996 there may have been over two hundred million of each of these balls produced—and we're talking about collecting balls? No, not these two names per se. However, during these years both companies changed their "trade dress," referring to the way the company name and the name of the ball is displayed on the ball. So, in addition to differences in the cover designs and number of dimples, the trade dress is another and very accurate method of assigning the period of time in which any one ball was produced. Unfortunately, neither this book nor any other one documents the trade dress of all golf balls in this century.

J. Gregory Sherry of the Spalding Company very thoroughly refused to give this author access to this information because of "deterioration" of their

Rapid change in Cayman Ball trade dress. In less than twenty years there are seven changes in trade dress and bramble-like covers. Originally owned by MacGregor and now by Troy Puckett, the inventor of the ball that goes only half the normal distance.

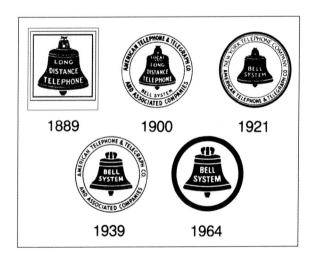

Dating by trade dress. A classic example of change in trade dress dating for telephone collectibles.

archives, and was abashed when shown a like-new bound copy of the *Spalding Store News* (dated 1915) that had been in an open display on a table in the waiting room. Some of this information is in *Olman's Golf Collectibles*, published in 1985. A great deal of it can also be obtained from the ads in old magazines such as *Golf Digest*, *Golf Magazine*, and even older ones in the collection at USGA in Far Hills, New Jersey, and to a limited extent in the Appendices of this book.

That's the bad news about collecting modern balls. The good news is that Part I of this book lists in detail innumerable balls which are today bringing well over several hundred dollars when one comes on the market. In November of 1992, Mike Daniels, a member of the Golf Collectors Society and an expert on golf balls, published a list of balls for sale, as follows: "Haskell remade bramble, the first rubber ball, minor iron marks, 95% paint, circa 1899—$450.00; Kempshall Flyer, rubber core bramble, circa 1902, 90% original paint, VG+ condition—$250.00; The Wonder Ball, unusual diamond pattern dimples, circa 1912—$100.00; Henley, mesh pattern, rubber core ball circa 1920s or 1930s, mint condition—$60.00." *Golf Week*, issue of February 19, 1993, reported that at a Phillips auction in Cheshire, England, a very rare bramble ball dated 1910 was knocked down to Manfried Shotten, a dealer, for about $5,200. In May 1996 at a McGrath auction a Stars & Stripes c. 1895 gutty was run up to $26,000.

Rare Stars & Stripes gutta percha ball made by Willie Dunn. Late 19th century.

Rare "Terrestial Globe" bramba gutta-percha ball c. 1905 in May 97 Phillips Auction. Estimate $10,000-$15,000.

Our research to date has uncovered several thousand different balls with different names and makers. Some of these would be extremely rare but unappreciated, and some extremely common. Collecting balls from 1900 to World War II offers any collector a real challenge, enough to keep him busy for many years. And finally, a collection does not have to be only old balls. There have been many interesting scarce balls produced in the last twenty-five years. For example: the Cayman Ball; the Polara; the first one-piece ball marked Bartsch, also PCR; PCR II; White Flash from Faultless; balls from Worthington; and many others, all previously illustrated. The value of these balls will increase in years to come as it has for the brambles and mesh balls. As in all collecting, experts advise buying the best examples you can afford, thereby concentrating on quality, not quantity, as being the most interesting and satisfying over the years. ❧

Feather Ball. See Value Guide A, Classification A, for price range.

Smooth Gutta Percha ball c. 1850. See Value Guide A, Classification A, for price range.

Paterson's Composite c. 1860. See Value Guide A, Classification A, for price range.

Hammered Gutta Percha c. 1860. See Value Guide A, Classification B, for price range.

Molded Gutta Percha c. 1870. See Value Guide A, Classification C, for price range.

Bramble Design c. 1900. Gutta Percha and three-pc. balls. See Value Guide A, Classification C, for prices.

Haskell three-pc. ball c. 1900. Molded and bramble designs. See Value Guide A, Classification D, for prices.

Mesh design new ball from old 1920 mold. For old mesh balls see Value Guide A, Classification E, for prices.

Dimple design balls 1910-1935. See Value Guide A, Classification F, for prices. For later, 1935-1997 use nominal prices in earlier Golf Ball Prices Table, Classification G, H, I.

VALUE GUIDE A TO NAMED GOLF BALLS

Date	Classification	Mint	Excel.	V. Good	Good	Fair	Poor
c. 1600 to 1860	A. FEATHER BALL		in thousands of dollars				
	Unnamed Balls	6-12	4-8	3-6	2-4	1-2	.5-1
	Named Balls	10-20	8-15	6-12	3-5	1-2	.5-1
c. 1850 to 1870	B. GUTTA PERCHA BALLS		in thousands of dollars				
	Hammered w/o Name	4-6	3-5	2-4	1-2	.5-1	.2
	Hammered with Name	6-10	4-8	3-6	2-4	1-2	.5
c. 1860 to 1910	C. GUTTA PERCHA BALLS		in hundreds of dollars				
	Molded w/o Name	4-8	3-6	2-4	1-2	1	.5
	Molded with Some Names	6-10	4-8	3-6	2-4	1-2	.5-1
c. 1900 to 1915	D. GUTTA PERCHA 3-PC WOUND BALLS		in hundreds of dollars				
	Bramble w/o Name	3-6	2-5	1-3	1-2	.5-1	.25-.3
	Bramble with Some Names	6-10	4-8	3-6	2-4	1-2	.5-1
c. 1910 to 1935	E. MESH 3-PC WOUND BALLS		in dollars only				
	Common Names & Designs	60-100	40-80	20-50	10-30	5-10	-
	Some Names & Designs	100-200	60-100	40-80	20-40	8-12	1
c. 1910 to 1935	F. DIMPLE 3-PC WOUND BALLS		in dollars only				
	Common Names & Designs	30-50	20-40	10-25	4-8	1-2	-
	Some Names & Designs	100-200	60-100	40-80	20-40	5-10	2
c. 1935 to 1970	G. DIMPLE 3-PC WOUND BALLS		in dollars only				
	Common Names & Designs	2-4	1-2	.50	-	-	-
	Some Names & Designs	3-25	2-10	1-5	-	-	-
c. 1967 to 1975	H. DIMPLE DESIGN BALLS		in dollars only				
	1-Pc Balls	5-25	3-20	2-5	-	-	-
	Early 2-Pc Balls	2-10	1-5	.50-2	-	-	-
c. 1970 to 1997	I. DIMPLE 2 & 3-PC BALLS*		in dollars only				
	Common Names & Designs	1-5	1-2	.50-1	-	-	-
	Some Names & Designs	2-10	1-5	.50-1	-	-	-

*Includes other than dimple cover designs

Note: See accompanying text for essential information before using this table.

*From a portrait of Bobby Jones in the Jones
Room, Golf House, USGA, Far Hills, NJ.*

Valuing Logo Balls: Grading & Pricing with the Value Guide

Bob Coyne is a very unhappy man because he accumulates logo balls for nothing. He doesn't even have to pay any delivery charges, since the balls are delivered right to his back yard, or, in many cases, right through the window into the bedroom. So far he hasn't been rendered unconscious by a delivery. He not only collects logo balls but he also gets a total of about 1,000 other practically new balls of every description every year. Bob receives these as a bonus for having built his house on the fifth hole at the Dunes Golf Club on Sanibel Island in Florida. They are donated very reluctantly by errant hackers who slice their drives off the fifth tee. Most of the rest of the logo ball collectors obtain balls under less traumatic circumstance, sometimes paying a good size sum.

The types of logo balls and sources have been adequately covered in the preceding pages. The Value Guide B to Logo Golf Balls on page 219 also gives collectors a very approximate range of values for the nine classifications previously described. After talking to dealers, collectors and reclaimers we are able to offer a tentative arrangement of values with the admonition that it be used with a great deal of latitude. If you are a beginner you can get these balls free by walking the course. You can buy them for less than one dollar at places listed in this book. Friends

An example of an "Unidentified, Only Symbol" golf ball. (See Value Guide B).

215

An effortless method of collecting golf balls.

will also pass some along. The more advanced collectors will have acquired an intuitive idea of what they think any logo ball is worth to them. That is what collecting is all about—buying something you like at a price you are willing to pay and enjoying it for years. If and when you sell it the going price may be a pleasant surprise.

The table at the end of Chapter 26 contains the values for named balls. The table at the end of this chapter accounts for the remaining nine suggested classifications for golf balls. The logo table is arranged in a format similar to that of the Named Ball Value Guide. The six columns on the right list ball conditions from mint to poor. Any logo ball not in very good condition is suspect as an adequate addition to any collection; it is not worth very much, and never will be. But never say never when collecting; it is full of surprises.

Visualize, if you will, that your Aunt Matilda is breaking up housekeeping and sending you your grandfather's golf bag and clubs. When it arrives you find eight balls which look pretty disreputable, but one has some writing on it. This turns out to be Bobby Jones's autograph, dated October 10, 1924, the day he won the first of his five USGA Amateur Open Championships at the Merion Cricket Club in Ardmore, Pennsylvannia. Now you buy the book and find that this ball, in fair condition, is worth twenty-five dollars. Don't believe it. You have a prize.

You might decide to put it in an auction which just might be attended by Karen Bednarski, new Curator of the World Golf Hall of Fame Museum, looking for additions, and/or Sid Mathews, the world's authority on Bobby Jones collectibles. Neither might have this ball. With two such bidders, the ball could probably bring a few hundred, or even many thousands of dollars. Only those two would decide.

Logo collectors can help to improve on this Value Guide to Logo Golf Balls for future editions if they will send their experiences and comments on values to the author, in care of the publisher ✍

1. Golf Course, Private.

2. Personalized, Original Signature, Gary Player.

2. Personalized, Portrait Ball.

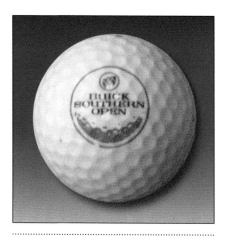

3. Commemorative, Undated.

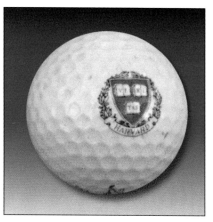

4. Organization, Uncommon.

5. Unidentified, Mixed Symbols and Letters.

6. Unidentified, Only Symbols.

7. Geographical, Common.

8. Novelty.

Picture numbers correspond to those on Value Guide B

1. Golf course, Public.

2. Personalized, Small Facsimile Signature.

3. Event, Dated.

4. Commemorative, Undated.

5. Organization, Common.

6. Unidentified, Only Symbols.

7. Geographical, Uncommon.

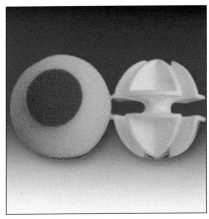

8. Novelty, Practice Balls.

9. Miscellaneous, Lord's Prayer.

Picture numbers correspond to those on Value Guide B

VALUE GUIDE B TO LOGO GOLF BALLS

No.	Classification	Mint	Excel.	V. Good	Good	Fair	Poor
				in dollars			
1	GOLF COURSES						
	Public	1-4	1-2	0-.50	-	-	-
	Private	1-20	1-10	50-5	-	-	-
2	PERSONALIZED						
	Printed Name	1-4	1-2	0-.50	-	-	-
	Small Facsimile Sig.	2-50	2-20	1-10	-	-	-
	Orig. Sig.	4-250	4-150	2-100	1-50	-	-
3	EVENTS						
	Logos Undated	1-25	1-10	.50-5	0-2	-	-
	Logos Dated	2-50	1-25	.50-10	.50-5	-	-
4	COMMEMORATIVE						
	Undated	1-50	1-25	.50-10	0-5	-	-
	Dated	2-100	2-50	1-25	.50-10	0-5	-
5	ORGANIZATIONS						
	Common	1-4	1-2	.50-1	0-.50	-	-
	Uncommon	2-10	1-5	1-2	.50-1	-	-
6	UNIDENTIFIED						
	Only Words	1-3	1-2	.50-1	-	-	-
	Only Symbols	1-6	1-3	1-1.50	.50-1	-	-
7	GEOGRAPHICAL						
	Common	1-4	1-2	.50-1	0-.50	-	-
	Uncommon	2-10	1-5	1-2	.50-1	-	-
8	NOVELTY						
	Any Example	1-10	1-5	.50-1	-	-	-
9	MISCELLANEOUS						
	All Other Logos	1-10	1-5	1-2	.50-1	-	-

Note: See accompanying text for essential information before using this table.

Frederic Remington's famous bronze sculpture "Coming Through The Rye." One of a very limited edition, c. 1910.

Reproductions, Plus and Minus: Caveat Emptor

Most collectors badmouth the word "reproductions," and for a very good reason. If you were Bob Rockwell, donor of the Rockwell Museum of Western Art in Corning, New York, who has an original Frederic Remington bronze entitled "Coming Through The Rye," worth perhaps several hundreds of thousands of dollars or more, you certainly would not be happy to see this ad in *The Antique Trader*: "For Sale, Frederic Remington's famous bronze 'Coming Through the Rye,' $1,500, The Sherman Trading Co. CA, Los Angeles CA." You would hate the idea of cheap reproductions flooding the market. Actually, Rockwell's original bronze is also a reproduction, but authentic: made, signed, numbered and documented from the original clay model by Remington. In fact, all currency and coin in your pocket is reproduced from the master plates and dies made from original art.

Fortunately, reproductions of golf balls are not the problems for collectors that Remington art, pattern glass, coins, Tiffany lamps, and hundreds of other collectibles are. Usually reproductions (later imitations of collectible items) are not produced until demand and price for a collectible spiral upward sufficiently to justify the expense of creating new replicas. Such reproductions may be just as serviceable and attractive as the original at a fraction of the original's price, but they usually depress, or at least stall, the market price of the originals. The featherie golf ball, made from a hat full of feathers stuffed into a sewn leather cover, is one of the balls that is very collectible and priced in the thousands.

A feathery ball in excellent condition. Made in Scotland c. 1840.

A feather ball reproduction by Phil Mason c. 1993.

The Anthology of Golf.

At the 1991 Annual Golf Collectors Society meeting and show in Dallas, the author was offered a featherie for twenty-five hundred dollars. Not being an expert on such high-priced merchandise he collared Frank, an authority on that type of ball, to render his opinion. When Frank appeared, so did several of his counterparts. No one seemed certain of the ball's authenticity. Frank said it could be genuine or it could be a very good later replica. As a result, no sale. Frank was following a very good rule: "When the price gets high, don't buy—unless you know the background of the seller, where he got it, what documentation is available, and what warranty goes with the item."

Actually, there are excellent reproductions of featherie balls made by Phillip Mason, a respected member of the Golf Collectors Society, and a collector/dealer who has learned to make playable copies. It takes him about three hours to make one, using the same meticulous methods and time that it took Allan Robertson 150 years ago in Scotland. The cost is about 50 dollars, a modest price when you consider the skill and patience required. The wages in Robertson's time were about a dollar a day, as compared to at least 40 dollars today at the minimum wage. A picture of one of Mason's autographed and numbered balls is illustrated here. When contacted, he was busy trying to fill an unusual order of several hundred balls to be used by a club on the East Coast about to stage a 150-year "throwback" tournament, using feather balls and old hickory-shafted clubs.

Another unusual limited edition set of reproduced balls was issued in a simulated skeleton book called *The Anthology of Golf*. Inside the book is a separate abbreviated story of the golf ball, and reproductions of twelve twentieth-century balls. When the Worthington Golf Company was revamping its plant in Elyria, Ohio, many old golf ball molds were discovered, dating back to 1900. Twelve representative molds were selected to reproduce a limited edition of representative examples from 1900 to 1990. These twelve golf balls are pictured on this page.

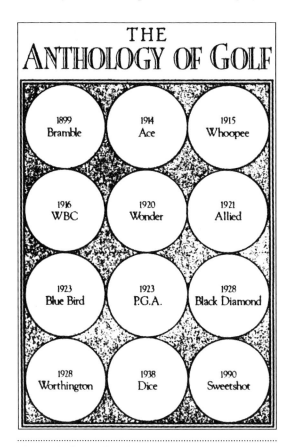

The Anthology of Golf

One dozen examples of balls remade from original molds over a period starting in 1900 by the Worthington Golf Co. in Elyria, OH.

A reproduction of Worthing's The Wonder Ball, originally introduced in 1920.

A reproduction such as Worthington's Anthology usually finds a niche as a worthwhile collectible in golf ball history. However, some of these balls are being sold separately. As long as they are sold as reproductions there is no problem. It behooves the buyer to beware.

CAVEAT EMPTOR

Further along there is an incident which illustrates the need for care. This also applies to old balls that are repainted and sold as Mint condition. A very careful examination will often reveal telltale giveaways.

While reproductions have their strong points and their weak points, they are sometimes misused and misrepresented. When that happens they acquire the very different, sinister name of "fake," "forgery," "false," or "fraudulent," for claiming to be something they are not. Sometimes this is done intentionally, sometimes unintentionally due to lack of knowledge. The intentional act of misrepresentation has resulted in some extended stays in jail.

Suppose one of the balls that Phil Mason made for the "throwback" tournament got lost in the underbrush and was not recovered for ten years. It was a weather-ravaged ball when found, and landed in a flea market. A knowledgable but unethical dealer spotted it for what it was, a reproduction, along with the opportunity to make a quick two thousand dollars by misrepresentation. His story was that he had purchased this from a relative of Allan Robertson, the early ball maker of St. Andrew's, Scotland. Such a scenario rarely happens, but it has and still may, if collectors do not use care in buying only from experienced, recognized dealers who document and warrant the sale. This is known in art galleries on upper Madison Avenue in New York City as the provenance, which in plain English means simply the authentic origin and ownership of the item. If big money is at stake, insist that the bill of sale says that you have seven days to authenticate the purchase and can return it within that time for full refund.

An example of the unintentional offer of some of the Anthology balls as original ones has already happened to an inexperienced and chagrined dealer. Two old balls were purchased at a garage sale by a member of the Golf Collectors' Society and advertised for sale in the *Society Bulletin* by their ball names —Wonder and Whoopee—for ten dollars. In a telephone call the owner described these as Mint condition. When he was told that these might be reproductions he apologized, saying he was unaware that they were not original. This offer to sell two such collectible balls for ten dollars showed his lack of knowledge of what he was offering.

With prices rapidly escalating on golf balls, especially those made from 1850 to 1950, more reproductions are likely to be discovered, and also more fakes, which could prove disastrous. Forewarned is to be forearmed when the seller and the origin of the golf ball are not known.

Timetable

225

c. 100 B.C.—Shepherds in southern Italy develop the "paganica," a leather ball stuffed with feathers, as a handball—believed forerunner of the latter-day "featherie," used by Europeans as a golf ball.

1340-1350—A stained-glass window erected in Gloucester Cathedral showing a man swinging a club at a ball.

1452—A golf ball in Scotland is sold for about ten shillings (five dollars today), the first recorded sale of a golf ball.

1502—King James IV buys clubs and balls from a bow-maker in St. Johnstoun (i.e., Perth).

1567—Murder of Lord Darnley. Queen Mary accused of playing golf and pall-mall in the fields of Seton House within a fortnight of her husband's death. Mary was perhaps the first to use on a golf course what was later termed a caddie.

c. 1600—The featherie, a leather-covered ball stuffed with feathers, replaces the wooden ball as the most popular type of golf ball. The feather ball period is sometimes described as from 1440 to 1848.

1618—A monopoly of ball-making rights granted to James Melvill. The price for each golf ball was fixed at four shillings.

1610

1642—Town council of Aberdeen issues "licence and tollerance to John Dickson to make gouff balls within this burgh during the councils pleasure, and his good carriage and behavior. . . ."

c. 1650—The Gourlay family of Leith and Musselburgh prominent in ball-making: it becomes fashionable to play with a "Gourlay" ball.

1682—First International Golf Match: the Duke of York (afterwards James II) and a shoemaker named John Patersone defeat two English noblemen at Leith.

1729—First golf clubs (or golf sticks) mentioned in America in an account of the estate of William Burnet, governor of New York and Massachusetts. (Among his possessions: "Nine Golf clubs, one iron ditto and seven dozen balls").

1744—First rules of the game (13) drawn up on one page. (Today the USGA Official Rules of Golf consist of a volume of 136 pages and a decision book of rulings and interpretation of 583 pages).

1764—The Royal and Ancient (R&A) Club at St. Andrew's becomes headquarters for the official governing body of the sport. An early decision: standard round set at eighteen holes instead of the previous twenty-two.

c. 1770—The boy carrying the golf clubs becomes known as the caddie.

1800—The featherie ball standardized by the R&A at 1.5 inches in diameter and between 26 and 30 pennyweights (16 to an ounce)—measurements slightly smaller than today's standards of 1.68 inches and 1.62 ounces

1811—First recorded Ladies Golf Competition at the Musselburgh Golf Club on January 9—conducted for fisherwomen ("fisher lassies") of this Scottish village. First prize was a creel and skull.

c. 1833—Allan Robinson became the first recognized golf professional when he succeeded his father, Davie (referred to as Senior Caddie).

1834—William IV confers the title of Royal and Ancient upon the Golf Club of St. Andrews.

1836—Frenchman Samuel Messieux hits the longest drive ever recorded—361 yards—using a featherie. This is a drive of more than twice the distance the average featherie travels off the tee—a questionable achievement (maybe off a mountain and with a hurricane tail wind).

1760   *1800*

1840—Allan Robertson turns out 1,021 featheries; in the following year 1,392.

1842—William Robertson, famous ball maker, remodels the St. Andrew's course.

1844—Allan Robertson of St. Andrews turns out 2,456 feather balls. He bitterly fought the introduction of the gutta-percha ball.

1845—The solid gutta-percha golf ball invented in Scotland—supposedly by Scottish divinity student Dr. Robert Adams Paterson. It was made of a rubberlike gum from the Far East, called gutta percha.

1848—The solid, molded gutta-percha ball replaces most featheries. The gutta-percha era lasts until about 1901, when it is superseded by the machine-made three-piece wound balls of the present day.

c. 1850—A white "complexion" in fashion for golf balls (and for snowy weather, a red one).

1858—Allan Robinson, a famous feather ball name, breaks the St. Andrews course record of 80 with a score of 79.

1860—Beginning of championship golf: the Prestwick Club offer a Championship Belt for an annual Professional Championship—a 36-hole stroke play tournament. The winner: Willie Park, Sr., who was one of eight

1815

1860

entrants. Thrown open also to amateurs this becomes the British Open Championship—won by "Old Tom" Morris in 1861.

1871—Ballmaker and professional golfer Willie Dunn first to make gutta-per-cha balls in molds, improving ball flight over smooth and hammered ones.

1876—Captain Duncan Stewart of England patents the "gutty composite," an improvement upon the gutta-percha ball. The new "gutty" is made of gutta percha, ground cork and metal filings, combined.

c. 1885—A yellowish composition guttie called "Eclipse" contains secret mix-tures of India rubber and cork.

1888—First permanent golf club in the United States opens in Yonkers, New York—set up at a dinner party November 14 for the "Apple Tree Gang" by British R&A member Jack Reid. The new body is called the St. Andrews Club of Yonkers.

1890s—Gutties manufactured in the brambled mold. Known as the "Agrippa," these balls featured raised bumps on the cover. Agrippas were found to be an aerodynamically superior ball.

—Mrs. John Reid is the first woman in the United States to play golf.

1891—The first real golf course in America is unveiled— shares sold at $100 apiece, and a club house planned. Shinnecock Hills, Southampton, Long Island, New York, becomes the nation's first duly incorporated golf club.

1892—English balls/clubs sold in United States by A.G. Spalding Co., Massachusetts

1893—Lady Margaret Scott wins first British Women's Open at St. Anne's (also won in 1894 and 1895).

—Harry Vardon plays in his first British Open, aged 23, at Prestwick.

—Shinnecock Hills creates separate nine-hole course sole-ly for use by wives and daughters of male members.

—According to Willie Fernie at the 1905 Haskell patent trial in Great Britain, in this year of 1893 his brother George had made and sold at least two dozen golf balls with rubber or cork cores and a gutta-percha cover, although the venture was not successful.

1894—Willie Park, Jr., from Scotland, plays a round at Tuxedo, New York using balls kept cool in ice water carried by his caddy. While they played better, Willie did not, and lost the match.

—The United States Golf Association was founded in New York City on December 22. Theodore Havemeyer was elected President.

1896—James Foulis wins first USGA Open at the 4,423-yard Shinnecock Hills Golf Course, with a score of 156 for eigh-teen holes. This was the first Amateur golf tournament of

1890

the USGA in which a black contestant was entered. The black contestant was John M. Shippen, the Club's 16-year-old caddie, whose score was 159.

1898—A.G. Spalding and Bros. produce the first ball made in the United States, a guttie called the Vardon Flyer.

1899—Americans Coburn Haskell and Bertram Work patent the "Haskell wound rubber-core"—hailed as "golf's greatest revolution": a solid center, wrapped with tightly wound rubber threads, covered by a layer of gutta percha.

—First golf tee invented by George F. Grant of Boston, Massachusetts: a wooden tee with a tapering base portion and a flexible tubular concave shoulder to hold the golf ball. Previously, damp sand from a sandbox on the tee was hand molded into a little pyramid on which to place the ball.

1900—Spalding calls its new "Vardon Flyer" the best gutty ball ever made. Harry Vardon tours United States, wins U.S. open at Chicago Golf Club using Flyer. Within five years, Flyer sold only for practice, due to popularity of wound (Haskell) ball.

—The estimated 100,000 golfers in the United States play 500 courses and spend an estimate of $10 million.

—Goodrich employee John Gammeter creates the thread-winding machine, eliminating hand-winding and improving quality in the process of making wound Haskell balls.

c. 1900—Around this time a number of factory-made gutties were on the market—including Eureka, Melfort, Henley (marked with St. Andrews crosses), O.K., Clan, Thornton, Ocobo, Musselburgh.

—First licensees under the Work-Haskell patent after Goodrich were the Kempshall Company of New Jersey, then Spalding, and then the Worthington Ball Co. of Elyria, Ohio.

1901—Introduction of the rubber-cored ball by Coburn Haskell: the Haskell wound ball beats the gutty. Australian Walter Travis uses one to win the United States Amateur Championships in Atlantic City, New Jersey.

1902—Kempshall receives patent #695,866 for the first two-piece ball with solid core and cover 65 years before Spalding introduces the same idea using Surlyn for a cover.

—Jack Jolly develops idea of liquid-core ball for the Kempshall Co.—injecting the rubber core of wound balls with liquid, making them more maneuverable.

—Kempshall requests patent for solid ball (invented and assigned to him by Francis R. Richards) made by stirring granules of leather or rubber, or both, into melted gutta percha.

1900

1903—Spalding "Wizard" (Haskell wound ball) introduced as a bramble design (small, raised pimples covering the surface). Spalding guaranteed in catalog that Wizard covers would not "crack open or break during eighteen-holes play."

—Some British residents build a nine-hole course in Kobe, Japan.

1903-1905—British ball makers start making wound balls similar to the Haskell Ball Co. "Eagle" and "Hawk" among the best.

1904—George Worthington builds a small shop for making golf balls, which grows over years into the country's oldest and largest manufacturer of golf balls exclusively—the Worthington Ball Co. One of his first inventions (four years before dimples and eight before mesh) was a diamond stud pattern raised within a diamond crater.

1905—Englishman William Taylor applies for a patent on a dimple-covered golf ball. (Dimples replace pimples).

—Balata, sap from the South American Bully Gum Tree, used by Spalding to cover three-piece balls—found more durable than gutta percha, it becomes widely used.

—Haskell finds competitors already in field in Britain, with brands such as "White Heather," "Tube Core," "Farsure Meteor," "Elastine," "Rompo," "White Imp," and a family called "Kite," "Eagle," and "Hawk," and begins an action for infringement of patent.

—Haskell patent declared invalid in Britain. Due to the help of Harry Fernie, British high courts ruled British manufacturer did not have to pay royalties—that the idea for the wound, three-piece ball originated in England during the 1870s.

1906—"Dot" is label for some Spalding balls; the Wizard ("Blue Dot") adds a line called Whites which included the "Red Dot."

—Kempshall rubber-cored balls echo a new bit of golf ball mystique expressed by the word "click."

1907—Spalding produces the first ball with "Taylor Dimples"—the "Glory," which proves to have superior flight qualities.

1908—Dunlop joins the rubber-core parade, producing the "Orange Spot," "Junior," and "V." Later balls (1912) would prove better.

—Frank Mingay of Scotland patents a way to make liquid golf balls; Spalding acquires rights.

—Patent #906,664 granted to James W. Smith for an invention which "consists primarily in providing yielding or resilient means for connecting together a pair of hemispherical shells made of suitable resilient material."

1909—Vardon gutty balls sold for two dollars per dozen for use as practice balls. They were being superseded by the Haskell wound ball.

—Introduction of Spalding's new Taylor-patent "Dimples" balls: the large floating "Glory"—red, white, and blue at its poles—and the Black & White, a slightly smaller sinker. Both were priced at an unprecedented nine dollars per dozen.

1910—Worthington Ball Company in Ohio introduces the Radium Ball, with a core containing the chemical radium.

—Patent issued to Arthur Knight of Schenectady for steel golf shafts (illegal in United States and Britain until 1926).

—St. Mungo of Glasgow buys out its American affiliate Kempshall and appoints Jack Jolly as operating vice president of its American subsidiary.

1911—Silvertown (once India Rubber Co., then British Goodrich, later British Tire & Rubber Co.) completes development of a distinctively-ridged rubber core to supersede its gutta-percha ball, names it Silver King.

1912—Albert Penfold of the Silvertown Ball Company patents the Silvertown Mesh pattern for the cover of the golf ball, to improve flight control—used into the 1930s.

—A lattice pattern introduced similar to the mesh—also used into the 1930s.

—Dunlop introduces better balls than its earlier tries: "29" and "31."

—Walter Hagen, 19, becomes head pro at the Rochester, New York Country Club, giving up the prospect of a professional baseball career for a $1,200 per year salary plus private lesson fees.

1913—First Spalding catalog devoted exclusively to golf.

—Domino family of balls introduced (four dots at each pole): the Black (big and heavy), the Blue (medium and heavy), and the Red (medium and quite light). Smallest of all were the Baby and Midget Dimples, the former with two red and two blue dots, the latter with two green and two orange. Baby was of medium weight.

—World's four great golfers—Vardon, Taylor, Braid and Ray—meet in tournament at Holylake, England, to determine better ball. Duo using Haskell ball wins easily, ending gutty ball, starting the rubber-core era.

1914—Wilson Co. (Chicago meatpackers) branches into balls supplied by Worthington; later shared with United States Rubber Co.

—American Walter Hagen wins U.S. Open with the greatest 72-hole round ever, shooting a 290 (2 strokes over par) at the Midlothian Golf Club in Blue Island, Illinois.

c. 1914—Albert Penfold succeeds in so refining gutta percha as to render it snow white.

1915—St. Mungo/Kempshall new plant in Newark, New Jersey produces 1,000 dozen balls per day. "Colonel" was Mungo name, but they also used thirty other names for distributors.

—Manufacturers produce different-sized balls—"small heavies," going farther, to large light "floaters."

—Spalding transfers Midget's manufacture to its new factory in London.

1916—United States professional golfers establish the PGA (Professional Golfers Association) to promote interest in the sport.

—Pneumatic ball, with compressed air in the core, introduced by Goodyear Tire and Rubber Company; does not last long—it has a tendency to explode.

—Haskell rubber-core patent expires.

—Bobby Jones is youngest player ever to qualify for the United States Amateur—at fourteen years, $5^1/_2$ months.

—First golfer to win both the U.S. Open and the United States Amateur in the same year was Charles ("Chick") Evans, Jr.: the national open championship (Minikahda Country Club, Minneapolis, Minnesota, June 27-30, and the amateur championship at the Merion Links, Philadelphia, Pennsylvania on September 9.

1917—Bradford survey of golf February 12, 1917 shows 1,200 courses, 300,000 players, and one-half million dozen yearly production of golf balls—which were selling for 50-85 cents each.

1918—United States Rubber introduces advanced-design ball with raised buttons, with wound rubber core, called United States Nobby.

1919—Dunlop secures the services of Albert Edward Penfold, who produces the "MaxFli," to rival his famous "Silver King."

—Spalding introduces the "Witch," a ball with glycerine injected into the core. (Balls also made with castor oil, honey, and mercury in the core).

—Spalding catalog lists various compression ratings.

1920—American dentist, William Lowell, invents another simplified golf tee, which in time replaces tees made by hand from wet sand, as well as Grant's 1899 model.

1921—The Royal and Ancient Club introduces the first limitation on the size and weight of the ball. The USGA and British R&A agree to a standard size ball measuring 1.62 inches and weighing 1.62 ounces.

—United States Rubber renames the United States Nobby the United States Royal; it has a steel ball in the center.

1922—Gene Sarazen wins his first U.S. Open at Skokie, Illinois, July 15—at the first Open to charge an admission fee.

—Dunlop introduces "MaxFli," developed by Albert Penfold, who joined them in 1919 with his 1912-patented lattice design.

—Walter Hagen first American to win the British Open (later he will win three more). Beginning of long series of American wins, remaining unbroken (except for Arthur Havers's win in 1922) until 1934.

1923—The Faultless Rubber Co. is issued a patent for a one-piece solid golf ball made of zinc oxide, sulfur, and glue whose durability and bounce-to-the-ounce might rival conventional balls. The concept failed at the time, but Faultless would later be part of the one-piece ball's return.

1920

—Wilson introduces first colored balls since the "Yellow Aster" in the 1890s. These are called the "Oriole Orange" and the "Canary Yellow."

1924—The English Silver King first ball to carry consecutive numbers (1-4) to reduce confusion in a foursome as to which ball was whose.

1927—The Far East Rubber Company becomes the first in Japan to manufacture golf balls.

1928—Two more Japanese golf-ball firms start—Seiko and Tani, using machinery purchased in Scotland from North British (whose plant A.E. Penfold had just redesigned).

—Dr. William Geer, Vice President for Research of Goodrich Rubber Co. improves method of vulcanizing balata ball covers by using an "accelerator," making the cover much tougher.

1930—In his own plant, Albert Edward Penfold produces mesh and lattice patterns on ball covers based on his earlier Silvertown patents.

—First awarding of the Chick Evans Scholarships, which by 1967 had put 894 ex-caddies through college and enrolled more than twice that in college programs.

—Grand Slam year for Bobby Jones, who climaxes his career by winning the U.S. Open and Amateur and the British Open and Amateur.

c. 1930—Spalding introduces Goodrich's Dr. Chauncey Geer-patented, cut-resistant cover formula, on its new Kro-Flite ball.

—Almost simultaneously Dr. Sidney Caldwell develops a similar process for United States Rubber.

—Spalding introduces "Top-Flite" ball with white solid cover—no paint required.

1931—The USGA breaks away from the R&A to standardize a larger, lighter ball (at least 1.68-inch diameter/1.55-ounce weight). This "balloon ball" standard was a short-lived attempt to tame what the USGA felt was out-of-control ball distance, due to the Geer, Campbell, and other innovations.

1932—USGA abolishes balloon ball. It is replaced with standard of 1.68 inch/1.62 ounce—which remains today's standard. British fixed their standards at 1.62 inch/1.62 ounce.

—Phil Young, Fred Bommer and Carl Saunders form the Acushnet Process Co., which begins manufacturing golf balls in New Bedford, Massachusetts—they would become industry leader, with the Titleist ball.

1930

—Stableford system of scoring was first used in England (instead of par). It used plus values for holes played under par and minus values for over par.

1934—Dunlop introduces "MaxFli 65," with thinner cover, still higher-tension windings, and more distance. The name commemorates a record-breaking round fired by Henry Cotton in the British Open at Sandwich.

—Bridgestone Tire and Rubber Co., largest in the Orient, opens ballmaking plant in Japan.

1935—Geer-Caldwell cover patents merged. Acushnet/Titleist starts using the cover and producing "Titleist."

—"Tournament" ball, with vulcanized cover, renamed with the famous "Dot" title, first used in 1906 by Spalding.

—P.S. Bush of the Round Hill Club, Connecticut, is President of the United States Golf Association; son George was to be President of the United States 1989-1993.

1938—USGA limits to fourteen the number of clubs a player may use in one round of golf.

1939—Dunlop builds a Japanese ball factory.

1942—Sam Snead wins his first Grand Slam Event, the PGA Championship at Seaview Gulf Club, Atlantic City, New Jersey. (Snead's career spanned 40 years, beginning in 1935—he won approximately 120 tournaments in those 40 years).

—Golf ball velocity limited by USGA to 250 ft. per second (plus $2^1/_2$%) at 70° F, sea level.

1947—First victory for an American player—Mildred ("Babe") Didrickson Zaharias—in the British Ladies' Championship (at Gullane).

1949—Record for longest straight hole-in-one by a woman is 393 yards by Marie Robie on the first hole of the Furnace Brook Golf Club, Wollaston, Massachusetts.

1950—Estimated eight million United States golfers, 4,500 courses and about twelve million dozens of balls produced. (In 1888 there were only about a dozen golfers).

—The Ladies Professional Golf Association—LPGA—is established.

c. 1950—Acushnet claims that "Titleist" has been played by more top pros and amateurs in major tournaments than any other ball—a claim still made today.

1950s—United States Royal tries to revive mesh-marking by having Dr. F. Martin design mesh marking with inverted four-sided pyramidal recesses, offering no lodgement for dirt. The "Royal Special" did not catch on.

1953—Ben Hogan enjoys one of his best seasons four years after his near-fatal accident—making a triple sweep of the U.S. and British Opens and the Masters. (His U.S. Open win at Oakmont Country Club in Oakmont, Pennsylvania was his fourth). This feat rated by some as equivalent to Jones's Grand Slam.

1954—Arnold Palmer wins United States Amateur, then turns professional, at age 25.

1958—Spalding, "The General Motors of Sport," sells its quarter-billionth golf ball.

1959—Gary Player, the 5'7", 150-pound son of a black mine supplier in Johannesburg, South Africa, wins first of three British Open titles.

—Bartsch's first rewound and recovered balls produced.

1960—Bartsch offers pro customers a line of custom-made and marked Bartsch balls ranging from $4.50 per dozen for light hitters up to $9 for sluggers.

1961—PGA drops Caucasian clause in its constitution, so for first time Blacks can become members.

—Number of golfers in the United States reaches ten million.

1950

—Charles (Chick) Evans, Jr. plays in his fiftieth United States Amateur tournament (his first was in 1907)—the record.

1963—James Bartsch, an MIT graduate chemical engineer from Stanhope, New Jersey, submits a patent for a solid one-piece golf ball he developed by crosslinking of thermoplastic polymers.

1965—Bob Mitera, 21, Omaha, Nebraska, scores history's longest hole-in-one on a straightaway hole on the 444-yard 10th hole at the Miracle Hills Golf Club course, Omaha. A 50- mph wind helps propel the big shot.

—Faultless becomes Bartsch licensee No. 1 on a non-exclusive "prior disclosure" basis, binding for $7^1/_2$ years.

1966—Japanese take option on the new American Bartsch one-piece ball.

—Worthington Ball Co. absorbed by Victor Comptometer Corp. and moved to Morton Grove, Illinois.

—Estimated United States production of more than sixteen million dozen balls per year.

1967—Bartsch is issued a patent for his one-piece ball on April 11, 68 years to the day after Haskell was granted the revolutionary patent for the three-piece wound ball.

—Spalding beats the first solid Bartsch balls to market with a one-piece product called "Unicore," and then with the same thing encased in a cover and named "Executive." This covered its Bartsch-like core with a synthetic polyurethane cover: more durable, superior to the Bartsch one-piece ball which was now overshadowed.

—DuPont Chemical Corporation develops and patents a synthetic thermoplastic resin later to be named Surlyn. Ram was first to use this material on a ball called Ramlon.

1968—The British R&A adopts the American standard ball, measuring not less than 1.68 inches in diameter by not over 1.62 ounces, for all British PGA events. They continue to use the 1.62 x 1.62 ball for the British Open and amateur tournaments.

—DuPont's Surlyn, as a cover material, proves to make a more durable, almost indestructible ball, and is used on over 80% of all golf balls.

—USGA officially recognizes the Modified Stableford Scoring System: +5 for double eagle, +5 for eagle, +2 for birdie, 0 for par, -1 for bogie, -3 for double bogie and over.

1971—Spalding introduces a new Top-Flite—a two-piece ball with Surlyn cover which revolutionizes the industry and sets the stage for the two-piece ball, soon to become more popular than the three-piece wound rubber core.

—United States Royal first company to deviate from standard "Atti" dimple design pattern, with the "Plus Six," having 252 dimples.

—First golf shot on the Moon (February). Captain Alan Shepard, Commander of the Apollo 14 spacecraft hit two balls with an iron-headed club which he presented to the USGA Museum in 1974.

—Bobby Jones dies.

1972—The USGA starts to list balls that conform to their standards, with sixteen different names and twenty-five different variations of ball types. By 1991 the list had grown to 215 primary names and over 1,500 differently-identified balls.

1973—Acushnet improves dimple design on their #1 Titleist ball with the new icosahedron pattern, which has 324 dimples. This was developed by Dr. William Gobush.

1975—Chemist David Nepala and Dr. Fred Homstrom, both of California, patent the "Polara" ball, with claims of reducing slices and hooks by 50%. USGA disallows it for tournament play.

1976—The USGA imposes the Overall Distance Standard, mandating that no ball can travel over 280 yards—plus 6% tolerance, or 296 yards in all—when hit by the USGA mechanical hitting machine.

1977—The Polara Ball is sold on the market by PGA Victor, despite its being deemed non-conforming by the USGA—as threatening, by reducing slices and hooks, to reduce the amount of skill required to play the game.

1970

1978—LPGA rookie Nancy Lopez wins nine tournaments, including an unprecedented five in a row, to become Player of the Year.

—Polara files a lawsuit against USGA and GBMA (Golf Ball Manufacturers Association) claiming that they conspired to keep the Polara ball off the market.

1981—Parliamentary handicapping for golf inaugurated in England.

—Record sale for a featherie golf ball made in London—ball by William Robertson, dating from about 1830, sold for £950, or about $2,000.

1982—Colored balls are reintroduced by Wilson, and gain up to 20% of the market. By 1992 they were available in more colors than the rainbow, used mostly by women golfers.

—Tom Watson takes his first U.S. Open at Pebble Beach, and his record fifth British Open, to win Player of the Year.

1983—The USGA adopts the symmetry standard, which states that all balls must have symmetrical cover designs. This prohibits balls that correct themselves in flight, such as the Polara.

—A line of longer balls introduced, including the Titleist 384 Tour, the Ram Tour 400, the Jack Nicklaus Muirfield, and the Max-Fli, with souped-up aerodynamics and more dimples than ever—some in the 400s.

1984—MacGregor introduces the Cayman, or "Short Ball," invented by Troy Puckett, that goes about one-half as far as a regular ball. (Jack Nicklaus builds a short course, "Britannia," on Grand Cayman Island, tailormade for the Short Ball.)

1985—Nancy Lopez shoots 268—10 under par—for the all time low record for 72 holes.

1986—Jack Nicklaus wins a record sixth Masters title.

—Spalding introduces a new cover material called "Zinthane," which is actually a blend of two types of Surlyn, and patents the mixture after the expiration of the basic Surlyn patent.

—PGA International inaugurated at Castle Rock Golf Course, Colorado, using the Modified Stableford Scoring System.

1989—The longest drive in officially regulated long driving contests over level ground—437 yards, 2 feet, 4 inches, by Jack L. Hamm (United States) at an altitude of 5,280 feet, on October 25, in Denver, Colorado.

1990—The Nite-Lite ball is introduced. This glow-in-the-dark ball touches off a new variation of the sport—night golf, with similarly energized course markers.

—Spalding and Acushnet, makers of the majority of American golf balls, announce a settlement of all lawsuits from 1981 to the present over the design and production of golf balls.

1991—Spalding introduces another cover material called Zylin, which is supposed to rival balata in softness—which by this time is a synthetic thermoplastic.

1992—The USGA List of Conforming Golf Balls contains 215 primary ball names and 1,584 different variations of ball types, from twelve countries and 97 suppliers.

—National Golf Foundation estimates about twenty-five million golfers and about fourteen thousand golf courses in United States. Production of golf balls estimated at forty-five million dozen, plus perhaps twelve million dozen recycled/reclaimed balls.

—Kasco receives approval from USGA. for their innovative DC492 dual core "smart ball," with twenty-one versions.

1993—In the Shell Formula One Long Drive Challenge, April 27, PGA Tour long-drive champion John Daly and Senior PGA Tour Champion Jim Dent competed for driving distance. Daly's drives measured 340 yards, winning over Dent's drives of 332 yards. Both used 44-inch drivers, Dent's lofted nine degrees, Daly's seven degrees.

—Ted Oh, 16, the youngest player to compete in a U.S. Open since 14-year-old Tyrell Garth, Jr. qualified in 1941.

—USGA introduces the first new handicapping system since 1911, called the "Equitable Stroke procedure." Golfers with a 0-9 handicap will post a maximum of 6 for any hole. Golfers with handicaps of 30-39 will post a maximum score of 9 on their cards.

—Spalding re-introduces an oversize ball named Magna, 1.72 inches in diameter, as a novel advancement. Actually, Lynx preceded this some years earlier in diameters of 1.74 inches and 1.80 inches.

—Asahi-Saisel Rubber Co. of Japan has a conforming one-piece ball named VR Hitjoy, with 432 dimples.

1994—Old golfers "don't fade away." Arnold Palmer has yearly earnings of $13,600,000 of which only $100,000 comes from playing golf. The balance is from endorsements and promotions.

1995—USGA celebrates in Centennial year with new men's Centennial Tournament and similar ones for women.

—USGA tests some new, unused balls seven years old, and finds a loss of only 1% in initial velocity compared to ones just made.

1996—Tiger Woods wins his fourth USGA Junior Amateur Open. He turns pro with reported 60 million dollars in contracts from Nike. Of his seven pro tournaments he wins three, and a total of $734,794, breaking all previous records, including Nicklaus' and Palmer's entries as pros in 1962 and 1955.

—Dunlop-Japan introduces a new one-piece ball named Flash (Dunlop in red), with 420 dimples.

—Spalding introduces an innovative ball named Strata with solid center and dual covers of different resiliency.

—USGA tests about 20,000 balls this year.

—USGA Conforming Ball List contains 140 variations for Titleist, 190 for Spalding, and about 180 for Bridgestone.

1997—An addition of the new "optimal" test may result in some balls exceeding 296.8 yards distance maximum.

—Several new balls have hurdled the 50 dollars a dozen barrier. This is more than four times as much as many playable "experienced" relatives.

—Tiger Woods, 21, wins the Masters Tournament, becoming the youngest Masters champion ever.

1998—This is the target year for the optimal distance standard to be effective.

Note: The above list was derived from over one hundred sources of varying degrees of authenticity. If you have documentation of any differences, please send them to the author, in care of the publisher, for addition to any future printings.

1997

Appendices

1. St. Andrews Golf Course in Scotland

2. Distribution of Golfers by Handicaps & The Silent Majority

3. Estimated 1997 Golf Ball Production by Source

4. Growth Trends of 20th Century Golf Activity

5. Golf Ball Sales in 1995

6. Surlyn Ball Covers Eclipse Balata Covers in 25 Years

7. Average Golfer Spending by Expenditure Category—1994

8. Demographic Profile of Golfers

9. Golf Courses: Distribution by State in 1995

10. Distance Range for Various Golf Clubs

11. A Comparative Test of Oversize Metal Wood and Traditional-Sized Drivers

12. Haskell patent No. 622,834-1899 For The Three-Piece Wound Ball

13. One of Kempsall's 92 Patents For Three-Piece Balls in 1902

14. "The Thirteen Rules of Golf"

15. Tentative List of Logo Ball Classifications

16. Over Fifty Ways Spalding Says "Flite"

17. Suggested Displays For Small Collections

18. Golf Smiles & Quotes

Royal & Ancient Golf Club of St. Andrews becomes headquarters of golf, 1764.

Note the common use of fairways in two directions starting at #2 and #16

Credit: Whiteholme (Publishers) LTD Dundee

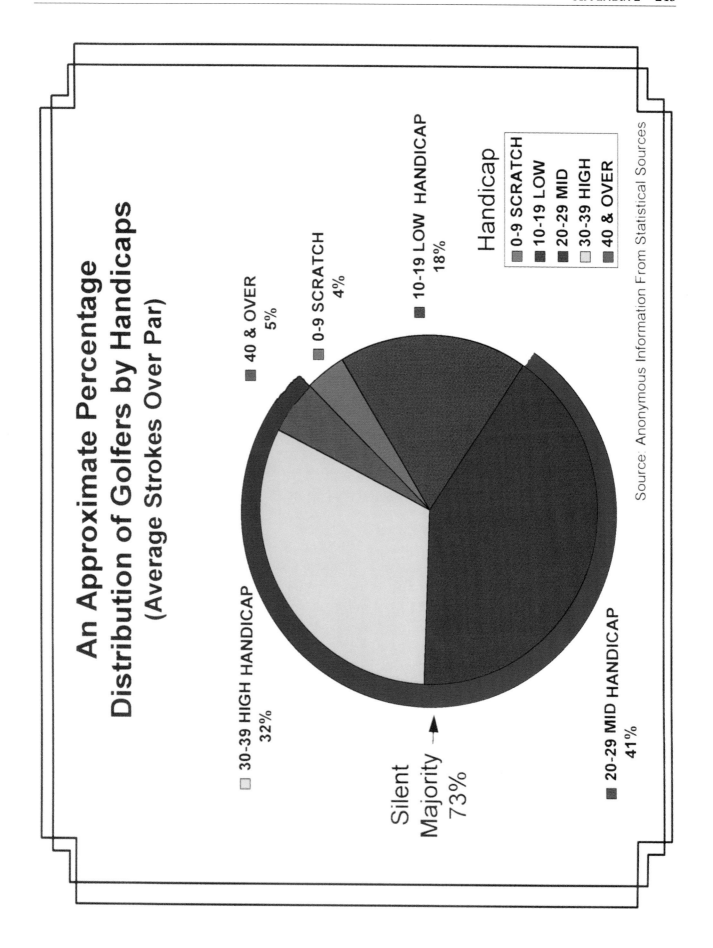

An Approximate Percentage
Distribution of Golfers by Handicaps
(Average Strokes Over Par)

40 & OVER
5%

0-9 SCRATCH
4%

10-19 LOW HANDICAP
18%

Handicap

- 0-9 SCRATCH
- 10-19 LOW
- 20-29 MID
- 30-39 HIGH
- 40 & OVER

30-39 HIGH HANDICAP
32%

Silent
Majority
73%

20-29 MID HANDICAP
41%

Source: Anonymous Information From Statistical Sources

Estimated 1997
Golf Ball Production by Source
Total - 50 Million Dozen

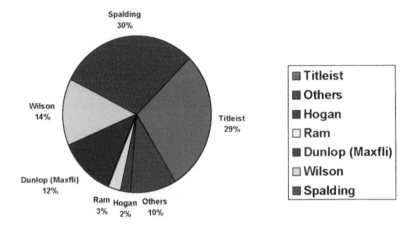

Estimated Asian, European, & Australian Production
20 Million Dozen

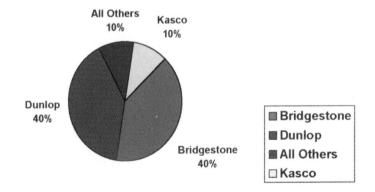

Estimated U.S. Balls Reconditioned and Sold

15 Million Dozen

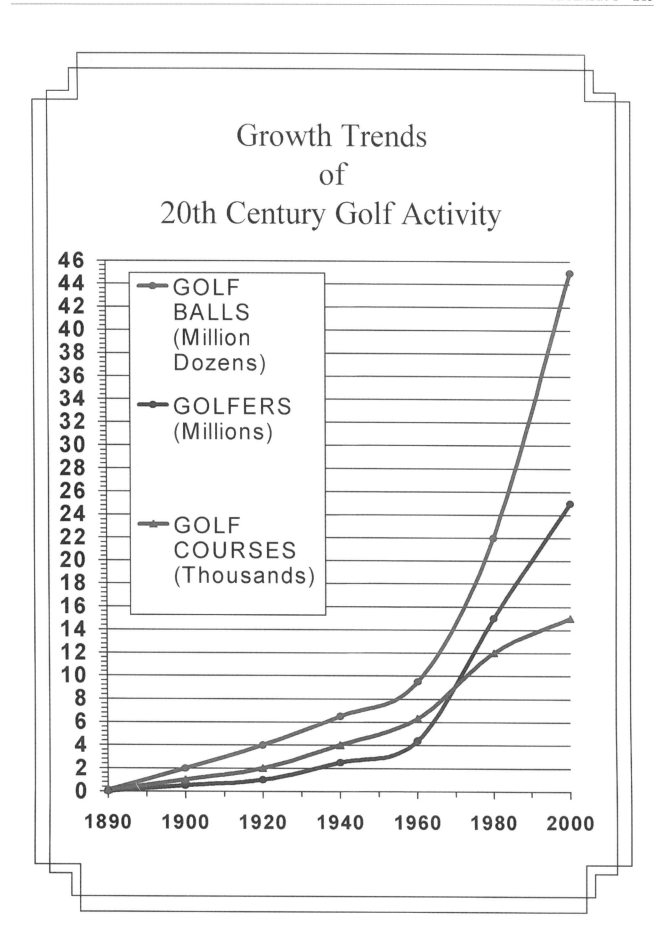

Growth Trends
of
20th Century Golf Activity

Titleist Still Tops
Golf Ball Sales in '95

Titleist	⚪⚪⚪⚪⚪⚪⚪⚪⚪⚪⚪⚪⚪⚪	**$265**
Spalding	⚪⚪⚪⚪⚪⚪⚪⚪⚪⚪⚪⚪⚪	**$245**.
Maxfli	⚪⚪⚪⚪	**$83**
Wilson	⚪⚪⚪⚪	**$80**
Bridgestone	⚪	**$21.8**
Nitro	◖	**$8**
Hogan	◖	**$5**
Bullet	◖	**$3.5**

(In Millions)

Source: Golf Pro Merchandiser

Does not include imports or reclamation ball value.

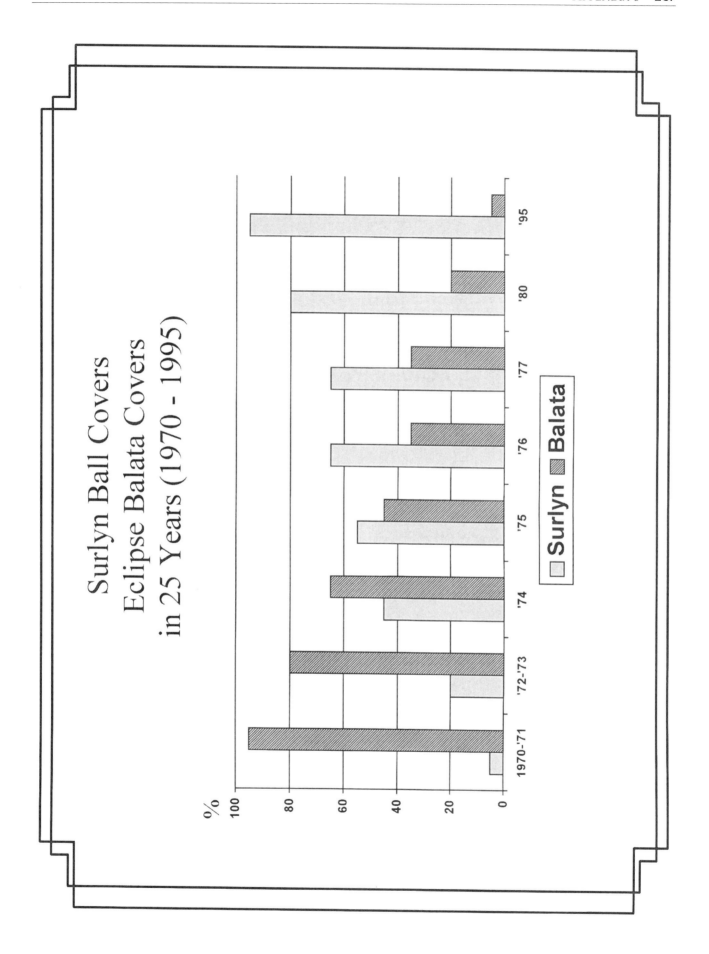

SPENDING BY GOLFER SEGMENT

	Percent of Golfers	Percent of Spending	Average Expenditure
Avid Golfers *	**24%**	**61%**	**$1,710**
Core Golfers **	26%	27%	719
Occasional Golfers ***	50%	12%	183

Source: Golf Consumer Spending in the U.S./NGF

Average Golfer Spending by Expenditure Category—1994

Expenditure Category	% of All Golfers Spending	Average Expenditure	Annual Expenditure
Fees			
Playing Fees	**91%**	**$335**	**$6,912**
Green Fees	83%	218	4,102
Guest Fees	18%	130	531
Golf Car Fees	59%	163	2,180
Pull Cart Fees	11%	20	50
Caddy Fees	2%	80	36
Membership Fees	**16%**	**$874**	**$3,170**
Initiation Fees	3%	498	339
Annual Dues	14%	867	2,752
Misc. Fees	**7%**	**$38**	**$60**
Locker Fees	3%	58	39
Handicap Fees	5%	20	23
Merchandise			
Golf Clubs	**37%**	**$266**	**$2,231**
Woods	26%	156	920
Irons	17%	230	886
Putters	9%	53	108
Specialty Wedges	16%	50	181
Sets of Clubs	278%	126	
Other Equipment	**75%**	**$134**	**$1,513**
Bags	17%	74	285
Balls	64%	44	638
Gloves	4%	24	234
Shoes	24%	68	370
Apparel	28%	122	774
Other Items	**43%**	**$47**	**$458**
Books	2%	34	154
Videos	5%	33	37
Golf Art	2%	97	44
Accessories	34%	29	224

Source: Golf Consumer Spending in the U.S./NGF

* 25+ Rounds per year
** 7-25 Rounds per year
*** 1-7 Rounds per year

DEMOGRAPHIC PROFILE OF GOLFERS

Participation Rate[1]
(Percent of Population Age 12+)

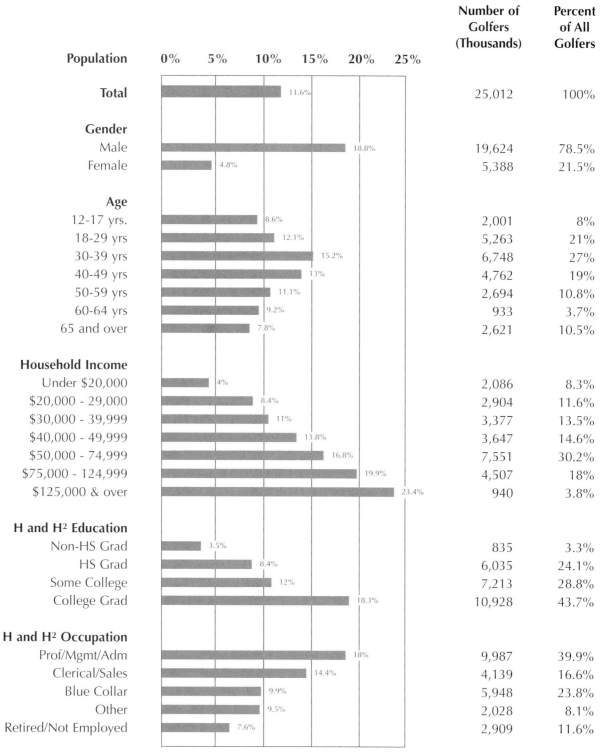

Population	Participation Rate	Number of Golfers (Thousands)	Percent of All Golfers
Total	11.6%	25,012	100%
Gender			
Male	18.8%	19,624	78.5%
Female	4.8%	5,388	21.5%
Age			
12-17 yrs.	8.6%	2,001	8%
18-29 yrs	12.1%	5,263	21%
30-39 yrs	15.2%	6,748	27%
40-49 yrs	13%	4,762	19%
50-59 yrs	11.1%	2,694	10.8%
60-64 yrs	9.2%	933	3.7%
65 and over	7.8%	2,621	10.5%
Household Income			
Under $20,000	4%	2,086	8.3%
$20,000 - 29,000	8.4%	2,904	11.6%
$30,000 - 39,999	11%	3,377	13.5%
$40,000 - 49,999	13.8%	3,647	14.6%
$50,000 - 74,999	16.8%	7,551	30.2%
$75,000 - 124,999	19.9%	4,507	18%
$125,000 & over	23.4%	940	3.8%
H and H[2] Education			
Non-HS Grad	3.5%	835	3.3%
HS Grad	8.4%	6,035	24.1%
Some College	12%	7,213	28.8%
College Grad	18.3%	10,928	43.7%
H and H[2] Occupation			
Prof/Mgmt/Adm	18%	9,987	39.9%
Clerical/Sales	14.4%	4,139	16.6%
Blue Collar	9.9%	5,948	23.8%
Other	9.5%	2,028	8.1%
Retired/Not Employed	7.6%	2,909	11.6%

[1] Percentage of the given population or demographic segment who are golfers.
[2] Head of Household

Source: National Golf Foundation/96

FACTS ON OVERSIZE METAL WOOD AND TRADITIONAL-SIZED DRIVERS

Table A

Shots tested at 95 mph

	Center Hits Two-piece ball		High Toe 1/2-inch, 1/4-inch high Two-piece ball		Low Heel 1/2-inch heel, 1/4-inch low Two-piece ball	
	Traditional	Oversize	Traditional	Oversize	Traditional	Oversize
Clubhead speed	93.5mph	93.7 mph	93.3 mph	92.8 mph	94.8 mph	94.0 mph
Initial velocity	142.7 mph	144.9 mph	139.1 mph	142.3 mph	140.5 mph	140.0 mph
Launch angle	9.3°	10.7°	10.5°	11.4°	7.3°	9°
Spin rate	3580 rpm	3630 rpm	3290 rpm	3260 rpm	4150 rpm	4080 rpm
Angle of apogee	11.2°	12.4°	12.2°	13.3°	8.3°	10.2°
Avg. carry distance	219.4 yds.	220.8 yds.	215.4 yds.	217.8 yds.	201.3 yds.	206.8 yds.
Longest carry	224.8 yds.	225.4 yds	218.8 yds.	223.2 yds.	205.6 yds	211.4 yds.
Shortest carry	214.4 yds.	216.9 yds.	211.0 yds.	2313.9 yds.	198.1 yds.	201.7 yds
Standard deviation	3.2 yds.	2.2 yds.	2.5 yds.	2.4 yds.	2.8 yds.	2.6 yds.
Dispersion	0.0 yds.	0.0 yds.	11.7 R yds.	9.1 R yds.	10.6 L yds.	1.4 R yds.

Table B

Shots tested at 108 mph

	Center Hits Two-piece ball		High Toe 1/2-inch, 1/4-inch high Two-piece ball		Low Heel 1/2-inch heel, 1/4-inch low Two-piece ball	
	Traditional	Oversize	Traditional	Oversize	Traditional	Oversize
Clubhead speed	107.2 mph	107.2 mph	104.9 mph	104.2 mph	108.7 mph	109.4 mph
Initial velocity	158.4 mph	148.6 mph	153.0 mph	156.6 mph	153.6 mph	152.9 mph
Launch angle	8.2°	8.8°	10.2°	10.5°	6.9°	7.5°
Spin rate	4260 rpm	4250 rpm	3620 rpm	3470 rpm	4500 rpm	4490 rpm
Angle of apogee	10.8°	12.2°	11.2°	12.0°	9.2°	9.9°
Avg. carry distance	249.0 yds.	254.8 yds.	248.3 yds.	256.2 yds.	225.8 yds.	233.4 yds.
Longest carry	252.0 yds.	263.1 yds.	251.7 yds.	260.2 yds.	228.4 yds.	238.8 yds.
Shortest carry	245.9 yds.	251.4 yds	241.3 yds.	249.6 yds.	220.7 yds.	229.9 yds.
Standard deviation	1.9 yds.	3.4 yds.	3.1 yds.	3.3 yds.	2.0 yds.	2.3 yds.
Dispersion	0.0 yds.	0.0 yds.	14.9 R yds.	3.3 L yds.	2.4 L yds.	0.5 L. yds.

SUMMARY: Distance - Oversize   +5 to 10 yds.
                 Dispersion -   Same
                 Spin Rate -   Same

OPINION: Dr. Dede Ownes, an instructor in Golf Digest Schools by way of Cog Hill near Chicago, says: "The mind plays a tremendous role in golf. And with this type of club, the weekend golfer feels kind of like David hitting Goliath. It is just too big to miss. With that in mind, he can relax, put a nice, easy swing on the ball and watch it travel a pretty good distance."

CONCLUSION: Mind Over Matter Wins

Source: *Golf Digest*

DRAWINGS FOR THE THREE-PIECE WOUND BALL

No. 622,834   Patented Apr. 11, 1899

B. G. WORK & C. HASKELL
BALL
(Application Aug 9, 1898)

Figure

Figure #1:   The cover pattern consists of shallow, narrow, grooves at right angles made in a two-part mold. This pattern was superceded by the raised bramble pattern (pimple) pattern and by 1910 with a variation of today's universal dimple pattern.

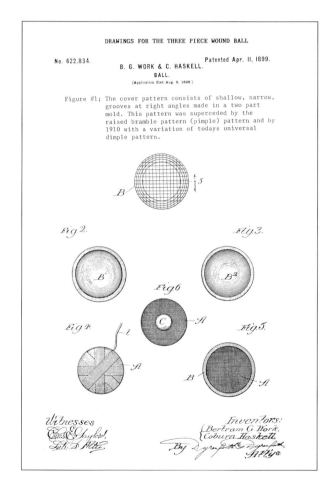

DRAWINGS FOR THE THREE PIECE WOUND BALL

No. 622,834.   Patented Apr. II, 1899.
B. G. WORK & C. HASKELL.
BALL.
(Application filed Aug. 9, 1898.)

Figure #1; The cover pattern consists of shallow, narrow, grooves at right angles made in a two part mold. This pattern was superceded by the raised bramble pattern (pimple) pattern and by 1910 with a variation of todays universal dimple pattern.

THE PATENT FOR THE REVOLUTIONARY

THREE PIECE WOUND BALL

UNITED STATES PATENT OFFICE.

BERTRAM G. WORK, OF AKRON, AND COBURN HASKELL, OF CLEVELAND, OHIO.

BALL.

SPECIFICATION forming part of Letters Patent No. 622,834, dated April 11, 1899.

Application filed August 9, 1898. Serial No. 688,153. (No model.)

To all whom it may concern:

Be it known that we, BERTRAM G. WORK, residing at Akron, in the county of Summit, and COBURN HASKELL, residing at Cleveland, 5 in the county of Cuyahoga, State of Ohio, citizens of the United States, have invented a new and useful Improvement in Balls, of which the following is a specification.

Our invention is in the nature of an im-10 proved ball for use more especially in the game of golf, though it may be used in other games where a ball of similar properties is desired.

Our object is to provide a ball for the above 15 purposes which shall possess the essential qualities of lightness and durability and which shall also have the property of being comparatively non-resilient under the moderate impacts incident to its use, but highly 20 resilient under the stronger impacts.

We accomplish the objects sought by making the main body of the core of rubber thread wound under tension into spherical form and providing the same with an adequately-thick 25 covering of gutta-percha or one of its substitutes, such as balata gum, the covering possessing the attributes, comparatively speaking, of inelasticity, toughness, hardness, and lightness.

30 The invention is illustrated in the accompanying drawings, in which—

Figure 1 is a view of the interior of the ball; Figs. 2 and 3, interior views of the two halves of the outer shell or covering laid open; Fig. 35 4, an outer view of the elastic core employed; Fig. 5, a section taken on line 5 of Fig. 1; and Fig. 6, a view, partly in section, of a modified form of the elastic core, showing the rubber thread, from which it is made, as wound upon 40 a central core-section of gutta-percha or the like.

The preferred manner of making the ball is by winding a rubber thread *t* upon itself, under a tension approximating the elastic 45 limit, to produce a spherical core A and covering this core with a gutta-percha shell of adequate thickness. The preferred method of applying the inclosing shell is by wrapping or inclosing the core in one or more sheets of 50 gutta-percha suitably cut and previously heated sufficiently to give it a certain de-gree of plasticity, as by dipping it in boiling water, and then placing the core thus wrapped in a mold and subjecting the whole to sufficient pressure to form it to the exact 55 shape desired, which shape is retained on cooling; but the shell may be produced by any other method which may be found practicable. The shell thus formed to be effective must be of such thickness as to remain 60 comparatively rigid under the moderate impacts to which the ball is subjected, as in the case of light blows with the golf-club or on striking the earth, but to yield under the more violent impacts, as in "driving," where- 65 by the force is brought to bear upon the elastic core.

B is the complete ball, and B' B² the halves of the comparatively unyielding shell which receives the elastic core A. The exterior sur- 70 face of the ball may be roughened, as shown in Fig. 1, by using a mold having intersecting ridges on its inner surface.

Fig. 5 shows a complete half-section of the ball, the core being shown as made simply by 75 winding a rubber thread upon itself to form a sphere.

Fig. 6 shows the rubber winding inclosing a small central-core-section C, which may be of any suitable material serving to facilitate 80 the winding and, if desired, to regulate to some extent the weight of the ball.

It is an essential feature of the construction that the core shall closely fill the interior of the shell and desirable that the core 85 be confined therein under some compression.

A core produced by winding a rubber thread under high tension into spherical form possesses a remarkably high degree of elasticity coupled with high rigidity in the sense of re- 90 sistance to deformation, which imparts to the ball the property of very great resilience. As the result of the described construction, therefore, our golf-ball has exceptionally high driving qualities owing to the fact that the 95 impact of a golf-club is capable of distorting it through the shell by reason of the adequate flexibility of the latter and little tendency to bound by reason of the fact that little, if any, distortion takes place upon con- 100 tact with the ground. The highest resistance to change in form, therefore, is attained when

ONE OF KEMPSHALL'S 92 PATENTS IN 1902

No. 6696,888

Patented Apr. 1, 1902

E. KEMPSHALL
PROCESS OF MAKING GOLF BALLS
(Application Dec. 12, 1901)

ONE OF 96 KEMPSHAL PATENTS IN 1902

No. 696,888.

Patented Apr. 1, 1902.

E. KEMPSHALL.

PROCESS OF MAKING GOLF BALLS.

(Application filed Dec. 12, 1901.)

(No Model.)

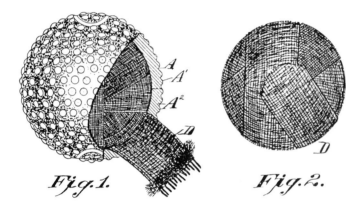

Fig.1.

Fig.2.

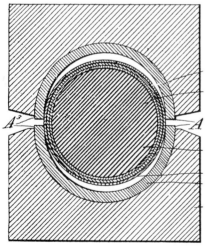

Fig.3.

Eleazer Kempshall, an English tire maker, jumped head first into golf ball making by obtaining over 40 patents between March 18th and May 6 1902 and a grand total of 92 for the year. A sample of #696,888 in Figure 1 shows an elastic webbing wound around the core.

Notice the small molded bumps on the cover called the bramble pattern. Pimples instead of today's dimples which were not invented until 1907

Witnesses:
F. E. Maynard
R. W. Pittman

Inventor:
Eleazer Kempshall.
By his Attorney,
F. H. Richards.

Eleazer Kempshall, an English tire maker, jumped head first into golf ball making by obtaining over 40 patents between March 18 and May 6, 1902 and a grand total of 92 for the year. A sample of #696,888 in Figure 1 shows an elastic webbing wound around the core.

Notice the small molded bumps on the cover called the bramble pattern. Pimples instead of today's dimples which were not invented until 1907.

"The Thirteen Rules of Golf"

Extract from *The Minute Book of*
The Honorable Company of Edinburgh Golfers, 1744

1. You must Tee your Ball within a Club's length of the Hole.*

2. Your Tee must be upon the Ground.

3. You are not to change the Ball which you strike off the Tee.

4. You are not to remove Stones, Bones or any Break Club for the sake of playing your Ball, Except upon the fair green & that only within a Clubs length of your Ball.

5. If your Ball come among Watter, or any wattery filth, you are at liberty to take out your Ball & bringing it behind the hazard and Teeing it, you may play it with any club and allow your Adversary a Stroke, for so getting out your ball.

6. If your Balls be found any where touching one another, you are to lift the first Ball, till you play the last.

7. At Holling, you are to play your Ball honestly for the Hole, and not to play upon your Adversary's Ball, not lying in your way to the Hole.

8. If you should lose your Ball, by its being taken-up, or any other way, you are to go back to the Spot, where you struck last, & drop another Ball, And allow your adversary a Stroke for the misfortune.

9. No man at Holling his Ball, is to be allowed, to mark his way to the Hole with his club or any thing else.

10. If a ball be stopp'd by any person, Horse, Dog, or anything else, the Ball so stop'd must be play'd where it lyes.

11. If you draw your Club in order to Strike to proceed so far in the Stroke, as to be bringing down your Club; If then, your club shall break, in any way, it is to be accounted a Stroke.

12. He whose Ball lyes farthest from the Hole, is obliged to play first.

13. Neither Trench, Ditch or Dyke made for the preservation of the Links, nor the Scholars Holes or the Soldiers Lines, Shall be accounted a Hazard, But the Ball is to be taken out, Teed and play's with any Iron Club.

*The Tee was less than one club length from the hole on the completed green and directed toward the next green.

TENTATIVE LIST OF LOGO BALL CLASSIFICATIONS*

Agriculture
Air Conditioning
Air Freight & Air Craft
Alcoholic Beverage
Aluminum Products
Animals
Automobiles
Automotive Products

Ball Boxes
Birds
Buildings

Carpet & Rugs
Caricatures
Chemical Products
Commemorative Balls
Communications
Computer Companies
Cruises & Tours

Data Systems

Ecology
Education
Electric & Electronic
Express—UPS

Familiar Food
Famous People
Famous Places
Farm & Orchard
Farm Equipment
Fast Food
Fastener Manufacturer
Fish & Fishing
Food Products
Food Service

Foreign Balls
Fraternal & Service Organiz.

Gas & Electric Utilities
Glass Products
Golf Balls
Golf Classics/Events
Golf Courses & Ranges
Golf Score Cards
Golf Societies
Golf Tees
Greetings & Slogans

Heating & Lighting
Hospitals & Resorts
Humor

Industrial Equipment
Insurance

Jewelry
Juices & Soft Drinks

Laboratories
Lady Golfers
Lawyers

Machinery Companies
Magazines
Meat Products
Medical Products
Metal Products
Military Post & Divisions
Mining & Drilling
Miscellaneous

Nature
Nature Newspapers

Oil Companies
Organizations

Paint Companies
Paper Products
Parks
Petroleum Products
Pharmaceutical
Photography & Pictures
Plastic Products
Portrait Balls
Presidential Balls
Pint Graphics
Range Balls
Research & Testing
Resorts
Restaurants
Retail Stores

Ships & Water Craft
Signature Events Balls
Sports Equipment
Sports Events
Stars & Space

Telecommunications
Textiles
Tire & Rubber
Tobacco
Tool & Die
Transportation
Toys

Unidentified Logos
Universities & Schools

* There is nothing official about the above list. It is merely a consolidation of the terminology a number of collectors have used. Some collectors have collections large enough to use as many or more categories. Others may have used only one or two such as Geographic, with subdivisions for states, countries, and regions. Use this as a check list for those categories that interest you.

OVER FIFTY WAYS SPALDING SAYS "FLITE"

An example of an actual specialized collection of balls on which Spalding issued their famous family of Flite Balls for some seventy years.

Accu-Flite	KRO-Flite 90	Strata-Flite
Air-Flite	KRO-Flite Floater	Super-Flite
Armour-Flite	KRO-Flite Pro	Super-Flite 492
Astra-Flite	Long-Flite (Orange)	Super KRO-Flite
Bullet-Flite	Par-Flite	Super-Flite II
Dura-Flite	Par-Flite Supreme	Tee-Flite
Fast-Flite	PGA KRO-Flite (Curved)	Top-Flite (Mesh)
Flite 100	PGA KRO-Flite (Mesh)	Top-Flite XL
Flite 280	Pin Flite	Top-Flite XL II
Flite 727	Pin Flite 100	Top-Flite
Flite Line	Power-Flite	Top-Flite C
Go-Flite	PRO KRO-Flite (Mesh)	Top-Flite II
Go-Flite II	Pro-Flite	Top-Flite Plus 492
High-Flite	Ram-Flite	Tour-Flite
K-Flite	Space-Flite	Tru-Flite
KRO-Flite (Mesh)	Speed-Flite	War-Flite
KRO-Flite 384	Star-Flite	World Flite

SUGGESTED DISPLAYS FOR SMALL COLLECTIONS

Above: A 7 x 12" special wooden plaque with recess for a ball used for a hole-in-one
Left: A shadow box with engraved plate & provision for a ball commemorating an event pictured above.

A highly polished metal stand which holds a ball that made a hole-in-one.

A novelty clock with provision to mount eight special balls.

A molded plastic frame with six vertical channels to hold thirty logo or antique balls.

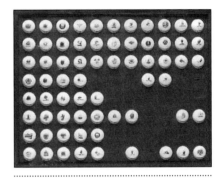

This eighty-eight ball display is backed by thick, dark green Styrofoam punched out to firmly hold each ball.

Two oak open cabinets holding seventy-two or twenty balls.

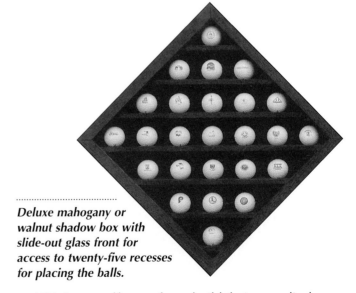

Deluxe mahogany or walnut shadow box with slide-out glass front for access to twenty-five recesses for placing the balls.

For examples of larger displays, see illustrations on page 187. Some golfers prefer to build their own displays similar to the two mentioned above.

GOLF SMILES & QUOTES

- Golf forever—housework whenever.

- He's on a golf diet—he just lives on greens.

- There's nothing extraordinary about a long hitter, the woods are full of them.

- 90% of the golf clubs are better than 90% of the golfers.—*Frank Thomas*

- My wife is going to leave me if I don't give up golf on New Years. I'm going to miss her next year.

- Chick Evans, famous amateur USGA Open winner in 1916, wished his partners "a long walk with a putter."

- Prominent Pro: "I have 6 different set of clubs. I can play equally as well with any of them, when I am playing at my best."

- Keith B. Marshal's book, *In Golf We Trust*.

- Arnold Palmer's reason why in the 1961 Los Angeles Open, he took 12 strokes on hole #5, "I missed the putt for an 11."

- One-upmanship occurred in the 1980 Masters by Tom Weiskoff's 13 on Raes Creek Par 3. Five successive balls in the water, and three putts.

- Sam Butterworth's comment on his driving distance "I'm hitting the woods just fine, but I'm having a hell of a time getting out of them."

- Forget the bad shot you just made and concentrate of the good one your about to make.

- Where there's golf, there's hope.

- Bobby Jones once said, "Without question, the most significant change in golf equipment since the inception of the game was the development of the wound ball."

- One of the old clichés that is better advice than it is poetry: Drive for show, putt for dough.

- The pre-game shoulder height drop test for levelyness is insufficient compression to be indicative.

- When the price gets high, refuse to buy—investigate.

- Buy the book—before you make the purchase.

- A Scotchman hired a new caddie, asking if he was good at finding balls, he received a very short reply, "Oh, yes. We'll go out and find one, and we'll start to play."

Sources

GOLF EQUIPMENT DEALERS
MAIL ORDER AND STORE FRONT

Austad's, 4500 E. 10th St., P.O. Box 5428 Sioux Falls, SD 57196: free catalog; golfing, balls and other equipment. 800-444-1234.

Duffer's Golf Depot, 1415 N. Federal Hwy., Ft. Lauderdale, FL 33304: free information; golf clubs and other equipment. 305-568-2489.

Foxbat Golf Equipment Outlet, 15105 Surveyor, Addison, TX 75244: free information with long SASE; discontinued and closeout golf equipment. 800-933-2775 or 214-239-5200 (in TX).

Golf Day, 135 American Legion Hwy. Revere, MA 02151: free catalog; bags and other equipment. 800-669-8600.

The Golfworks, P.O. Box 3008, Newark, OH 43055: free catalog; supplies how-to books, and video and audio tapes. 800-848-8358.

Larry's Golf Discount Center, 21 W. 35th St., New York, NY 10001: free information; golf equipment. 212-563-6895.

Las Vegas Discount Golf & Tennis, 5325 S. Valley View Blvd., Suite 10, Las Vegas, NE 89118: free catalog; equipment, clothing and shoes for golf. 702-798-7777.

Nevada Bob's Pro Shops, A giant chain of 275 store front shops. Some are company owned but most are franchises. Some also sell by mail. For the store nearest you, call toll-free 888-348-2627.

Pennsylvania Sporting Goods, 1360 Industrial Hwy., P.O. Box 451, Southampton, PA 18966: free information; golf balls, ball retrievers, ball washers and other equipment. 800-535-1122.

Pro Shop World of Golf, 8130 N. Lincoln Ave., Skokie, IL 60077: free catalog; golf equipment and shoes. 800-323-4047 or 608-675-5286.

SGD Company Inc., P.O. Box 8410, Akron, OH 44320: free information; golf balls, ball retrievers, ball washers and golf course equipment. 216-239-2828.

Wittek Golf Supply Co. Inc., 3650 N. Avondale, Chicago, IL 60618: free information; golf course equipment, grips, head covers, tubes, clubs and balls. 312-463-2636.

World of Golf, 147 E. 47th St., New York, NY 10017: free catalog; equipment for men and women. 212-755-9398.

World of Golf Equipment, 8130 N. Lincoln Ave., Skokie, IL 60077: free information; equipment for men, women and juniors. 800-323-4047.

GOLF-RELATED MAGAZINES

Executive Golfer, (Country Club Golfer) Pazdur Pub. Corp., 2171 Campus Dr., Irvine, CA 92715-1422. Tel #714-752-6474, Fax # 714-752-0398.

Fairway, Golf Magazine Properties, 2 Park Ave., New York, NY 10016. Tel #212-779-5200, Fax # 212-481-8085. The official magazine of the LPGA Tour. Articles cover all aspects of ladies golf.

Golf Canada, Canadian Golf Press Inc., 24 Mercer St., Ste. 200, Toronto, On M5V 1H3. Tel # 416-596-1555, Fax # 416-596-1520. Information about Canadian golfing and golfers.

Golf Collectors Society Bulletin, P.O. Box 200546, Dayton, OH 45420. Tel # 513-256-2474. Published quarterly for members. Informative articles, editorials, book reviews, upcoming events and classified ads by members for Wants and For Sale items.

Golf Digest, New York Times Mag. Group, 5520 Park Ave., Trumbull, CT 06611. Tel # 203-373-7000, Fax # 203-373-2102. Reports golf instruction, service and articles. Coverage of golf courses and equipment.

Golf Journal, U.S. Golf Assn. Golf House, P.O. Box 708, Far Hills, NJ 07931-0708. Tel # 908-781-5497, Fax # 908-781-1112. Articles on course design, clubs, history, equipment, humor, championships and rules.

Golf Magazine, Times-Mirror Magazines, Inc., 2 Park Ave., New York, NY 10016. Tel # 212-779-5000, Fax # 212-779-5465. Devoted to interest of average recreational golfer with particular emphasis on instruction from top teachers.

Golf Product News, Golf Publishing Ent., Inc. 11-15 River Rd. Fair Lawn, NJ 07410. Tel # 201-795-6031, Fax # 201-796-5206. Products and service through professional golf shops, practice ranges and club repair shops.

Golf Shop Operations, New York Times Mag. Group., 5520 Park Ave., Trumbull, CT 06611-0395. Tel # 203-373-7232, Fax # 203-371-2102. Concerned with coverage of successful golf shops, merchandising aids, buying and selling and teaching.

GolfWeek—America's Golf Newspaper, (Florida Golfweek) Golfweek L.P., 7657 Commerce Center Dr., Orlando, FL 32819. Tel # 407-345-5500, Fax # 407-345-9404. Serves paid subscribers as well as individuals within golf-related organizations.

Golf for Women, Meredith Corp., 1716 Locust St., Des Moines, IA 50309-3023. Tel # 515-284-3000, Fax # 515-284-3343.

LPGA Player Guide, Ladies Professional Golf Assn. of America, 2570 Volusia Ave, Ste. B, Daytona Beach, TX 32114-7103.

Minnesota Golfer, Minnesota Golf Assn., 6550 York Ave., Ste. 211, Ednia, MN 55435. Tel # 612-522-1200, Fax # 612-881-2172. Golf in the state of Minnesota.

North Texas Golfer, Golfer Magazines, Inc., 9182 Old Katy Rd., Ste. 212, Houston, TX 77055-7444. Tel # 713-464-0308, Fax # 713-464-0129. Covers golf and golfers in North Texas.

Ohio Golfer Magazine, Ohio Golfer, P.O. Box 509, Reynoldsburg, OH 43068-0509. Tel # 614-447-9001, Fax # 614-447-9044. For golf players and fans in Ohio.

PGA Magazine, Quarton Group Publishers, Inc. 888 Big Beaver Rd., Ste. 600, Troy, MI 48084-4737. Tel # 810-362-7400, Fax # 810-367-7425. Association new instruction techniques, methods of merchandising and golf shop operation, promotional ideas, golf equipment, etc.

Senior Golfer, Vandenburgh Pub. Co., 1 Execter Plaza, Boston, MA 02116-2831. Tel # 617-266-2600, Fax # 614-437-0030. Tips and articles for golfers 50+ in age who play at least 25 rounds of golf a year.

Sports Illustrated Golf Edition, Time Inc., 1271 Ave. of the Americas, Rockefeller Center, New York, NY 10020. Fax # 212-765-2699. Golf news and info for enthusiasts, both players and spectators.

Tour, Times-Mirror Mag. Inc., 2 Park Ave., New York, NY 10016. Tel # 212-779-5200, Fax #212-481-8085. Golfing info with interviews, course reviews and yearly highlights.

GOLF COLLECTORS SOCIETY
ANNUAL SHOWS & MARKETS

A great opportunity for ball collectors to buy is at the annual Golf Collectors Society meetings and shows having some two hundred tables displaying a panorama of golf collectibles. Only members qualify to sell but all collectors are welcome to buy—and about five hundred do at this autumn event.

This master show is supplemented by numerous regional shows throughtout the year at various locations, at which all collectors are welcome. Some of the long runnning ones are listed below. A pre-show attraction is a day devoted by members having fun playing golf with pre-1930 hickory-shafted clubs, some of them dressed in appropriate vintage knickers, argyle socks or perhaps John Henry and others will be there in traditional kilts.

SEASON	LOCATION	FREQUENCY
February	Southwest, FL	Once per year
Early Spring	Farhills, NJ *	Once per year
March	Dunedin, FL	Once per year
March/April	Irving, TX	Once per year
Winter	Dayton, OH	Once per year
May	Rolling Meadows, Chicago, IL	Once per year
June	Kansas City, Omana or Iowa	Once per year
Sept/Oct	Annual Meeting	Once per year
Nov/Dec	Southern California	Once per year
Various	Carolinas	Twice per year
Various	Washington, D.C. area	Four per year
Various	Toronto, Canada area	Three per year

* United States Golf Association—Golf House Museum Library (10,000 books) and Technical Center.

NOTE: You may call a month or two in advance for exact dates by contacting the Golf Collectors Society office, P.O. Box 20546, Dayton, OH at Tel # 937-256-2474 or Fax # 937-256-2974.

Golf Ball Recyclers

Raven Golf Ball Co.   51270 Milano Dr., Macomb, MI 48046
Tel # 800-238-0009. Over the counter and mail order sales of various grades and makes. Minimum order is 6 doz. Call for a price list.

Birdie Ball Company   266 North State Rd. #7, Margate, FL 36063
Tel # 800-333-6271. Over the counter and mail order sales. Wide range of quality and brands. Minimum order 3 doz. Call for extensive price list.

Golf Ball Paul's   2423 Early Street, Kansas City, KS 66103
Tel # 800-466-4271. Over the counter and mail order sales. Send for price list of brands and different quantities available. Minimum order 3 doz.

Port Supply Group   1901 Diplomat Street, Dallas, TX 75234
Tel # 800-624-8337. Sold only to retail stores.

In addition to the above and other mail-order outlets, there are many shops selling only recycled balls ranging from shag balls to almost mint balls. They are packaged by brand names such as Titleist DT. Similar in bulk or packaged balls are available in golf equipment stores and on course pro shops. These may be found in the yellow pages under "Golf Equipment and Supplies—Retail."

SAMPLE OF TYPICAL PRICES PER DOZEN

BRAND	AAA	AA	A
Titleist Professional	$16.00	$12.95	$6.00
Maxfli HT Balata	$16.00	$12.95	$6.00
Top Flite Z-Balata	$16.00	$12.95	$5.50
Titleist—DT, Wound & Two-Piece	$9.95	$7.95	$4.95
Maxfli—All Models Except DDH	$10.95	$8.50	$4.95
Ultra—All Models Except Balatas	$7.95	$6.50	$4.25
Wilson Staff	$8.50	$6.25	$4.50
**Special Buy—50 Balls Mixed Brands	$33.25	$25.95	$16.50
** Special Buy—100 Balls Mixed Brands	$63.00	$49.25	$33.00
Practice Balls—Three Dozen	$7.20		

"AAA" balls are perfect to near-perfect condition balls.
"AA" balls are near-perfect balls with a slight abrasion or discoloration.
"A" balls are playable balls with an abrasion and or discoloration.

USA Companies Making Golf Balls

Golf ball manufacturers all have customer service departments that welcome your questions.
Call the toll-free 800 numbers listed below.

Ben Hogan Company
8000 Villa Park Drive
Richmond, VA 23228
800-225-8500

Bridgstone Sports Inc. (Precept)
15220 Industrial Park Blvd., NE
Covington, GA 30209
800-358-6319

Bullet USA Headquarters
2803 South Yale Street
Santa Ana, CA 92704
800-842-3781

Cayman Golf Co.
1705 Radium Springs Rd.
Albany, GA 31705
800-344-0220

David Geoffrey & Associates (Slazenger)
P.O. Box 7259
Greenville, SC 29611
800-766-2615

Dunlop Golf Division (Maxfli)
P.O. Box 3070
Greenville, SC 29602
800-476-5400

Hansberger Precision Golf (Ram)
238 Industrial Circle
Pontooee, MS 38863
800-647-8122

Karsten Manufacturing Corp. (Ping)
2201 W. Desert Cove
Phoenix, AZ 84029
800-528-0650

MacGregor Golf Company
3651 Clearview Place
Atlanta, GA 30340
800-941-4358

American Ball (Nitro)
1225 Tappan Circle
Carolton, TX 75006
800-96-NITRO

Spalding Sports Worldwide (Top Flite)
425 Meadow Street, Box #901
Checopee, MA 01021-0901
800-642-5004 or 800-443-3776

Titleist Worldwide
P.O. Box 965
Fairhaven, MA 02719-0965
800-225-8500

Wilson Sporting Goods Co. (Ultra/Staf)
8700 W. Bryn Mawr Ave.
Chicago, IL 60631
800-622-0444

MUSEUMS

American Golf Hall of Fame
Foxburg C.C. Box 305 Harvey Road, Foxburg, PA 16036. Tel # 412-659-3196. Collection of balls, books and clubs.

British Golf Museum
St. Andres, Bruce Embankment Fife, KY 169AB, Scotland. Excellent displays and content. Second only to private museum in Royal and Ancient Golf Club.

Country Club of Rochester
Rochester, NY 14610. Private, please call for availability.

Cypress Lake Country Club
Ft. Myers, FL 33908. Private, Patty Berg Collection. Call for availability.

James River Country Club
New Port News, VA 23606. Private, call for availability.

Royal Canadian Golf Assoc.
R.R. #2, Oakville, Ontario Canada L6J423. Clubs, balls, books and memorabilia.

U.S. Golf Assoc.
Farhills, NJ 07931. Library of over 10,000 books and catalogs on golf. Displays of all phases of golf, research lab and test driving of balls. Allan Shepard's club that was used on the moon is also displayed here. Andy Mutch, Curator. Tel # 908-234-2300.

World Golf Hall of Fame
World Golf Village, St. Augustine, FL. Under construction now, scheduled to open Spring of 1998. Supersedes Old Pinehurst PGA Museum and includes much, much more. Karen Benarski, Curator.

LIBRARIES

The only library most of readers will need for their enjoyment and research, is the one nearest to them. It may be a small one-story house-size structure with a few thousand volumes like the one in Quogue on Long Island, New York or the giant New York City Public Library on 5th Ave. at 42nd Street with untold number of volumes.

The introduction of inter-library loans was made possible with the advent of the computer. Just call your library for the book you want; if it is in the stacks, go in and pick it up. If they don't have it, request an inter-library search and 99 times out of 100, you'll get a call in two or three weeks to come in and pick it up. It's faster, less effort, more flexible and the price is right—no charge!

Like all good things, there are exceptions. Books in private collections are not available for circulating like the 10,000 plus volumes in the USGA Museum and Library in Far Hills, New Jersey. The exception also applies to reference books most libraries have. These special books can only be used in the library.

Bibliography

Part 1

A History of Golf in Great Britain
Bernard Darwin, Sir Guy Campbell, et al.

A History of the Royal & Ancient Golf Club
H.S.C. Everard

A History of Golf: The Royal & Ancient Game
Robert Browning

Fifty Years of American Golf
H.B. Martin

The Story of American Golf
Herbert Warren Wind

Golf: Its People, History and Events
Will Grimsley

Golfiana Miscellanea
James Lindsay Stewart

Perkinsiana, Vol II
Ralph Perkins

History of the United States Rubber Co.
Glenn D. Babcock

The World of Golf
Charles Price

Only on Sunday
Henry Longhurst

Old files of *Golf Illustrated*
(London weekly)

Recent files of *Golf Digest*
(Norwalk, Conn. monthly)

Catalogs of A.G. Spalding & Bros., Inc.
(1896-1941)

U.S.A. and British patent files

Encyclopaedia Britannica

Parts 2 & 3

The American Golfer
Charles Price, Random House, 1954

Antique Golf Ball References & Price Guide
Leo M. Kelly Jr., Old Chicago Shop, 124 pages, many in color

The Badmington Library Book on Golf
Horace G. Hutchinson, 1890 and later editions

The Complete Golfer
Herbert Warren Wind, Simon and Schuster, 1954

Duffer's Handbook of Golf
Rice & Clare Brigg, Grantland, 1926, Rebul. 1989.

The Encyclopedia of Golf Collectibles
John & Morton Olman, Books Americana, 1985

Golf, A Guide to Information Sources
Joseph S.F. Murdoch & Janet Seagle, Gale Research, 1979.

Golf Antiques & Other Treasures with Prices
John & Morton Olman, Market St. Press, 1993, 201 pages.

Golf in America—First 100 Years
Geo Pepper, Ed Abrams, 1987

Golf in the Making
William Henderson & David Stark, 1979
(Contact used-book dealer)

Golfing Curios and the Like
Harry B. Wood, 1910
(Contact used-book dealer)

A History of Golf
Robert Browning, 1955
(Contact used book dealer)

History of Golf
A history of golf in Britain, 1952

The Story of American Golf
Herbert Warren Wind, 1948

Strictly Balls
Louis G. Caschera Jr., Progressive Pub., 1995.
Performance test on over 100 balls.

List of Illustrations

Chapter 16

Chapter 17

Chapter 18

Chapter 19

Chapter 20

Chapter 21

Chapter 22

Chapter 23

Chapter 24

PART 3

Chapter 25

Chapter 26

Chapter 27

Chapter 28

Timetable

Index